# Burton Anderson's
## guide to
# *Italian Wines*

*Revised Edition*

D0914846

Simon and Schuster
New York

## Key to symbols

| | | |
|---|---|---|
| r. | red | |
| p. | rosé | |
| w. | white | |
| am. | amber | In parentheses means |
| dr. | dry | relatively unimportant |
| s/sw. | semisweet | |
| sw. | sweet | |
| fz. | *frizzante* | |
| sp. | sparkling | |

| | |
|---|---|
| ★ | everyday wine |
| ★★ | above average |
| ★★★ | superior in its category |
| ★★★★ | grand, exceptional |
| ★★ | usually good value in its class |

| | |
|---|---|
| DOC | name and origin controlled |
| DOCG | name and origin controlled and guaranteed |
| Ag. 1 yr. etc. | aging required under DOC |
| 74 75 etc. | recommended years. Where red, rosé and white are indicated the red is intended unless otherwise stated. |
| DYA | drink the youngest available |
| NV | vintage not normally shown on label |

See p. 5 for more information.

| | |
|---|---|
| | 200 meters |
| | 500 meters |

Edited and designed by
Mitchell Beazley International Ltd.
Artists House, 14–15 Manette Street, London W1V 5LB
© Mitchell Beazley Publishers 1982
First edition 1982
Revised edition 1984
© Mitchell Beazley Publishers 1984
Text © Burton Anderson 1982, 1984

Published by Simon and Schuster
A Division of Simon & Schuster, Inc.
Simon & Schuster Building
Rockefeller Center
1230 Avenue of the Americas
New York, New York 10020

Library of Congress Cataloging
in Publication Data
Anderson, Burton.
The Simon and Schuster pocket guide
to Italian wines.
Includes index.
1. Wine and wine making    Italy.
I. Title. II. Title: Pocket guide
to Italian wines.
TP559.I8A56        641.2′22′0945        82-3340
ISBN 0-671-53022-4        AACR 2

Maps by Illustra Design Ltd., Reading
Typeset by Servis Filmsetting Ltd., Manchester
Printed and bound in Italy by New Inter Litho, Milan

*Executive editor* Chris Foulkes
*Editors* Alison Hancock, Anita Wagner

# Contents

# Foreword

Italy has always stood in the central piazza of civilization like a great baroque fountain, rather battered by time and small boys, spewing forth a torrent of wine of all colours and kinds. The Italians were happy to fill their pitchers at it and relatively unconcerned about whether the tourists joined them. To post notices round the fountain explaining the contributions of myriad farmers in scores of regions seemed absurd. Besides it would spoil the view.

But now things are different. The public, and particularly the public abroad, is intensely interested in precisely who makes what wine where. It wants to identify the wine of each region, to enjoy it with the region's food. It wants to celebrate the individual winemakers and get the feel of their land – and to understand why some wines are inherently better than others.

Italy is so vast and various that it takes a certain kind of mind to plot its ramifications. It must be methodical – but not Germanically so. It needs patience – oh what patience! Dedication is essential and a sense of humour a *sine qua non*. It must be someone who cares about people – because that, emphatically, is what Italians do.

The model guide, in fact, turned out to be a reformed American newspaperman who lives in Tuscany. He broke cover with his book *Vino* in 1980. My first reading convinced me that this author knew what he was talking about. When I met him I realized that he judges wine as well as he describes it and the men who make it. I was delighted to have found a kindred spirit, and I am delighted to introduce him, and the fruit of his Herculean labours, to you.

The toast is – Burton Anderson.

Hugh Johnson
*April, 1982*

# Introduction

Italy produces more than a fifth of the world's wine and ships nearly two fifths of the world's exports. But perhaps more often awesome than the scope is the intricacy of it all.

How many Italian wines are there? Two to five thousand, as some censuses have suggested? Undoubtedly more. Given the freelance inclinations of so many winemakers, it might even be said that there are 1,605,785 wines in Italy, or one for every registered vineyard. In compiling a handbook, though, the exercise was not so much in counting as in deciding which count.

The renaissance in Italian wine, initiated by the laws of controlled name and origin (DOC) of 1963, continues to expand – and with it the numbers of qualified wines and producers. Already it has brought about the most thorough transformation in history of any nation's wine industry, after millennia in which the making of wine was often left to nature.

Consumers have not been slow to recognize that Italian wine is the best overall value on the world market. What is harder to grasp is that the nation exports only about a quarter of an annual production of 7.9 billion liters, much of which is bulk blending wine for France and West Germany, and that most of the best Italian wine is drunk at home. This is not because Italians are reluctant to share the wealth, but rather because non-Italians have been hard to convince that there is so much there. Only recently have foreigners lifted the lid off Italy's enological treasure chest after overcoming fears that they might be opening another Pandora's box of cheap wine in straw flasks, painted crockery and fishy amphorae.

Now that the lid has been lifted, the problem is picking the gems. The profusion of colors, scents, and flavors that make modern Italian wine so alluring is partly screened by the jumble of names – of grape varieties, wine types, places, people, and trademarks – which can, even if inadvertently, create confusion and inhibit sales. For example, the nearly 220 DOC zones approved by mid-1984 take in more than 500 distinct wines. Yet DOC represents only 10–12% of total production – supposedly the cream of the crop, but not always. Some of Italy's finest wines fly their own colors.

Today the most exciting progress is taking place at the upper levels, where the potential for producing great wines is only just beginning to be fulfilled. Grape varieties that thrive in Italy's unsurpassed conditions of soil and climate are being selected by skilled winemakers to create wines of outstanding quality.

Most Italian wines of importance are described in the A–Z section, which considers all 20 regions in alphabetical order. Though an encyclopedic listing may have seemed handier, it would have put the subject out of focus. Italian wines come into context only when related to their homes – to the geography, climate, customs, foods and people of their own regions.

This handbook is a buyer's guide, compact enough to take along for reference to a shop or restaurant anywhere. It is also designed to be a tour guide with maps, travel tips, local food specialities and recommended restaurants, an ideal companion for discovering the intricacies of Italian wine at first hand.

# How to read an entry

The top line of each entry indicates in abbreviated form:

1. If the wine is DOC or designated as DOCG. If not, whatever its class, its authenticity is not officially controlled.
2. Whether it is red, rosé, white, amber, dry, semisweet, sweet, *frizzante* (lightly bubbly), sparkling, or several of these.
3. Rating of general quality:
   * ★ everyday wine
   * ★★ above average
   * ★★★ superior in its category
   * ★★★★ grand, exceptional

   These rankings weigh status consigned by recognized critics and experts against personal experience. The context is strictly Italian. Four stars (applied cautiously) indicate wine of the top echelon in Italy without hypothesizing international status. One reason for this is that some exceptional Italian wines are hardly known elsewhere. One star indicates the ordinary, but bear in mind that what some Italians drink daily would be prized in other nations. Because so many Italian wine names cover various colors and types and represent a multitude of producers, quality may vary considerably within a single denomination, indeed by as much as ★→★★★★. A box ☐ signals generally good value, though prices, too, may fluctuate among wines of the same name.
4. Recommended recent vintages. Each description mentions in principle when the wine should be at prime. If, for example, 80 is recommended and prime is in 5–8 years, ideal drinking should be from 1985 to 1988. Remember, though, that vintage information is relative. Some producers make good wine in off years, and wine from certain vintages and winemakers may age better than wine from others. No matter what the charts say, your taste and experience of a wine are the final arbiters in deciding when to drink it. The abbreviation DYA suggests that the wine should be drunk within months or, at the most, a couple of years, but that doesn't exclude the possibility that it could hold up well for longer. The term NV usually applies to non-vintage sparkling or fortified wines.

If a wine is subjected to aging under DOC, the required time is mentioned, as is specified barrel aging, where it applies. Special designations, such as *vecchio* and *riserva*, signify further aging; these, too, are indicated.

Producers (listed after each entry) have been screened for reliability against every source I could find. Single listings of producers are given in zones with more than one wine because it would be beyond the limits of a handbook to cite each producer with each type of wine. (Of the 17 wine types with the Alto-Adige appellation, for instance, some producers make a dozen or more.)

Some Italian wines sold on foreign markets carry bottler, shipper or importer brands or names used only in countries where sold. Most such wines, however qualified they might be, are not considered. The focus is on wines whose grape compositions and origins are verifiable in Italy.

The information under *Wine & Food* at the end of each regional section is intended mainly to aid travelers in Italy, though home cooks and diners in Italian restaurants in other lands may also find it useful. Wine suggestions with each speciality are intended to be indicators, not requisites. Others will prefer to make their own choice, based on the selection of wines available.

# Glossary

These terms may help you to read a label or be of use while traveling through a wine zone.

**Abboccato** Lightly sweet, literally "mouth-filling."

**Acidità** Acidity.

**Acidulo** Acidulous, acidic.

**Alcool** Alcohol.

**Amabile** Semisweet, literally "amiable," a shade sweeter than *abboccato* or *pastoso*.

**Amaro** Bitter.

**Amarognolo** The almond-like bitter undertone detectable in many Italian wines.

**Ambrato** The amber hue noted in many dessert or aperitif wines.

**Annata** Year of vintage.

**Aroma** The odor of certain amply scented (*aromatico*) wines, such as Moscato or Traminer.

**Asciutto** Bone dry.

**Auslese** German term permitted on labels in Alto Adige for wines from select grapes.

**Azienda agricola, azienda agraria, azienda vitivinicola** Terms for farm or estate winery.

**Bianco** White.

**Bicchiere** Drinking glass.

**Blanc de blancs** French term for white wine from light grapes only, sometimes used on labels of Italian sparkling wine.

**Botte** Cask, barrel.

**Bottiglia** Bottle.

**Brut** French term for dry sparkling wine, also used in Italy.

**Cantina** Wine cellar or winery.

**Cantina sociale** or **cooperativa** Cooperative winery (abbreviated to C.S. in producer listings).

**Casa vinicola** Wine house, usually in reference to one that processes purchased grapes.

**Cascina** Farm or estate, usually in northern Italy.

**Cerasuolo** Cherry red, used to describe certain rosés.

**Charmat** The French-originated method of refermenting sparkling wines in sealed vats, used frequently in Italy.

**Chiaretto** Though it means *claret*, it describes certain dark rosés.

**Classico** Classic, used to define zones of long-standing tradition within a DOC (i.e. Chianti Classico, Orvieto Classico) and the wine from grapes grown there.

**Consorzio** Voluntary consortium of growers and producers set up to supervise and control production and to promote wine.

**Degustazione** Wine tasting.

**Dolce** Sweet, technically in reference to wines with 5–10% residual sugar.

**Enologia** Enology, the study of wine.

**Enologo** Enologist. Italian graduate enologists are known as *enotecnici* or wine technicians.

**Enoteca** Literally wine library, applied to both public and commercial establishments with wines on display.

**Etichetta** Label.

**Ettaro** Hectare, or 2.471 acres, the standard measure of vineyard surface in Europe.

**Ettolitro** Hectoliter, or 100 liters, equivalent to a *quintale*, or 100 kilograms, the standard measure of wine volume in Europe.

**Fattoria** Farm or estate, usually in central Italy.

**Fermentazione** Fermentation. Wine made bubbly through natural processes is often labeled as *fermentazione naturale*.

**Fiasco** Flask, i.e. the straw-based, bulbous Chianti container.

**Frizzante** Lightly bubbly, *pétillant*, but not with enough pressure to qualify as sparkling.

**Frizzantino** refers to wine with a barely noticeable prickle.

**Fusto** Cask, barrel.

**Gradazione alcoolica** Alcohol grade (%) by volume.

**Gusto** Flavor (not in the English-language sense of "gusto," however).

**Imbottigliato da** Bottled by.

**Invecchiato** Aged.

**Liquoroso** Wine of high-alcohol grade, possibly, though not necessarily, fortified.

**Litro** Liter, equivalent to 1.056 U.S. quarts or 0.908 British quart.

**Marchio depositato** Registered brand name or trademark.

**Marsalato** or **maderizzato** Refers to wines which through oxidation take on flavors reminiscent of Marsala or

Madeira, favorable when controlled in certain dessert wines, undesirable in most table wines.

**Metodo champenois** or **metodo classico** Italian ways of referring to the classical Champagne method (*méthode champenoise*) of bottle-fermenting sparkling wines.

**Passito** Strong, usually sweet wine from the concentrated musts of semidried, or *passito*, grapes.

**Pastoso** Mellow, off-dry.

**Podere** Farm or estate.

**Produttore** Producer.

**Profumo** The perfumed, flowery odor of certain wines.

**Riserva** Reserve, applied only to DOC or DOCG wines that have undergone specified aging. *Riserva speciale* denotes even longer required aging.

**Rosato** Rosé.

**Rosso** Red.

**Rubino** Ruby color.

**Sapore** Flavor.

**Secco** Dry.

**Semisecco** Medium sweet, *demisec*, usually used to describe sparkling wines.

**Spumante** Sparkling wine. The term applies to dry as well as sweet wine.

**Stravecchio** Very old, a term permitted for very few DOC wines.

**Superiore** Denotes DOC wine that meets standards above the norm (higher alcohol, longer aging, a special subzone, etc.), though conditions vary.

**Tappo di sughero** Cork top.

**Tenuta** Farm or estate.

**Uva** Grape.

**Uvaggio** Mixture of grapes, as in a composite wine like Chianti or Valpolicella.

**Vecchio** Old. Certain DOC wines may carry the term after a set amount of aging.

**Vendemmia** The grape harvest, sometimes also used for vintage.

**Vigna, vigneto** Vineyard.

**Vignaiolo, viticoltore, coltivatore** Grape grower.

**Vino da arrosto** Robust, aged red wines that go with roast meats, e.g. Barolo, Brunello.

**Vino da pasto** Everyday table wine.

**Vino da taglio** Blending wine, usually produced in southern Italy and shipped north.

**Vino da tavola** Table wine. See explanation under *Laws & Labels* on p. 8.

**Vino novello** New wine, usually red, in the *Beaujolais nouveau* style.

**Vite** Vine.

**Vitigno** Vine or grape variety.

# Temperature

Wine expresses its best only when at the right temperature. All other arguments about serving – breathing, decanting, proper glass, etc. – are secondary. The chart indicates, with some leeway for personal preference, the best serving temperature for each type of wine.

| | °F | °C | |
|---|---|---|---|
| | 66 | 19 | Big aged reds: Barolo, |
| Chianti *riserva*, Cabernet, | 64 | 18 | Brunello, Amarone, Taurasi, |
| Corvo *rosso*, Rosso Piceno, | 63 | 17 | Torgiano *riserva* |
| Montepulciano d'Abruzzo | | | |
| | 61 | 16 | Merlot, Valpolicella, Barbera, |
| Bardolino *rosso*, Dolcetto, | 59 | 15 | Oltrepò Rosso, Sangiovese di |
| young Chianti, Grignolino, | 57 | 14 | Romagna |
| Marsala Vergine | | | Caldaro, Lambrusco *secco*, Vin |
| | 55 | 13 | Santo, Port-like reds, Marsala |
| Most rosés and new wines: | 54 | 12 | Superiore, Recioto della |
| Castel del Monte *rosato*, | 52 | 11 | Valpolicella |
| Bardolino Chiaretto | | | |
| | 50 | 10 | Delicate, fruity whites: Fiano |
| Most dry whites: Soave, Gavi, | 48 | 9 | di Avellino, Nosiola, Sylvaner, |
| Frascati, Pinot Grigio, Tocai. | 46 | 8 | Moscato d'Asti |
| Best sparkling champenoise | | | |
| | 45 | 7 | Most dry and semisweet |
| Fortified dessert wines: | 43 | 6 | sparkling wines: Asti |
| Moscato di Pantelleria, Picolit, | 41 | 5 | Spumante |
| Greco di Bianco | | | |
| | 39 | 4 | |

# Laws & Labels

Italian wine production is governed by national and regional authorities in compliance with European Economic Community policy. If exported, the wine and label must also meet standards imposed by the importing nation. The legal details involved, from buying land, selecting and planting (only EEC approved) vines to making wine and selling it, are increasingly complicated. Bureaucracy has made labeling, particularly for table wines, a heavy and often unnecessary burden for producers. Yet, in a way only those intimately involved comprehend, wine production in Italy works with a reasonable degree of discipline.

Though the way is open for a four-level system of classifying Italian wines, only one category is fully in effect: *denominazione di origine controllata*, or DOC, which applies to only 10–12% of production. Most other still, dry wines, no matter what their class or style, must be called *vino da tavola* (table wine), though lightly bubbly (*frizzante*), sparkling (*spumante*), and strongly alcoholic or fortified (*liquoroso*) wines can be thus labeled.

*Vino da tavola* applies to many things, including wines of unspecified origin with names like Lacrima del Paradiso. The recently instituted category of *vino da tavola con indicazione geografica* specifies references to color and place (Rosso di Bellagio) or, where approved, grape variety and place (Moscato di Strevi). Authenticity is implied if not strictly controlled. Some such table wines with place names will one day qualify as *vini tipici*, a loosely defined category similar to France's VDQS and *vins de pays*.

For the moment, wording on the labels of *vino da tavola* and non-DOC *frizzante*, *spumante*, or *liquoroso* can be no more reliable than the producer's reputation. The bottle may contain something strictly mediocre or, indeed, one of Italy's best wines. More than a few wines labeled *vino da tavola* rate three or four stars here.

The category DOC applies to wines from specified grape varieties grown in delimited zones and processed and aged following set methods in order to meet prescribed standards of color, odor, flavor, alcohol content, acidity, etc. All of these processes favor quality but do not guarantee it. In 1984, nearly 500 distinct varieties or types of wine were produced in the nearly 220 DOC zones.

Details of each DOC are determined by producers in the zone (often grouped in a *consorzio* that helps supervise production) guided by the national DOC committee, whose approval must be confirmed by presidential decree. The program is relatively new (the first DOC was instituted in 1966), but reforms are being made constantly to improve quality and bring winemaking up to date. Overall, despite some dubious choices, DOC has done more than anything else to improve the status of Italian wine worldwide.

*Denominazione di origine controllata e garantita*, or DOCG, the highest category, has been instituted after years of delay. Of the four wines originally covered, Vino Nobile di Montepulciano came out in 1983, followed by Barbaresco and Barolo in 1984. Brunello di Montalcino was to follow in 1985 and Chianti in the near future. But questions among producers, administrators and consumers about the purpose of DOCG have given rise to doubts about the program's effectiveness.

Italian DOC and DOCG wines rate the Common Market designation VQPRD (for quality wine produced in determined regions) or, for sparkling wine, VSQPRD. Such wines now must pass chemical and taste analysis before being sold.

Labeling of all wines, DOC and otherwise, has been restricted by the EEC to pertinent data presented in a set order in which the wording and even the type sizes are controlled. Obligatory on all labels are: the wine name; its category (DOC, VQPRD, *vino da tavola*, etc); the producer or bottler's name and place of bottling; volume (a standard 750ml bottle must carry the letter **e**); the alcohol by volume. Labels may also carry the producer's trademark, coat of arms or other illustration and a vintage date (obligatory on all DOCG and many DOC wines). Also permitted are mention of awards (but only for the wine and vintage contained), a *consorzio* symbol and number, data on vineyards and (for DOC and DOCG only) the number of bottles produced.

Further information may be given on a back label or an attached card or scroll, though this must be verifiable and cannot include such terms as *speciale*, *riserva*, *extra*, and *vecchio* unless the wine qualifies for them under DOC and DOCG. Most Italian terms found on labels are defined in the *Glossary*.

Wines exported to the United States must have the official INE mark either on the cork or a neck label and must be described in English (e.g. Red Table Wine, Product of Italy). Net contents, alcohol percentage by volume and importer must also be given.

## Anatomy of Italian wine

Italy produces more than a fifth of the world's wine. Its average of 7.9 billion liters a year surpasses the combined output of all nations outside Europe. France once rivalled it in volume, but in recent years Italy has established a clear lead over its neighbor.

Why this mass of vines in a relatively small country somewhat cramped for space? Vines and wines obviously suit the nature of the land and its people, even though that nature varies to extremes. As for space, there's plenty: Italy's endless hillsides are better suited to vines than any other type of agriculture.

Mountains play a decisive role in Italian viticulture. The Alps shield the temperate climate from the damp cold of central Europe and the Apennines shape weather patterns from Piedmont to Calabria. Sicily and Sardinia also have snowy peaks. What makes it all so complex is the way in which the myriad microclimates correlate with the different types of soil.

Although generalizations can be made about growing conditions in various sections of the country, exceptions abound. For instance, low-lying zones in the Veneto and Friuli-Venezia Giulia in the far north have longer, hotter seasons than do Sicily's Etna or Calabria's Donnici in the mountains of the deep south. In short, in this land that is 39.7% hills and 38.7% mountains, altitude is often more important than latitude.

Still, the north is well ahead of the rest of Italy in quality wine production. The eight northern regions produce more than half the nation's DOC wine in the vast arc formed by the Alps and Apennines around the broad valley of the Po. The cool climate in hills of glacial moraine, limestone, and clay, favors slow ripening for perfumed young wines and aged reds of rarefied bouquet.

Native varieties – Nebbiolo, Barbera, Dolcetto, Schiava, Tocai, Albana, Cortese, Traminer, Garganega, among many –

compete for space with such imports as Cabernet, Merlot, the Pinots, Chardonnay, Sauvignon, and Riesling. As in other places, much new planting is in varieties for dry white and sparkling wines. Major wine schools at Alba in Piedmont, San Michele all'Adige in Trentino, and Conegliano in the Veneto have upgraded viticulture and enology to levels comparable with those of France, West Germany, and California.

As winemakers in privileged zones of northern Italy (the hills of Alba, Asti, Oltrepò Pavese, Fruilis, Trentino-Alto Adige, and the Veneto, for example) complement their skills with new commitment to top quality at any cost, their wines will become more prominent among the world's elite. But this will involve further reduction of grape yields and use of only the best equipment.

A national trend, most visible in the north, was to make wines of all colors for early consumption, following market demands and the need to clear stocks. The ultimate expression was *vino novello*, the Beaujolais-style "new wine" made by carbonic maceration.

Central Italy, the six regions from Tuscany south to Latium and Molise, produce about one-third of the DOC wine (Chianti alone makes up about one-sixth of the national total). But Chianti's lagging sales have made it the most worrisome example of overproduction in a nation plagued by wine surpluses.

Despite the intrinsic advantages of temperate climate in its sunny hills, central Italy lags behind the north in technique and ambition (though there are plenty of individual exceptions). Relatively few grape varieties are used in the major wines. All the DOC reds of Tuscany and most of Umbria and the Marches are based on Sangiovese. The other important dark variety is Montepulciano d'Abruzzo, prominent in the Abruzzi, Marches, Latium, and Molise. Central Italian whites derive chiefly from Trebbiano and Malvasia in their various clones (Orvieto and Frascati are the best-known examples). Tuscany has many whites based on Trebbiano, though the region's best whites stem from other varieties. The Marches has Verdicchio, whose innate class has been squandered by its popularity.

Southern Italy (six regions including Sicily and Sardinia) makes a fair share of the nation's wine, but only about 7% of the DOC. Cooperatives dominate production, particularly in Sicily, Apulia, and Sardinia, where surpluses are most severe in the blending wine field.

Progress has been more dramatic in the Mezzogiorno (south) than elsewhere, but, ironically, southern wines have been neglected by consumers despite low price and improved quality. Some examples of how good southern wines can be are provided by Basilicata's Aglianico del Vulture; Campania's Fiano, Greco, and Taurasi; Apulia's Favonio, Torre Quarto, Rosa del Golfo, and several DOC reds; Sicily's Regaleali, Corvo, Etna, and Marsala; Calabria's Cirò and Greco di Bianco; and Sardinia's Cannonau, Vermentino, and non-DOC wines of Alghero.

The surplus, aggravated by declining domestic consumption (from 110 liters a head to less than 90 in a decade), had engendered a crisis in Italian wine in the 1980s that seemed certain to bring radical change. Clearly, less emphasis on quantity and more on quality was needed. The situation was really nothing new. Domitian removed vines in parts of the Roman Empire in the 1st century BC to combat excess production.

Despite rapidly rising winemaking costs, Italian middle-class wines have retained their competitive edge over those from most other nations. At the top, continuing quality improvements signal increasing prices, but at that level, too, Italians can continue to capitalize on natural advantages.

# Grape varieties

Before the scourges from America struck Italian vineyards around the turn of the century, Italy grew thousands of types of vines, some universally recognized, but most so localized that their features, like their names, varied from one village to the next. For example, in Lombardy's Oltrepò Pavese in the mid-19th century, some 260 different varieties were recorded growing in an area smaller than Burgundy's Côte d'Or. Phylloxera reduced the numbers, though the ensuing tendency in much of Italy to plant heavy-bearing varieties did little for quality. In the last two decades, the steady conversion from mixed crops to uniform vineyards has brought new order and increased plantings of outstanding varieties, both native and imports (most of which were present in Italy in the last century). Still, the numbers and names of Italian grape varieties remain staggering. Listed are 83 of more than local interest.

## Dark Grapes

**Aglianico** An aristocrat of Greek origin, epitomized in Campania's Taurasi and Basilicata's Aglianico del Vulture.

**Aleatico** Makes attractive dark dessert wines in Latium (Aleatico di Gradoli), Apulia (Aleatico di Puglia), Tuscany, and Umbria.

**Barbera** Hearty Piedmont native, most prominent in varietals and blends in NW Italy. Vies with Sangiovese as the nation's most widely planted vine for red wine.

**Bombino Nero** Source of Apulia's Castel del Monte *rosato*.

**Bonarda** Strain of Croatina used for varietals and blends in Lombardy, Piedmont, and Emilia.

**Brachetto** Makes bubbly, semisweet red wines in Piedmont around Acqui and Asti.

**Brunello di Montalcino** The special clone of Sangiovese Grosso that carries the same name as Tuscany's vaunted red wine.

**Cabernet** Bordeaux native most prominent in NE Italy, where Cabernet Franc has been favored, though Cabernet Sauvignon is gaining in many places in Italy both as a varietal and in composites.

**Calabrese** or **Nero d'Avola** Noted in Sicily as a source of both DOC Cerasuolo di Vittoria and table wines.

**Cannonau** Sardinia's main dark variety – apparently France's Grenache introduced v.. Sp... is used for dry and sweet wines of strong character.

**Carignano** The Carignan of France and Spain is grown in Sardinia.

**Cesanese** Most respectable native of Latium, where it is used in DOC varietals and blends.

**Clinton** Native of New York state, popular in NE Italy for use in strawberry-scented wines, even though banned for not being, technically speaking, a wine grape.

**Corvina Veronese** Chief component of Veronese reds (Valpolicella, Recioto, and Bardolino) along with Rondinella, Molinara, Negrara, and Rossignola.

**Croatina** Used heavily in Lombardy's Oltrepò Pavese, mainly in composites with Barbera and Uva Rara. See Bonarda.

**Dolcetto** Treasured in S Piedmont, where it makes supple, appealing varietals in seven DOC zones.

**Freisa** Makes unique wines, often bubbly, in its native Piedmont.

**Gaglioppo** Source of most Calabrian reds, including Cirò. It has numerous synonyms.

**Grignolino** Once prominent, this Piedmontese variety is still admired in light red wines around Asti.

**Guarnaccia** Chief grape of Ischia *rosso*, found in other wines of Campania.

**Lagrein** Source of distinctive reds and rosés in Trentino-Alto Adige.

**Lambrusco** Abounds in Emilia's plains, where its several subvarieties make bubbly wines – red, pink, even white – DOC and otherwise.

**Malbec** or **Malbeck** Usually secondary in Bordeaux composites, it is sometimes a protagonist in the Veneto and Apulia.

**Malvasia Nera** Dark versions of the wide-ranging Malvasia family make DOC reds in Piedmont and Alto Adige. Prominent in Apulia.

**Marzemino** Popular variety in Trentino and Lombardy.

**Merlot** The Bordeaux native is extremely popular in NE Italy as a source of varietals. One of the nation's most heavily planted vines, it is used both alone and in mixes in many regions.

**Monica** Spanish origin, grown in Sardinia for both sweet and dry wines.

**Montepulciano d'Abruzzo** Dominant dark variety of the Abruzzi, gaining favor in other regions for fine varietals and blends.

**Nebbiolo** Noble progenitor of Piedmont's greatest red wines – Barolo, Barbaresco, and Gattinara – and a host of others elsewhere in Piedmont, Lombardy, and Valle d'Aosta. Among many synonyms are Spanna, Chiavennasca, and Picutener.

**Negroamaro** Apulian variety that dominates the big reds of the Salento peninsula.

**Nerello Mascalese** Worthy Sicilian, most noted as source of Etna *rosso* and *rosato*.

**Petit Rouge** Used in some of Valle d'Aosta's distinguished reds, including Enfer d'Arvier and Torrette.

**Piedirosso** or **Per'e Palummo** Prominent in Campanian reds, notably of Ischia.

**Pinot Nero** Burgundy's Pinot Noir is used for red wines, especially in N Italy, with mixed results. It has been more successful in white and pink sparkling wines. Known as Blauburgunder in Alto Adige.

**Primitivo** or **Primativo** Apulian source of powerful table, dessert, and blending wines. Possibly related to California's Zinfandel.

**Raboso** Makes interesting reds in its native Veneto.

**Refosco** Makes fine varietals in Friuli. Known as Mondeuse in France.

**Rossese** Source of DOC Rossese di Dolceacqua and good table wines in Liguria.

**Sangiovese** Mainstay of all Tuscan DOC reds (Chianti, Brunello di Montalcino, Vino Nobile di Montepulciano, and more), it is one of Italy's most widely planted vines, though in various strains, including Sangiovese Grosso, Brunello, Prugnolo, and Sangiovese di Romagna.

**Schiava** Important vine of Trentino-Alto Adige, its various clones account for such wines as Santa Maddalena and Caldaro. Known as Vernatsch in German.

**Teroldego** Grown only in Trentino, where it makes the admired Teroldego Rotaliano.

**Tocai Rosso** or **Nero** Dark version of the Friulian vine, makes DOC red in Veneto's Colli Berici.

**Uva di Troia** Fine variety from N Apulia, where it dominates several DOC wines.

**Vespolina** Often blended with Nebbiolo in the Novara-Vercelli hills of Piedmont, it also makes a varietal table wine.

## Light Grapes

**Albana** Native of Romagna's hills, where it makes both dry and semisweet wines, still or bubbly.

**Arneis** Gaining stature in the Alba area of Piedmont after it almost disappeared.

**Biancolella** Campanian vine prominent on Ischia as a varietal and a partner of Forastera in Ischia DOC *bianco*.

**Blanc de Valdigne** Source of Blanc de Morgex and Blanc de La Salle, grown in Italy's highest vineyards in Valle d'Aosta.

**Bombino Bianco** Main grape of Apulia's San Severo *bianco*; grown in Abruzzi as Trebbiano d'Abruzzo.

**Bosco** Prime ingredient of Cinqueterre in Liguria.

**Carricante** Chief grape of Etna *bianco* in Sicily.

**Catarratto** Prevalent in W Sicily, where it figures in Marsala, Bianco Alcamo, and in many other wines.

**Chardonnay** Aristocratic Burgundian, often confused with Pinot Bianco and incorrectly called Pinot Chardonnay, is more widely planted in Trentino-Alto Adige, Veneto and Friuli than previously estimated. Increasing source of varietal wine in many regions.

**Cortese** Piedmont's popular whites, notably Gavi, derive from this native variety also found in Lombardy's Oltrepò Pavese.

**Fiano** Known as Apianum to the ancient Romans, it makes Campania's fine Fiano di Avellino.

**Forastera** Campanian variety mixed with Biancolella in Ischia *bianco*.

**Garganega** Mainstay of Soave is grown mostly in the Veneto.

**Gewürztraminer** A superior clone of Traminer, developed in Alsace, is widely planted in NE Italy, where it is often confused with its common cousin.

**Greco** Vines of this name, probably of Greek origin, are grown in several parts of Italy, notably Campania (Greco di Tufo) and Calabria (Greco di Bianco). Vines known as Grechetto (which gives impressive results in Umbria) and Grecanico may be related.

**Grillo** Once the chief grape of Marsala (still considered the best), it now usually supplements Catarratto.

**Inzolia** Grown throughout Sicily for use in white wine, including Marsala and Corvo *bianco*.

**Malvasia** Name applied to a vast range of S European vines, also known as Malvoisie and Malmsey. Light varieties are grown throughout Italy, conspicuously in Latium (for Frascati, Est! Est!! Est!!!, etc.), though something of the name can be found in nearly every region, used for both dry and sweet, and still and bubbly wines.

**Moscato** Muscat vines are found throughout Italy and usually used for white or golden wines, generally with some degree of sweetness and distinct aroma. Basic styles are sparkling and *frizzante* – as in Piedmont's Asti Spumante and Moscato d'Asti – and richly sweet, as in Sicilian Moscato. There is also some red Moscato.

**Müller Thurgau** The Riesling-Sylvaner cross is catching on in Italy, making wines of unexpected class in Trentino-Alto Adige and Friuli.

**Nuragus** Ancient Sardinian vine, source of Nuragus di Cagliari.

**Picolit** Native of Friuli long rendered Italy's most prized dessert wine. It is now coming back after decades of decline.

**Pigato** Grown only in SW Liguria, where it makes fine table wines.

**Pinot Bianco** Burgundy's Pinot Blanc is grown throughout N Italy, where it is sometimes confused with Chardonnay. It makes both still and sparkling wines, often DOC, in Friuli, Veneto, Trentino-Alto Adige, and Lombardy. Known as Weissburgunder in Alto Adige.

**Pinot Grigio** France's Pinot Gris is increasingly popular in Italy, especially in the Tre Venezie and Lombardy, where it is often DOC, though much Pinot Grigio is not. Known as Ruländer in Alto Adige.

**Prosecco** Prominent in E Veneto for sparkling, *frizzante*, and some still wines, usually a touch sweet. The most respected is Cartizze.

**Riesling Italico** Not a true Riesling and probably not even native to Italy. It sometimes stands alone and occasionally alternates with Riesling Renano in DOCs. Known as Welschriesling in Alto Adige.

**Riesling Renano** The Johannisberg or White Riesling of the Rhine, increasingly respected in N Italy, where it is often interchanged with Riesling Italico. Known as Rheinriesling in Alto Adige.

**Sauvignon** The outstanding promise of this Bordeaux native has begun to be realized in certain parts of N Italy, where it makes DOC varietals.

**Sylvaner** Limited, but it makes remarkable wines in Alto Adige's heights.

**Tocai Friulano** Friuli's beloved vine also makes DOC whites in the Veneto and Lombardy. Gaining interest elsewhere.

**Traminer** Native of Alto Adige, this progenitor of Gewürztraminer is more productive but less distinguished.

**Trebbiano** Vines of the name abound through Italy, though they may vary markedly in character. Trebbiano Toscano is most diffused; the Romagnan strain is also widespread.

**Verdeca** Important Apulian variety, used with Bianco d'Alessano in Locorotondo, Martina Franca, and other southern whites.

**Verdicchio** Predominant light grape of the Marches.

**Verduzzo** Friuli grape, used in Veneto for dry and dessert wines.

**Vermentino** Makes DOC white in Sardinia and good table wines in Liguria.

**Vernaccia di Oristano** Used exclusively around Oristano in Sardinia for a Sherry-like dessert wine.

**Vernaccia di San Gimignano** Ancient vine used for the white of Tuscany's famous towered town.

# Abruzzi

## Abruzzo

*Bacchus amat colles*, as the Romans observed, so the wine god must adore the Abruzzi. Between the Adriatic Sea and the Apennines, which reach their highest point in the snow-capped Gran Sasso range above the regional capital of L'Aquila, there is little else but hills. The microclimates of these sun-drenched slopes vary from warm maritime to alpine, so if you pick your spot carefully, you can find conditions suited to nearly any type of vine. But growers in the Abruzzi have chosen to work almost exclusively with grapes for two regional DOCs: Montepulciano d'Abruzzo, which comprises both a red and a pink Cerasuolo, and the white Trebbiano d'Abruzzo. Montepulciano d'Abruzzo *rosso* (not to be confused with Vino Nobile di Montepulciano of Tuscany) has been drawing praise in Italy and abroad for its naturally robust breed. Trebbiano d'Abruzzo, usually neutral as Trebbianos tend to be, has less to offer, though it is capable of inspiring a surprise or two.

**Wine Zones**
1 Montepulciano d'Abruzzo
2 Trebbiano d'Abruzzo

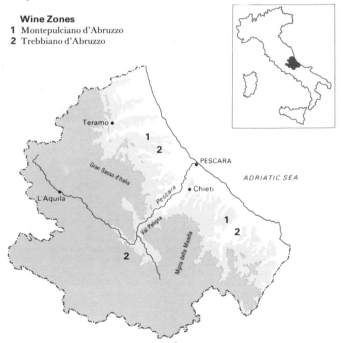

The Abruzzi, easily accessible from Rome via the *autostrada* to L'Aquila and the Adriatic port of Pescara, has fine beaches and some of Italy's grandest mountain scenery, including the wilderness area known as the Abruzzi National Park. Wine tourism has not been explicitly introduced in the region, but the coastal hills between Teramo and Chieti have numerous wineries and country inns where local wines can be tasted. In Pescara, the *Enoteca Europea* provides a good choice of the region's wines.

## Recent vintages

Red Montepulciano d'Abruzzo improves with moderate aging, usually 3–6 years, occasionally more. Some producers also age Trebbiano d'Abruzzo for 5 years or more.

1983   Abundant crop of satisfactory quality or better.
1982   Heat and drought took toll, but select wines good to very good.
1981   Reduced; fine, perfumed wines from select grapes only.
1980   Big crop, satisfactory quality.
1979   Generally very good wines.
1978   Good to excellent year.
1977   Meager harvest, but some outstanding wines.
1976   Mediocre.
1975   Abundant harvest, good wines.
1974   Exceptional red wines for aging.

**Abruzzo** r. p. w. dr.   ★ DYA
Simple table wines made in many parts of the region, the red and rosé from Montepulciano and Sangiovese, the white from Trebbiano.

**Cerasuolo d'Abruzzo**
See Montepulciano d'Abruzzo Cerasuolo.

**Montepulciano d'Abruzzo** DOC
Red and rosé from Montepulciano d'Abruzzo with up to 15% Sangiovese grown in choice vineyards through the coastal hills and in valleys in the uplands around L'Aquila.

– **Cerasuolo** p. dr.   ★→★★   80 81 82
The rosé version is vinified only briefly with the skins. Cherry pink, fresh and tasty, it is a good, all-purpose wine, if rarely distinguished. Drink in 1–3 years.

– **Rosso** r. dr.   ★★→★★★   74 75 77 78 79 80 81 82 83
Deep ruby, robust, round, lightly tannic, with 3–6 years of age – and from certain producers – it can be one of central Italy's smoothest and most attractive red wines. Made in significant quantity (about 20 million liters a year), it seems to have a highly promising future.
Ag. *vecchio* 2 yrs.

| | |
|---|---|
| Barone Cornacchio | Masciarelli |
| Nestore Bosco | Paolo Mezzanotte |
| Cantalupo (Di Giulio) | Antonio Monti |
| C.S. di Tollo | Camillo Montori |
| Casal Thaulero | Nicodemi |
| Santoro Colella | Emidio Pepe |
| Duchi di Castelluccio | Gaetano Petrosemolo |
| Dario D'Angelo | Rosso della Quercia |
| Dino Illuminati | Scialletti |
| Vittorio Janni | Edoardo.Valentini |

**Moscato** w. sw. fz. sp.   ★ DYA
Dessert wine, often sparkling or *frizzante*, made from Moscato Bianco grapes in various places. The best Moscato, noted for its fruity Muscat aroma, is from Torre de' Passeri, near Pescara.

**Rubino** r. dr.   ★★ 80 81 82 83
Like Montepulciano DOC, except that it contains 20% Sangiovese. Bright ruby, finely scented, generous, and warm, it is best in 2–4 years.
Tenuta S. Agnese (Acciavatti)

**Rustico** r. dr.   ★ DYA
Thick mountain wine, in keeping with its name, made from Montepulciano and Sangiovese in the high Val Peligna.

**Spinello** w. dr.   ★★ DYA
Fine, light table wine from Trebbiano grapes, made at Città Sant'Angelo, near Pescara.
Tenuta S. Agnese (Acciavatti)

**Trebbiano d'Abruzzo** DOC w. dr. (fz.)   ★→★★   DYA
White from Trebbiano d'Abruzzo and/or Trebbiano Toscano grown in designated vineyards in coastal hills and upland valleys. Usually bland in odor and flavor, bone dry, and pale straw in color, it may also be

*frizzante.* From one producer, Edoardo Valentini, from certain vintages, it can attain a luxuriant (★★★) tone of fine white Burgundy while retaining an appealing fruitiness for 5–6 years.

| | |
|---|---|
| Casal Thaulero | Camillo Montori |
| Barone Cornacchia | Nicodemi |
| Dario D'Angelo | Emidio Pepe |
| Duchi di Castelluccio | Scialletti |
| Dino Illuminati | Edoardo Valentini |

**Val Peligna** r. w. dr. ★→★★ DYA
Besides the standard varieties in this mountain valley, one winemaker has been experimenting with such unfamiliar vines as Pinot Grigio, Riesling Renano, Traminer, Veltliner, and the hybrid Sejve Villard 12,375 in limited quantities.
Santoro Colella

**Vin Cotto** am. dr. or sw. ★★
Rare fortified wine made by cooking down musts of light grapes and fermenting them with freshly pressed grapes. This "cooked wine," with its burnished color, syrupy texture and bitter or bittersweet prune-like flavor is reputed to aid digestion (18–20% alcohol). But you'll have to try it privately because it's banned from commerce.

Wine & Food

When it comes to eating, the people of the Abruzzi don't mince matters; they like strongly flavored food and lots of it. Though the Adriatic is full of fish, even coastal dwellers look to the land for sustenance. Historically an abode of shepherds, the Abruzzi's favored meats are lamb and mutton. Ewe's milk is the source of *pecorino* cheese. Pork is popular, too, either fresh or in preserved *salame*, sausages, and *prosciutto.* The seasoning is often hot, peaking in the chili-flavored *diavolino.* The Abruzzi's "national dish" is pasta: *maccheroni alla chitarra.* Once, before girth went out of style, the Abruzzesi celebrated with *la panarda,* a feast that ranged upward from 30 courses. Today, most young people have never heard of it, let alone eaten their way through one.

**Agnello alla diavola** Lamb sautéed with chili peppers and white wine.
    ★★ Cerasuolo.
**Brodetto pescarese** The Pescara version of Adriatic fish soup, this one cooked with green peppers.
    ★→★★ Trebbiano.
**Maccheroni alla chitarra** Pasta noodles cut into quadrangular sticks on a stringed instrument (the "guitar") and served with either tomato sauce or meat *ragù.*
    ★★ Cerasuolo (with tomato sauce), ★★ Montepulciano (with *ragù*).
**'Ndocca 'ndocca** Pungent stew of pig's innards, ribs, feet, and head with peppers, rosemary, and vinegar, a speciality of Teramo.
    ★★ Montepulciano *rosso.*

**Rosticini** Lamb or pork grilled on skewers and served at street stalls.
    ★★ Montepulciano *rosso.*
**Scrippelle 'nfuss** or **'mbusse** Pancake-like fritters or crêpes served in broth.
    ★★ Cerasuolo.
**Stracci** Baked timbals of meat, béchamel, cheese, and vegetables, a speciality of L'Aquila. Known as *fregnacce* around Teramo.
    ★★→★★★ Montepulciano *rosso* (fairly young).
**Virtù** or **le sette virtù** Legendary soup of Teramo that once took seven damsels each using seven different ingredients seven days to put together. Today the "seven virtues" soup is less romantic, but still good.
    ★★ Cerasuolo.

### Restaurants

Recommended in or near wine zones: *Le Salette Aquilane* at Coppito near L'Aquila; *Beccaceci* at Giulianova Lido; *Le Tre Marie* at L'Aquila; *Ranieri* at Lanciano; *La Bilancia* near Loreto Aprutino; *Guerino* and *Da Duilio* at Pescara; *Onofrietto* at Popoli; *Golfo di Venere* at San Giovanni in Venere; *Vecchia Silvi* at Silvi Alta; *Il Duomo* at Teramo; *Il Corsaro* at Vasto.

# Apulia

## Puglia

Apulia probably has a denser concentration of vines in its 7,469 square miles than any other place on earth. Not long ago, the region produced more wine than any other in the rust-colored soil of its plains and low plateaus that stretch from the spur to the heel of the Italian boot. But production has declined lately as emphasis has switched from blending wines to dry table wines of moderate strength. Meanwhile, Apulia continues as Italy's leading supplier of table grapes.

Apulian wines are better than ever, but they have not realized merited success in bottle. Of 20 DOCs, only a handful of names are recognizable to outsiders, and just 2% of the annual output of nearly a billion liters is officially classified. Several of Apulia's better wines are not DOC.

Production follows two basic patterns divided geographically by a line drawn across the region from the port of Taranto, on the Ionian Sea, to Brindisi, on the Adriatic. Southeastwards lies the hot Salento peninsula with Italy's easternmost point at Capo d'Otranto, long the source of strong, dark blending wines based on Negroamaro and Primitivo grapes (the latter possibly related to California's Zinfandel). New techniques have reduced the strength but retained the remarkable robust character in red table wines. Rosés here show elegance rarely equaled elsewhere.

North of the Taranto–Brindisi line, the climate is warm and dry along the coast near the regional capital of Bari, becoming relatively cool in the interior. The whites, noted for their neutral nature that makes them ideal for vermouth, are beginning to show some fruitiness when processed at low temperature. Some reds and rosés from Uva di Troia, Montepulciano, and Bombino Nero have the delicately perfumed qualities of northerly wines. Such outside varieties as Malbec, Cabernet Franc, Pinot Bianco,

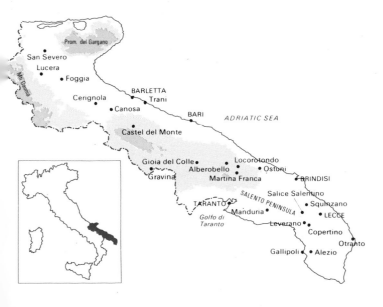

and Chardonnay have been introduced with unexpected success.

As Italy's perennial gateway to Greece, Apulia has remnants of Hellas along with reminders of innumerable other peoples. Of particular interest are the *trulli* dwellings in the Itria valley. The octagonal Swabian structure that gave Castel del Monte its name is also worth a visit, as is the Salento peninsula with its ancient Greek cities of Lecce and Gallipoli.

Select Apulian wines are on display at the *Enoteca Puglia* in Alberobello and the *Enoteca De Pasquale* in Bari.

## Recent vintages

Apulian reds are noted for longevity, as are certain rosés of Salento, though as a rule pink and white wines should be drunk young. The hot Salento peninsula tends to have more consistent harvests than do more temperate northern zones.

1983   Despite heat and drought, Castel del Monte and Salento recorded a good harvest.
1982   Reduced crop due to drought and hail, and heat caused problems with acidity. Where irrigation was possible good wines made.
1981   Meager harvest; excellent quality in Castel del Monte, generally satisfactory elsewhere.
1980   A good crop, bountiful in Salento, reduced in the north.
1979   The best in a series of fine vintages in Salento, good to excellent in the north. Red wines to keep.
1978   Good to excellent year in Salento; above average if light in north.
1977   Generally very good harvest of wines to lay down.
1976   Subpar vintage.
1975   Excellent, except in isolated sections of the north.
1974   Spotty north and south; excellent in Castel del Monte.
1973   Generally fine harvest for long-lived wines.
1972   Below average.
1971   Best vintage of the decade in Salento; also good in the north.

**Aleatico di Puglia** DOC r. sw. ★★   77 78 79 80 81 82 83
Smooth, warm, garnet-violet dessert wine from Aleatico di Puglia grapes in two types: *dolce naturale* (of 15%) and the fortified *liquoroso dolce naturale* (of 18.5%). Produced throughout Apulia, but only a little is made.
Ag. *riserva* 3 yrs.

| | |
|---|---|
| Felice Botta | Nuova Vinicola Picardi |
| Francesco Candido | Riforma Fondiaria |
| Lippolis | |

**Alezio** DOC r. p. dr. ★★→★★★   83
New DOC for red and rosé from Negroamaro and Malvasia Rossa grapes grown E of Gallipoli on the Salento peninsula. The *rosso* is ample in color and body, warm, suited to aging. The brand names Doxi Vecchio and Portulano will qualify. The *rosato* is coral pink, fragrant and attractively flavored, among Italy's finest rosés. The DOC will include Lacrima di Terra d'Otranto and Rosa del Golfo.
Ag. *riserva (rosso)* 2 yrs.

| | |
|---|---|
| Giuseppe Calò | Niccolò Coppola |

**Apulia** r. dr. ★★   75 77 78 79 81 83
Dynamically robust red table wine made at Martina Franca from Primitivo, Negroamaro, and Malvasia Nera. It tends to develop smoothness and bouquet after about 6 years.
Vinicola Miali

**Bianco di Gravina**
See Gravina.

**Brindisi** DOC r. p. dr. ★→ ★★★   75 77 78 79 81 83
*Rosso* and *rosato* from Negroamaro grapes at 70% or more grown inland from the port of Brindisi towards Mesagne. The rosé can be pleasant. The red, though powerful, can be smooth and elegant at 5–10 years old or more. Cosimo Taurino's Patriglione stands out.
Ag. *riserva* 2 yrs.

| | |
|---|---|
| Santachiara (Medico) | Cosimo Taurino |

**Cabernet Franc**
See Favonio.

**Cacc'e Mmitte di Lucera** DOC r. dr.  ★→★★  DYA
The dialect name – one interpretation is "toss it down and fill it up"
(your glass presumably) – is more colorful than the wine. It derives from
a staggering mix of grapes: the dark Uva di Troia, Montepulciano,
Sangiovese, and Malvasia Nera, and the light Trebbiano Toscano,
Bombino Bianco, and Malvasia Bianca grown around Lucera in N
Apulia. Results fall somewhere between unusual and nondescript.

Lorenzo Carapelle                   Riforma Fondiaria
Federico II

**Castel del Monte** DOC r. p. w. dr.  ★→ ★★★   73 75 77 79 81 83
Apulia's best-known DOC is named after the octagonal castle of
Emperor Friedrich II von Hohenstaufen. The general good quality is
due to relatively cool climate and grower discipline. The *rosso* from Uva
di Troia with some Bombino Nero and Montepulciano is well-rounded
with deep ruby-garnet color and a capacity to improve, as *riserva*, with
5–10 years of aging, sometimes more. The *rosato* is the trio's bestseller,
understandably, with its pretty roseate color and finesse in scent and
flavor. It comes mainly from Bombino Nero. The *bianco*, from
Pampanuto and other grapes, has little to say. See also Il Falcone.
Ag. *riserva* 3 yrs (*rosso*).

Felice Botta                         Riforma Fondiaria
Bruno                                Rivera
Fattoria Torricciola                 Giuseppe Strippoli
Vittorio Jatta                       Torre Sveva
Gennaro Marasciuolo                  Vini Chiddo
Nuova Vinicola Picardi               Vinicola Palumbo

**Castel Mitrano** r. dr.  ★★→★★★   75 77 79 80 81 83
Elegant red table wine from Negroamaro and Malvasia Nera grown at
Mitrano near Brindisi. Dry, tannic, and warm, it needs 4–5 years before
starting to show its impressive bouquet.
Tenuta di Mitrano

**Chardonnay**
See Favonio.

**Copertino** DOC r. p. dr.  ★★→★★★   75 77 78 79 80 81 83
Red and rosé from Negroamaro primarily grown at Copertino. The *rosso*
can be one of Salento's finest reds, especially the *riserva*. Deep ruby,
velvety, rich in aroma and flavor, it has a nicely bitter undertone and
improves with 4–10 years. The *rosato* is salmon pink and finely scented.
Ag. *riserva* 2 yrs (*rosso*).
Barone Bacile di Castiglione

**Don Carmelo** r. p. dr.  ★★   78 79 80 81 83
Table wines from Negroamaro with Malvasia Nera grown at Cellino San
Marco near Brindisi by the popular singer Albano Carrisi. The *rosso* is
smooth and perfumed, best in 3–6 years. The *rosato* is to drink young.
Albano Carrisi

**Donna Marzia** r. p. w. dr.  ★★→★★★   75 77 78 79 80 81 83
Impressive red and white table wines made at Leverano on the Salento
peninsula. The *rosso*, based on Negroamaro, is rich and warm,
developing a smooth bouquet over 5–8 years, sometimes more. The
*bianco*, from Malvasia Bianca, has a fine aroma and more suavity than
you'd expect in a hot-climate dry white. Its straw-yellow color deepens
as it develops character over 2–3 years or more.
Conti Zecca

**Doxi Vecchio**
See Alezio.

**Favonio** r. w. dr.  ★★→★★★   78 79 80 81 82
The wines called Favonio made by Attilio Simonini defy (with
astonishing success) Apulian viticultural traditions. Though grown in
vineyards irrigated by a drip system on the hot, dry plain E of Foggia,
the white Pinot Bianco and Chardonnay can be as crisp and as fruity as
northern wines of those names. The full-blooded Cabernet Franc, with
its distinct bell pepper scent and flavor, equals nearly anything from the

Tre Venezie. The Pinot Nero and Trebbiano are less convincing.
Attilio Simonini

**Five Roses** p. dr.  ★★  73 75 77 78 79 80 81 83
Italy's first bottled rosé (in the 1930s), the name was given by U.S.
officers in Salento during World War II, a translation of the place it is
grown: Cinque Rose. Another curiosity is its longevity: after 5–6 years in
cask, it can hold up that long in bottle. Light cherry red, delicately
scented, its uniquely dry flavor doesn't betray its years – or strength of
13.5%.
Leone De Castris

**Galatina** r. dr.  ★★  81 83
From Malvasia and Negroamaro grown in the Salento town of Galatina,
this light table wine has a pale ruby color, fruity fragrance, best in 2–3
years.
Giuseppe Strippoli

**Gioia del Colle** r. dr.  ★→★★  77 78 79 81 82 83
Big, strong (14–16%) table wine from Primitivo grown around Gioia del
Colle, S of Bari. Dry but fleshy, it becomes redolent of berries and spices
like some of the similarly boisterous California Zinfandels. Takes 5–10
years of aging. Also known as Primitivo di Gioia.
Giuseppe Strippoli

**Gravina** DOC w. dr.  ★  DYA
New DOC for a white based on Verdeca grapes grown at Gravina near
the border of Basilicata SE of Bari.

**Il Falcone** r. dr.  ★★★→★★★★  73 75 77 79 81 83
Though sold as Castel del Monte *riserva*, this luxuriant red contains more
than the 35% Montepulciano specified by DOC. Needs 7–8 years.
Rivera

**Lacrima di Terra d'Otranto**
See Alezio.

**Leverano** DOC r. p. w. dr.  ★→★★  77 79 80 81 83
Recent DOC of Salento, the *rosso* and *rosato* come from Negroamaro. The
red, warm and smooth, is capable of aging. The rosé, fresh and fruity, is
to drink young. The *bianco*, from Malvasia, can be interesting.
C.S. Leverano                          Conti Zecca

**Locorotondo** DOC w. dr. (sp.)  ★→★★★  DYA
Made from Verdeca and Bianco d'Alessano grapes grown around the
whitewashed town of Locorotondo in the Itria valley. As made by the
local cooperative this may be the best DOC white of Apulia. Pale straw
green, subtly fruity, it is a briskly satisfying fish wine. However, some
look and taste almost bleached. A *spumante* version is permitted.
Borgo Canale                           Renna
C.S. di Locorotondo                    Riforma Fondiaria
Distante Vini                          Rivera
Leone De Castris                       Giuseppe Strippoli

**Lupinello** w. dr. fz.  ★★  DYA
Snappy pale yellow wine from grapes grown in N Apulia – in the new
style of light (10.5%), dry and fizzy.
Federico II

**Martina Franca** or **Martina** DOC w. dr. (sp.)  ★→★★  DYA
Almost identical to Locorotondo in grapes and personality, from around
one of Apulia's prettiest towns. The zone extends along the Itria to
Alberobello, capital of the conical *trulli* dwellings. A *spumante* is
permitted.
C.S. di Alberobello                    Miali
De Felice                              Riforma Fondiaria
Di Gregorio                            Giuseppe Strippoli
Lippolis                               Villa Valletta

**Matino** DOC r. p. dr.  ★  78 79 80 81 83
The southernmost DOC of Salento, Matino's *rosso* and *rosato* are based
on Negroamaro. Similar to other Salento wines, they are rarely seen.

**Mitrano** p. dr.  ★→★★  DYA
Tasty, light rosé based on Negroamaro grapes grown near Brindisi.
C.S. Mitrano                           Tenuta di Mitrano

**Moscato di Trani** DOC w. sw. ☐**★★** 77 78 79 81 82 83
Rich, golden dessert wine from Moscato Reale grapes grown inland from
the port of Trani as far as Cerignola. Luscious and velvety, it rates as one
of the better southern Italian Moscatos in two versions: *dolce naturale*
(15%) and *liquoroso* (18%).

Felice Botta                          Nuova Vinicola Picardi
Mauro De Cillis                    Rivera
Gennaro Marasciuolo

**Nardò** r. dr. ☐**★→★★** 79 80 81 83
Good table wine from Negroamaro and Malvasia Nera grown near
Lecce. Robust and warm with grapy aroma, it is best in 3–6 years.

Cantine Riunite del Salento          Giuseppe Strippoli

**Negrino** r. sw. **★★★** 67 70 75
Port-like red dessert wine made from semidried Malvasia Nera and
Negroamaro grapes and aged in barrels for at least a decade. Warm,
alcoholic (16%), and moderately sweet with bitter undertone, it
becomes velvety with great age. Recommended for convalescents.
Leone De Castris

**Negroamaro** or **Negramaro** r. p. dr. **★** 79 80
Red and rosé table wines from Negroamaro grapes of Salento.

C.S. de Lizzano                    Romano Luccarelli
Distante Vini                        Luigi Ruggeri

**Ostuni** DOC
The ancient town of Ostuni NW of Brindisi makes two distinct wines:
– **Bianco** w. dr. **★** DYA
Straw-yellow, delicate fish wine from Impigno and Francavilla grapes.
– **Ottavianello** r. dr. **★** 81 83
Light ruby, almost rosé, this subtly flavored wine from the Ottavianello
grape adapts to a range of foods. Drink in 2–3 years.
C.S. di Ostuni

**Pinot Bianco di Puglia** w. dr. **★★** DYA
Made experimentally from Pinot Bianco grown in the Castel del Monte
zone, the '83 was fruity, balanced and well-scented, promising an
interesting future.
Rivera

**Portulano** r. dr. **★★→★★★** 75 77 80 82
Fine dry table wine from Negroamaro and Malvasia Nera grown near
the Salento town of Alezio. Bright ruby with ample body, it develops a
generous bouquet and elegant tone with long finish after 5–6 years of
aging. It should now qualify as Alezio DOC.
Giuseppe Calò

**Primitivo di Gioia**
See Gioia del Colle.

**Primitivo di Manduria** DOC r. dr. sw. **★→★★** 75 77 78 79 81 83
Once used almost entirely for blending, Primitivo from around
Manduria E of Taranto is now occasionally made into varietal DOC
wine. It may be either dry or sweet, always big in body and strong with
deep purple color and blackberry-like flavor. The normal version may be
either dry or slightly *amabile*, a wine suited for heroic dishes. The sweet
versions are somewhat reminiscent of California Port. *Dolce naturale* must
have 16% alcohol, *liquoroso dolce naturale* 17.5%, and *liquoroso secco* 18%
(all with residual sugars). The normal and *dolce naturale* age from 3 years
to well over a decade. The *liquoroso*, which may not be sold for 2 years
after being fortified with alcohol, can last almost indefinitely. See also
Rosso di Sava.                          Giovanni Soloperto
Romano Luccarelli                  Vinicola Amanda

**Rosa del Golfo** p. dr. **★★★** DYA
One of Apulia's (and Italy's) best rosés; a table wine from Negroamaro
and Malvasia Nera grown near Alezio in Salento. Made by the ancient
"teardrop" system of soft crushing, it is bright cherry pink with flowery
scent and dry, harmonious, exquisite flavor. It now qualifies as Alezio
DOC.
Giuseppe Calò

**Rosato del Salento**
See Salento.

**Rosso Barletta** DOC r. dr.  ★→★★  80 81 83
Made from Uva di Troia grown around the N Apulian port of Barletta,
this ruby-garnet wine is usually refreshing if unremarkable young,
though it can develop something resembling style within 3–4 years.
Ag. *invecchiato* 2 yrs.

| | |
|---|---|
| C.S. di Barletta | Nuova Vinicola Picardi |
| Fattoria Torricciola | Giuseppe Strippoli |

**Rosso Canosa** DOC r. dr.  ★→★★  77 79 80 81 83
Red of sturdy structure from Uva di Troia and other varieties grown
around Canosa in N Apulia. Fresh and fruity when young, it shows some
finesse with age. It may also be called Canusium after the Roman name.
Ag. *riserva* 2 yrs.

| | |
|---|---|
| C.S. Nicola Rossi | Giuseppe Strippoli |

**Rosso del Salento**
See Salento.

**Rosso di Cerignola** DOC r. dr.  ★★  77 79 81 83
One of N Apulia's better reds, it is based on Uva di Troia and
Negroamaro grown around Cerignola. Ruby turning to brick red with
age, its fine bouquet and robust flavor support 4–8 years admirably.
Ag. *riserva* 3 yrs.
'Cirillo-Farrusi'

**Rosso di Sava** r. dr. or sw.  ★★→★★★  75 77 78 79 81 83
Name used by Librale Amanda for red wines from Primitivo grown at
the town of Sava. Dry or sweet, they qualify as Primitivo di Manduria
DOC and are the best wines of that name.
Vinicola Amanda

**Salento** r. p. w.  ★→★★★  80 81 82 83
Table wines from the Salento peninsula. The Rosso del Salento and
Rosato del Salento, both based on Negroamaro and Malvasia grapes,
are widely noted. The strong red can age well, the rosé can be
attractively fragrant and tasty. The white is rarely as good.

| | |
|---|---|
| Francesco Candido | Notarpanaro (Taurino) |
| Cantine Riunite del Salento | Santachiara (Medico) |
| Distante Vini | Giovanni Soloperto |
| Leone De Castris | Vinicola Venturi |
| Baroni Malfatti | Ubaldo Zanzarella |

**Salice Salentino** DOC r. p. dr.  ★★→★★★  75 77 78 79 80 81 83
Fine red and rosé from Negroamaro primarily grown around Salice
Salentino W of Lecce. The *rosso*, rich and velvety with bitter undertone
and impressive durability, stands out among Salento wines. The *rosato*
also has depth and, following tradition, is sometimes aged.
Ag. *prodotto invecchiato* 1 yr (*rosato*); *riserva* 2 yrs (*rosso*)

| | |
|---|---|
| Leone De Castris | Cosimo Taurino |
| Baroni Malfatti | |

**San Severo** DOC r. p. w. dr.  ★  81 83
Undistinguished wines from the Capitanata plain take this name.

| | |
|---|---|
| D'Alfonso Del Sordo | Aldo Pugliese |
| Federico II | Riforma Fondiaria |

**Spumante** p. w. (sw.) sp.  ★→★★  DYA
The mania for sparkling wines is spreading south, though Apulia so far
uses the *charmat* method. The local was Leone De Castris with white Don
Piero and pink Donna Lisetta. Rivera has a pink Rivera Brut.

| | |
|---|---|
| Leone De Castris | Rivera |

**Squinzano** DOC r. p. dr.  ★→★★★  77 78 79 80 81 82 83
Sound wines from Negroamaro grown at the Salento town of Squinzano.
The *rosso* needs a couple of years to develop robust goodness, the *riserva*
about 5 years. The *rosato* is bright coral pink, fresh, and tasty.
Ag. *riserva* 2 yrs (*rosso*).

| | |
|---|---|
| Renna | Villa Valletta |
| Giuseppe Strippoli | |

**Torre Alemanna** r. dr.  ★★  77 78 79 81 83
Red table wine of character from Malbec, Negroamaro, and Uva di

Troia grown near Cerignola. Deep garnet, dry, and balanced, will age.
Riforma Fondiaria

**Torre Quarto** r. p. w. dr.  ★→★★★  71 73 74 77 79 81
The vast estate of the Cirillo-Farrusi family near Cerignola makes some
of Apulia's finest red wine for aging. From Malbec, Uva di Troia, and
Negroamaro, it has a ruby-violet color taking on *pelure d'oignon* with age
as it develops a warm bouquet on a sturdy structure that can hold up
well over a decade from some vintages. *Rosato* and *bianco* are more
modest.
Cirillo-Farrusi

**Torre Saracena** r. dr.  ★★  77 78 79 81 83
Fleshy red table wine of sound character made from Malvasia Nera and
Negroamaro just outside Taranto. Deep ruby, it has a hint of sweetness
in its otherwise dry flavor. Ages 5–8 years.
Teodoro Caiulo

**Trani** r. dr.  ★  79 81 83
Sound table wine from Uva di Troia, with some aging capacity.
Giuseppe Strippoli

## Wine & Food

Balance seems built in to the Apulian diet, probably because the
region, if not perennially rich, has never lacked for nutritive
elements. The northern plains provide grain for pasta and bread;
the plateaus lamb, sausages, and cheese; the Adriatic and Ionian
seas fish. Everywhere there are vegetables, herbs, fruit, olive oil.

**Agnello al cartoccio** Lamb chops
baked in paper with green olives
and *lampasciuoli*, a wild, bitter-
tasting bulb similar to onion.
  ★★→★★★  Torre Quarto *rosso* or
  ★★  Rosso di Cerignola.
**Burrata** Soft, buttery cheese from
the town of Andria.
  ★★  young Castel del Monte *rosso*.
**Cavatieddi con la ruca** Conch-
shaped pasta served with *ruca*
(rue), tomato sauce and *pecorino*.
  ★★  Copertino *rosato*.
**Cozze alla leccese** Mussels
cooked with oil, lemon, and
parsley, one of dozens of ways of
preparing this favored shellfish.
  ★★  Martina Franca.
**Frisedde** Hard rolls softened with
water and served with fresh
tomato, oregano, and olive oil.
  ★★  Five Roses.
**Gniumerieddi** Lamb innards

flavored with *pecorino*, lard, lemon,
and parsley, rolled, skewered, and
cooked over coals.
  ★★  Primitivo di Manduria *secco*.
**'Ncapriata** Dried fava beans
boiled, peeled, and mashed with
chicory, pimentones, onion, tomato,
and lots of olive oil.
  ★★  Squinzano *rosato*.
**Orecchiette con cime di rapa**
Small, ear-shaped pasta served
with boiled turnip greens and chili.
  ★  Brindisi *rosato*.
**Ostriche alla tarantina** Fresh
oysters cooked with oil, parsley,
and breadcrumbs.
  ★★  Locorotondo.
**Tiella** Versatile baked layer
concoction, always containing
potatoes, usually rice, and
vegetables, with meat, cheese, or
seafood, a heritage of Spain.
  ★★  Castel del Monte *rosato*.

### Restaurants

Recommended in or near the wine zones: **North** *Ostello di Federico*
adjacent to Castel del Monte; *Cicolella* in Foggia (two restaurants);
*Cristoforo Colombo* at Trani. **Center** *Il Poeta Contadino* at Alberobello; *Casa
Mia* near Locorotondo; *Le Terrazze* at Martina Franca; *Da Renzina* at
Fasano; *Il Fagiano Da Gastone* at Selva di Fasano. **South** *Marechiaro* at
Gallipoli; *Da Guido & Figli* at Lecce; *Al Gambero* at Taranto.

# $\mathcal{B}asilicata$
## Basilicata

Basilicata lacks nearly every benefit that could rate it some sorely needed attention. It has no major monuments to its Greek and Roman past; two meager strips of seacoast; few exploitable natural resources; pleasant but hardly spectacular upland scenery; and not so much as a restaurant of renown.

That the region has only one DOC would seem to fit the pattern of deprivation, except that Aglianico del Vulture is one thing about Basilicata that isn't innately underprivileged. Had the fates been a little kinder, it might be universally recognized for what it is – one of Italy's great red wines. The Aglianico vine was brought to Monte Vulture by the Greeks; its name is a corruption of Hellenico. This late-maturing variety performs best in the heights of Basilicata and Campania.

Bàsilicata, whose alternative name is Lucania and whose capital is Potenza, is not a tourist paradise. But these days obscurity in itself is worth something. The ancient city of Matera has Greek-like charm, and wine lovers looking for out-of-the-way places will find them on Monte Vulture near the Naples-Bari *autostrada*.

### Recent vintages

Though Aglianico del Vulture has extraordinary aging potential, only in the last decade have producers in the zone improved vinification and aging techniques to realize the optimum.

1983 Some good wine, but rain marred the harvest, bringing uneven results.
1982 Drought, then rain and hail resulted in a spotty, subpar crop.
1981 Down by 40% but exceptional, certainly the best since '73. Wines to lay down.
1980 Fair to good, though earthquakes ruined the late harvest.
1979 Excellent, abundant vintage. Start to drink in the late 1980s.
1978 Uniformly good year.
1977 Outstanding crop of long-lived wines. Good, getting better.
1976 Poor.
1975 Very good wines for medium-long aging.
1974 Average quality; not wines to keep.
1973 Some exceptional wines nearing prime.
1972 Poor.
1971 Good, but getting old.

**Aglianico dei Colli Lucani** r. dr. (s/sw.) (sp.) ★→★★ 75 77 78 79 81
Table wine from Aglianico grown in E Basilicata, notably around towns of Irsina and Tricarico in Matera province. Similar to Aglianico del Vulture when young (also in *amabile* and *spumante*), but it fails to rival the sheer grandeur of the DOC wine, though it does well with 5–6 years, often more, of aging. Also made in Apulia.
Vinicola Miali

**Aglianico del Vulture** DOC r. dr. (s/sw.) (sp.) ★★→★★★★ 73 75 77 78 79 81
From Aglianico grapes grown on the E slopes of Monte Vulture and hills to the SE past Venosa to Genzano. Though it may be sold after a year as a dry wine or a lightly *amabile spumante*, it's the aged Aglianico that stands in the front rank of Italian wines. Deep ruby to garnet, taking on orange reflections with age in barrel and bottle, its bouquet heightens as it becomes richly smooth with unusual depth of flavors. The better grapes come from volcanic soil high up around Rionero and Barile where microclimates are similar to those in alpine regions. Potential

production of 700,000 bottles a year is rarely realized. The **★★★★** rating applies to '73, '77, '79 and '81 vintages from Fratelli D'Angelo, though others can approach that level. The DOC permits vinification in Apulia. Ag. 1 yr; *vecchio* 3 yrs (2 in barrel); *riserva* 5 yrs.

| | |
|---|---|
| Botte | Miali |
| Consorzio Viticoltori | Fratelli Napolitano |
|   Associati del Vulture | Paternoster |
| Fratelli D'Angelo | Torre Sveva |
| Armando Martino | |

**Asprino** or **Asprinio** w. dr. fz.  **★  DYA**
Curiously acidic, fizzy white from Asprinio grapes grown around the town of Ruoti. Most is sent with haste to Naples.

**Malvasia del Vulture** w. or am. dr. sw. sp.  **★  DYA**
Virtually the same as Malvasia della Lucania but restricted to the Vulture zone, where it is usually sweet and sparkling.

| | |
|---|---|
| Fratelli D'Angelo | Paternoster |
| Armando Martino | Sasso |

**Malvasia della Lucania** w. or am. dr. sw. (sp.)  **★  DYA**
Ancient Malvasia vines grown in various places, notably Val Bradano, render dry, sweet, fortified, and often sparkling wines. The dry versions, of various yellow shades, are to drink quickly. The sweet, from semidried grapes, are golden to amber and can keep. *Spumante* is usually sweet.

**Metapontum** r. w. dr.  **★  81 83**
Table wines from the Ionian coastal plain around Metaponto: the *rosso* from Sangiovese, Negroamaro, Malvasia Nera, the *bianco* from Malvasia Bianca and Trebbiano.
C.S. del Metapontino

**Montepulciano di Basilicata** r. dr.  `★→★★`  79 81 83
Table wine from Montepulciano grapes grown near Metaponto. Robust, round, well-scented, it is good for 2–6 years.
C.S. del Metapontino

**Moscato del Vulture** w. sw. sp.  `★→★★`  DYA
Dessert wines, usually sparkling, from Moscato grapes of the Vulture zone. Golden yellow, sweet, aromatic, low in alcohol, and best young.

| | |
|---|---|
| Botte | Armando Martino |
| Consorzio Viticoltori | Paternoster |
|   Associati del Vulture | Sasso |
| Fratelli D'Angelo | |

*Wine & Food*

The cooking of Basilicata may be as lean and spare as the landscape, but it has a warmth that comes directly from the summer sun. Appetites are satisfied with ample servings of beans, pasta, soups, potatoes, and bread. Vegetables play a starring role in stews cooked with olive oil and plenty of herbs and spices. Pimento (known as *diavolicchio*) goes into a sauce called *piccante*, fiery enough to live up to its name and more. In the old days, meat was used thriftily in, for example, preserved pork products: *soppressata*, *coppa*, or the piquant *luganighe* sausages.

**Cazmarr** Stew of lamb's innards, *prosciutto*, cheese, and wine.
**★★→★★★** Aglianica del Vulture *vecchio*.

**Ciammotta** Peppers, potatoes, eggplant, tomato, and garlic – first fried, then stewed.
**★** Malvasia della Lucania *secco*.

**Lasagne e fagioli** Lasagne and beans laced with pepper and garlic.
**★** Metapontum *rosso*, young.

**Minuich** Hand-made pasta rolled into cylinders around a slim metal stick, sometimes served with cabbage greens.
**★** Malvasia del Vulture *secco*.

**Pignata** Lamb marinated with vegetables, hot peppers, cheese, and wine in a sealed earthenware pot (*la pignata*) and left to simmer on the hearth for hours.
**★★** Aglianico dei Colli Lucani.

### Restaurants
Recommended near Monte Vulture: *La Pergola* at Rionero; *Al Fusillo* and *Grottino dell'Arco* at Avigliano.

# Calabria

Calabria

Once a garden of the Greeks, who favored its wines over others of Enotria, Calabria is striving gamely to recapture its antique vinicultural luster. They say Calabrian athletes returning in triumph from an early Olympiad were hailed with Krimisa, which, if not the "world's oldest wine," as some contend, was probably among the earliest in Europe. Krimisa was made where Cirò is made today, on the Ionian coast between the sites of the Greek cities of Sybaris and Kroton.

Cirò remains the paragon of Calabrian wines, the only well-known name among the 8 DOCs. Cirò *rosso* and *rosato* derive from Gaglioppo, as do most Calabrian reds, though the others, if sound and flavorful, rarely show the breed of the aged Cirò. White Cirò comes from Greco Bianco, a lively relic capable of both bright, modern dry wines and luxuriant, old-style dessert wines, the sweetest and best being Greco di Bianco.

The toe of the Italian boot is so mountainous that most vineyards are confined to rugged, relatively cool hillsides – probably a blessing because big yields are out of the question and the alternative is the pursuit of quality. Most Calabrian wines, Cirò excepted, can be found only on their home grounds. Several are well worth seeking out.

Calabria's tourist attractions are mostly natural: the Sila Massif (Italy's "Little Switzerland") in the north around Cosenza and Catanzaro (the region's capital); and the Aspromonte range in the south, overlooking Reggio di Calabria and, across the straits, Sicily's Mount Etna. Remnants of the Greeks are evident along the coasts, the most scenic of which is the Calabrian Riviera between Reggio and Gioia Tauro.

**Wine Zones**
1 Lamezia
2 Pollino
3 Savuto

## Recent vintages

The chart applies to Cirò, though it serves as a guideline to other Calabrian wines, such as Donnici, Pollino, Savuto, and Melissa.

1983   Despite drought, Cirò was up in quality and quantity.
1982   Drought reduced crop of middling to good wines.
1981   Small harvest of generally good wines, notably Cirò.
1980   Some acceptable wines from select grapes.
1979   Fine, abundant crop of durable reds.
1978   Generally excellent, long-lived wines.
1977   Mixed results, some good wines.
1976   Poor.
1975   Good, normal vintage, for medium aging.
1974   Very good, durable wines.
1973   Excellent wines, Cirò in prime form now.

**Cerasuolo di Scilla** p. dr. or s/sw.  ★ DYA
Cherry-pink local wine of Scilla (the legendary Scylla at the top of the Straits of Messina) made from a mix that includes Alicante.

**Cirò** DOC r. p. w. dr.  ★→★★★   73 74 77 78 79 81 83
A name of ancient renown applied to three colors of wine from the Ionian coastal hills around Cirò and Cirò Marina. The *rosso*, from Gaglioppo with 10% of light Greco or Trebbiano permitted, is ample and strong (13.5%), with deep bouquet and velvety texture. With 5–8 years of age, sometimes more, it develops a distinct ruby-amber color. The *rosato*, from the same grapes as the red, can be a good all-purpose wine. The *bianco*, from the worthy Greco Bianco grape, was often lackluster, but cold fermentation and other techniques have immensely improved the white from certain producers. Wines from the heart of the zone may be labeled *classico*.
Ag. *riserva* 3 yrs (*rosso*).

C.S. Caparra & Siciliani          Antonio Librandi
C.S. Torre Melissa               Antonio Scala
Fratelli Caruso                  Tenute Pirainetto (Nicodemo)
Vincenzo Ippolito

**Donnici** DOC r. dr.  ★→★★   81 83
Medium ruby to light red from Gaglioppo and Greco Nero grapes grown in hills adjacent to Cosenza. Fruity, fragrant, and unimposing, it is good fairly young and fresh.
Pasquale Bozzo                   Opera Sila C.S. di Donnici

**Greco di Bianco** DOC w. sw.  ★★→★★★★   75 77 78 79 81 83
Made from Greco grapes grown around the SE Calabrian seaside town of Bianco, this can be one of Italy's outstanding dessert wines. Golden, velvety, and luscious but not cloying, it has an entrancing orange blossom aroma and about 17% alcohol. With great age it tends to become drier and more richly scented, though its balance seems best in 4–8 years. Rare, expensive, and consistently excellent from Umberto Ceratti, who used to call the wine Greco di Gerace. New plantings promise more of this newly tapped DOC wine.
Ag. 1 yr.
Cacib                            Francesco Saporito
Umberto Ceratti

**Lacrima di Castrovillari** r. dr. sw.  ★★   81 83
Full-flavored table wine from Lacrima Nera and Gaglioppo. *Secco* or *amabile*, it has deep ruby-violet color, fresh, richly fruity flavor and strength (14%). Drink in 1–3 years.
Alia                             C.S. Vini del Pollino

**Lametino** w. dr. (sw.)  ★ DYA
The white version of Lamezia, which is DOC only in *rosso*. Made from Greco and Malvasia, when dry it is soft and easy, when *amabile* mouth-fillingly rich.
C.S. di Sambiase

**Lamezia** DOC r. dr.  ★ DYA
Dry red from Nerello Mascalese, Nerello Cappuccio, Gaglioppo, and Greco Nero grown around Lamezia Terme, Sant' Eufemia, Sambiase,

and Filadelfia, W of Catanzaro. Cherry red, sometimes almost rosé, refreshingly uncomplex, it is best young.
C.S. di Sambiase

**Mantonico di Bianco** am. dr. or s/sw. ★★→★★★  75 77 78 79 81 83
Made from semidried light Mantonico grapes grown around Bianco, it becomes a strong (15–16%) amber wine that needs barrel age to develop a Sherry-like style. Whether dry or slightly sweet, it retains a tannic, lightly bitter almond undertone and a curiously citrus-like aroma.
Cacib                                    Francesco Saporito
Umberto Ceratti

**Melissa** DOC r. w. dr.  ★→ ★★  78 79 81 83
Recent DOC from the Ionian coast around Melissa, Strongoli, and Crotone–adjacent (and similar) to Cirò. The *rosso*, based on Gaglioppo, is dry, rather full, capable of becoming interesting in 5–6 years. The *bianco*, based on Greco Bianco, can be dry and crisp, good with fish.
Ag. *superiore* 2 yrs (*rosso*).
C.S. Torre Melissa                       Giuseppe Ippolito

**Moscato** w. s/sw. sw. (sp.)  ★→★★  DYA
Dessert wines made in many places from Moscato grapes, often semidried. Golden, aromatic, sometimes lightly sweet and sparkling but more often rich, strong and smooth.
Alia

**Nicastro** r. w. dr. (sw.)  ★  DYA
Recognized table wines from the town of Nicastro. The *rosso*, from Nerello and Gaglioppo, is a fruity wine, similar to the neighboring Lamezia. The *bianco*, usually dry, is based on Malvasia Bianca.

**Pellaro** r. p. dr.  ★→ ★★  79 81 83
Red and rosé table wines from Alicante and other varieties grown on the Pellaro promontory S of Reggio di Calabria. Light in color (cherry red to pink), it is robust, strong (up to 16%), and can improve over 3–5 years.
Vincenzo Oliva                           Pasquale Scaramozzino
Cristoforo Pastorino

**Pollino** DOC r. dr.  ★→ ★★  78 79 81 83
Sturdy red from Gaglioppo and Greco Nero grown in the Monti Pollino around Castrovillari and Frascineto. Light, almost rosé in color, it has fruity fragrance, good body, and can show class with 2–5 years.
Ag. *superiore* 2 yrs.
C.S. Vini del Pollino                     Basilio Miraglia

**Sant'Anna di Isola Capo Rizzuto** DOC r. dr.  ★  DYA
Inconsequential but tasty red from Gaglioppo and a host of other varieties grown on the Ionian coastal hills SW of Crotone near the town of Isola di Capo Rizzuto. Roseate red, it is best young and cool.
C.S. Sant'Anna

**Savuto** DOC r. p. dr.  ★★  79 81 83
One of Calabria's better reds, from Gaglioppo and Greco Nero principally, grown on steep hills along the Savuto River S of Cosenza. Light ruby and fragrant, it can develop charm with 3–5 years of age.
Ag. *superiore* 2 yrs.
C.S. Vini di Savuto (G. Longo)           Istituto Professionale di Stato
                                         F. Todaro

**Squillace** w. dr.  ★→★★  DYA
Fragile but convincing white from Greco Bianco, Malvasia, and others grown at Squilláce SW of Catanzaro. Young (and on the spot) it is pale gold with a hint of sweetness, though it qualifies as dry.

**Villa Santelia** w. dr.  ★★  DYA
Good white table wine based on Greco grown in the Cirò area.
Fratelli Caruso

## Wine & Food

Calabria, behind its mountain barriers, has always lived in splendid isolation. Its cooking, although drawing on standard southern Italian ingredients, expresses this independence. Pork is so important that the pig has been called Calabria's "sacred cow." The great peasant tradition (which survives in home kitchens if rarely in restaurants) relies on soups, pastas, and vast arrays of vegetables. When not in season, peppers, zucchini (courgettes), artichokes, eggplant, and mushrooms are preserved in olive oil, of which the region is a major producer. Besides the usual range of shellfish, Tyrrhenian waters provide swordfish and tuna. Calabrians adore sweets, often based on citrus and other fruit, either candied or dried, such as figs filled with chocolate.

**Alalonga in agrodolce** Tender small tuna caught in Calabrian waters cooked sweet-sour.
   ★ Cerasuolo di Scilla.
**Cicirata** Christmas pastries flavored with either honey or cooked grape must and lemon.
   ★★★→★★★★ Greco di Bianco.
**Melanzane a polpetta** Eggplant stewed with eggs, garlic, pepper, and breadcrumbs.
   ★ Sant'Anna di Isola Capo Rizzuto.
**Mursiellu alla catanzarese** Rich stew of various pieces of pork, tomatoes, and peppers.
   ★★ Savuto or ★★ Cirò *rosso*.
**Mùstica** Newborn anchovies with oil and lemon.
   ★★ Squillace.
**Pesce spada** Swordfish, a speciality of Bagnara on the Calabrian Riviera, with peppers, lemon, garlic, capers, and herbs.
   ★★ Cirò *bianco*.
**Pitta chicculiata** Calabrian pizza – a sort of pie filled with tuna, tomato, anchovies, black olives, and capers.
   ★ Cirò *rosato*.
**Sagne chine** Festive lasagne baked with as many ingredients between the layers as possible, usually pork, peas, artichokes, and mushrooms.
   ★★ Savuto or ★★ Donnici.

## Restaurants
Recommended in or near wine zones: **Cirò-Melissa** *Il Gabbiano* at Cirò Marina; *Il Girrarosto* at Crotone; *Concordia* at Torre Melissa; **Donnici** *La Calavrisella* at Cosenza; **Lamezia** *Pesce Fresco* at Gizzeria Lido; **Pollino** *Alia* at Castrovillari.

# Campania

Campania

Both Greeks and Romans knew that vines thrived as nowhere else in the volcanic soil of Campania. The Greeks introduced vines now known as Aglianico and Greco and the Romans celebrated the wines of Avellino, Vesuvius, and Falernum. Sadly, Campanian viticulture has never fully recovered from a decline that began with the fall of the Roman Empire. Today, the region of Naples produces much less wine than conditions would permit. But what really lacks is a sense of quality; 99.6% of production is outside DOC. Though some table wines are admirable, many reinforce the notion that Campanian wines are lightweights masquerading under touristy, melodramatic names.

Interestingly, though, what little serious wine there is confirms the wisdom of the ancients. Campania's best wines today come from Aglianico, Greco, and Fiano (a Roman flavorite) in the hills of Avellino. One winery there stands out, Mastroberardino, which is also striving to restore the ancient luster of Vesuvius. The volcano's wines are burdened with the legendary but overworked name of Lacryma Christi (Christ's Tear), one reason why the long overdue DOC still wasn't in effect by 1982.

Falernum or Falernian is not what it used to be, and just as well as modern palates wouldn't tolerate resin, salt water, and honey. However, a red called Falerno (from Anglianico) proves that the Romans understood the privileged nature of the place.

Though most wines of maritime Campania, from the Gulf of Naples to Sorrento and Salerno, are laughable at best, exceptions include certain wines of the island of Ischia and the resort town of Ravello on the Amalfi coast.

Campania's fabled tourist sites – Capri, Pompeii, Herculaneum, Sorrento, Amalfi, Ischia, Paestum, and Naples – need no further promotion. Wine lovers, who should find Ischia rewarding in the off-season, might be even more excited by the wines around Avellino and Benevento. The *Enoteca Partenopea* in Naples provides a discriminating selection from Campania and other regions.

**1** Falerno
**2** Greco di Tufo
**3** Lacryma Christi
**4** Taurasi

## Recent vintages

The chart applies to wines of Avellino. Recommended years for others are shown with each entry.

1983  Latest in a series of fine vintages in the hills.
1982  Sharply reduced due to drought, but wines were very good.
1981  Exceptional harvest, slightly reduced but for Taurasi probably the best since the memorable '68.
1980  Latest harvest in memory resulted in excellent Fiano and Greco, but earthquakes crippled Taurasi's production.
1979  Great but limited harvest for Fiano and Greco; rain spoiled Taurasi's promising start, though a little fine wine was salvaged.
1978  Fine, abundant harvest; start drinking Taurasi about 1985.
1977  Very good year for the whites, exceptional for Taurasi to drink in the late 1980s.
1976  Damp and cool; fair wines at best.
1975  Very good year; drink Taurasi now.
1974  Average crop, not for aging.
1973  Excellent harvest; long-lived Taurasi approaching top form.
Earlier fine vintages: '71, '68, '61, '58.

**Amber Drops** am. sw.  ★★  77 78 79 81 83
Sherry-like sweet wine from raisined Biancolella grapes of Ischia. Amber yellow with rich, woody aroma after aging in *barriques*, it becomes soft and smooth over 7–10 years.
D'Ambra Vini d'Ischia

**Asprino** w. dr. fz.  ★  DYA
Fizzy, fragile, acidic, lemon-yellow wine served over the counter in Naples as a thirst quencher. Most of this light (8–9%) wine comes from Asprinio grapes grown in Caserta province.

**Barbera** r. dr.  ★→★★  81 82 83
The Piedmont grape is used for table wines in several areas, notably the Sannio and Irpinia hills around Benevento and Avellino, where it is also blended with others. Dark and robust, the wines are best in 1–3 years.
La Vinicola Ocone

**Biancolella** w. dr.  ★★  DYA
Table wine from Biancolella grapes of Ischia. Light golden yellow and nicely scented, it is sharply dry but well textured. Good young.
D'Ambra Vini d'Ischia

**Capri** DOC r. w. dr.  ★  DYA
Simple wines designed to appeal to visitors of the lovely but touristy isle, though grapes for their extremely limited production may also come from certain spots on the mainland as well as Capri. The *rosso*, from Piedirosso and others, is medium-ruby, dry, and drinkable if you're lucky. The *bianco*, from Falanghina and Greco, can be drunk with fish.
De Rosa

**Cilento** r. (p.) (s/sw.) (sp.)  ★→★★  79 81 83
Red, occasionally rosé, wines in various styles, even *amabile* and *spumante*. The red from Primitivo, Guarnaccia, and others is often used for blending, but it can also be a fine table wine with 3–5 years of aging.
C.S. di Cilento

**Don Alfonso** r. p. w. dr.  ★→★★  79 81 83
Good table wines of Ischia made from composites of the island's dark and light varieties. The name comes from Don Alfonso Perrazzo, founder of a leading winery.
Perrazzo

**Falerno** r. w. dr.  ★→★★★  77 78 79 80 81 83
Italianized name for Falernum, the Roman favorite. The *rosso* from Aglianico grown around the NW Campania coastal town of Mondragone, is a fine, full-bodied table wine that improves with 4–6 years or more. The *bianco*, from Falanghina, is of little note.
Michele Moio                    Villa Matilde

**Fiano di Avellino** DOC w. dr.  ★★→★★★★  79 80 81 82 83
Exceptional dry white wine from Fiano – a derivation of Apianum, the

Roman name that acknowledged the bees' (*Apis*) attraction to the grape
– grown in hills surrounding Avellino. Light straw, smoothly textured,
with a scent of pears and hazelnuts, it has a dry, elegant, lingering flavor.
Wine from the community of Lapio, considered the most privileged part
of the DOC zone, may use Fiano di Lapio as a subdenomination.
Production is about 40,000 bottles a year.
Mastroberardino                          Scuola Enologica Avellino

**Forastera** w. dr.  ★  DYA
Pale straw table wine from Forastera grapes of Ischia – dry and fresh.
D'Ambra Vini d'Ischia

**Gragnano** r. dr. (s/sw.) fz. sp.  ★→★★  81 83
Refreshing purplish table wine, often *frizzante* or *spumante*, sometimes off-
sweet. Made from various combinations of grapes, which may include
Aglianico, Olivella, and Per'e Palummo, grown near the town of
Gragnano in the hills of the Sorrentine peninsula.
Saviano

**Greco di Tufo** DOC w. dr. (sp.)  ★★★  81 82 83
Fine dry white from Greco grapes of antiquity grown around the village
of Tufo in the hills of Irpinia N of Avellino. Pale straw to medium yellow,
both its bouquet and flavor suggest almond. Mastroberardino's
Vignadangelo, from a special vineyard, has the character to evolve
favorably over 3–4 years. The *spumante* is rarely seen.
Mastroberardino

**Ischia** DOC r. w. dr.  ★→★★  82 83
Light reds and whites from the resort island on the Gulf of Naples. Most
are common, but those from a couple of producers have deservedly wide
followings. The *rosso*, from Guarnaccia and Per'e Palummo, is a good all-
purpose wine, young and fresh. The *bianco*, from Forastera and
Biancolella, is a light refresher. Ischia *bianco superiore*, a very good fish
wine, comes from the same grapes grown in select parts of the island. It
may be fermented briefly with the skins and refermented with musts of
semidried grapes to give it character.
D'Ambra Vini d'Ischia                    Perrazzo

**Lacrimarosa d'Irpinia** p. dr.  ★★  DYA
Delicate rosé from Aglianico grapes of Irpinia processed under the
*lacrima* or teardrop system, which gives it a topaz-pink color and dry,
crisp, clean flavor.
Mastroberardino

**Lacryma Christi del Vesuvio**
See Vesuvio.

**Lettere** r. dr.  ★★  DYA
Round, refreshing table wine of special drinkability, made from a
labyrinthian mélange of grapes, including Aglianico, Olivella, and Per'e
Palummo, grown at Lettere near Sorrento. Dry and supple, served cool
it goes with many dishes. Growers have requested DOC.
Antonio Pentangelo

**Per'e Palummo** r. dr.  ★★  79 81 82 83
Good table wine of Ischia made from Per'e Palummo with some
Guarnaccia. Well-structured, medium-ruby, it develops bouquet and
smooth flavor with 3–5 years.
D'Ambra Vini d'Ischia

**Ravello** r. p. w. dr.  ★★→★★★  77 78 79 82 83
Fine table wines, the best of the Amalfi coast, from the lovely town of
Ravello. The *rosso*, from Per'e Palummo, Aglianico, Merlot, and others,
is dry, balanced, elegant, and capable of 5–10 years of aging (Episcopio
*rosso* is a superior example). The *rosato*, from the same grapes as the red, is
burnished pink, clean, and easy. The *bianco*, from Coda di Volpe, San
Nicola, Greco, and others, is a fish wine of more than usual character.
Episcopio (Vuilleumier)                  Gran Caruso

**Solopaca** DOC r. w. dr.  ★→★★  81 82 83
Unsung DOC zone named after a town in the Sannio hills W of
Benevento. The *rosso*, from Sangiovese with some Aglianico and
Piedirosso, is ruby red and pleasantly soft, good in 2–4 years. The *bianco*,

from Trebbiano Toscano and Malvasia, is common.
C.S. La Guardiense                          La Vinicola Ocone

**Sorrento** r. p. w. dr.  ★ DYA
Simple table wines from various grapes grown on the Sorrento peninsula.
Usually served locally from the latest vintage.
De Rosa

**Taurasi** DOC r. dr.  ★★→★★★★  73 75 77 78 80 81 82 83
One of Italy's great aged red wines (most notably from
Mastroberardino) made from the late-maturing Aglianico grape grown
in the cool Irpinia hills NE of Avellino around the village of Taurasi.
Deep ruby when young, it takes on an onion-skin color with age as its
bouquet enhances and its youthful robustness tones down to a velvety
austereness. Rich, complete, and highly personal, it excels with roasts.
Ag. 3 yrs (1 in barrel); *riserva* 4 yrs.
Mastroberardino                          Saviano

**Vesuvio** DOC r. p. w. (sw.) (sp.)  ★→★★★  83
Finally approved as DOC in 1983, Vesuvio takes in *rosso*, *rosato* and *bianco*
of rather common stature and Lacryma Christi del Vesuvio in superior
versions. The red wine comes from Piedirosso and Olivella grapes, the
white from Coda di Volpe primarily grown on the lower slopes of Mt
Vesuvius or nearby. Lacryma Christi can become a notable, generous
garnet red, capable of 3–6 years of aging or more. The white can be dry,
semisweet, or sweet (also *liquoroso*) and may be sparkling.
Mastroberardino                          Saviano

## Wine & Food

It is hard to imagine that Naples was once a gastronomic capital
– under the Romans and again under various monarchs between
the late Middle Ages and Italy's unification. The sumptuous
dining of the past has since been replaced by the culinary
improvisations that perfume the alleyways of Naples: onions,
garlic, and herbs stewing with tomatoes for a *pommarola* sauce;
pastries frying in hot grease; steaming *espresso*; and fresh fish.
That many of Campania's specialities can be eaten standing up
should not detract from their inherent worth.

**Capretto in agrodolce** Sweet-
sour kid, a speciality of Irpinia.
Lamb is also done that way.
★★→★★★★  Taurasi.
**Cianfotta** Peppers, onions,
tomatoes, eggplant, and zucchini
stewed in oil and eaten cold.
  ★★ Ravello *rosato* or *bianco*.
**Mozzarella in carozza**
*Mozzarella* sandwiches coated with
batter and deep-fried in olive oil.
  ★★★★ Fiano di Avellino
or  ★★★ Greco di Tufo.
**'Mpepata di cozze** Fresh mussels
served in their cooking water with
lemon, pepper, and parsley.
  ★ Ischia *bianco*.

**Parmigiana di melanzane** or
**melanzane alla parmigiana**
Campanian classic: eggplant
baked with tomato sauce,
*mozzarella*, and Parmesan.
  ★★ Lacrimarosa d'Irpinia.
**Pizza napoletana** The original,
with tomatoes, oregano, and fresh
basil – or, with *mozzarella* and
Parmesan added as a Margherita.
  ★ Asprino or  ★ Vesuvio *bianco
secco*.
**Spaghetti alla puttanesca**
"Strumpet's spaghetti" dressed
with tomato, pepper, capers,
olives, and anchovies, a speciality
of Ischia.
  ★★ Biancolella.

### Restaurants
Recommended in or near wine zones: **Amalfi-Sorrento** *Cappuccini
Convento* near Amalfi; *La Canonica* at Lettere; *Antico Francischiello da Peppino*
and *Maria Grazia* at Massalubrense; *Buca di Bacco* and *La Cambusa* at
Positano; *Caruso al Belvedere* and *Da Palumbo al Confalone* at Ravello; *La
Spagnola al Porto* at Salerno; *O'Parrucchiano* at Sorrento; **Avellino** *Barone*
and *La Caveja* at Avellino; **Capri** *Aurora* and *La Pigna*.

# Emilia-Romagna

Emilia-Romagna

Bologna "the fat" dotes over a region that sometimes carries its plenitude to excess. Wine isn't usually thought of as a product of the flatlands, but here in the broad Po Valley there is no ignoring it. Lambrusco is one of numerous plains wines that contributed to Emilia-Romagna's 1.281 billion liter harvest of 1980 – a record for an Italian region that also surpassed the output of such wine nations as Portugal, West Germany, and Yugoslavia.

Lambrusco's conquests in America (where it accounts for about half of Italian imports) steal the show while even worthier products of the Apennine foothills (which stretch along the region's southern flank from Piacenza to the Adriatic) wait in the wings. Emilia, the western sector, makes Lambrusco, as well as Gutturnio and some remarkably good innovations in the hills of Bologna and Piacenza. Romagna, between Bologna and the Adriatic, has three improving DOC varietals that bear its name – Albana, Sangiovese, and Trebbiano – and a host of little known table wines that can be every bit as worthy.

**Wine zones**
1 Albana di Romagna
2 Colli Bolognesi
3 Colli di Parma
4 Colli Piacentini
5 Lambrusco di Sorbara
6 Lambrusco Grasparossa di Castelvetro
7 Lambrusco Reggiano
8 Lambrusco Salamino di Santa Croce
9 Sangiovese di Romagna
10 Trebbiano di Romagna

Emilians and Romagnans delight in bantering over their differences, which indeed exist, if less so now than in the past. Both have a distinct range of vines and work them in their own way. Emilians prefer their wines bubbly, Romagnans tend to like theirs still, but both drink them young because they've learned that the richest, most glorified cooking of Italy is complemented by youthful freshness. Wines for aging are exceptions here.

Emilia-Romagna's prosperous small cities hold treasures of art and architecture. Of special interest are Bologna, Ravenna, Parma, Ferrara, Modena, and Piacenza. The Adriatic Riviera is overwhelmingly popular in summer, especially Rimini. Wine tourism is being developed in the region, notably in Romagna, through the *Ente Tutela Vini Romagnoli* (its symbol is the bearded *Passatore* in tilted hat, whose image graces bottles of approved wines). The wine house, a Romagnan institution, has been revived at Bertinoro (*Ca' de Bé*), Predappio Alto (*Ca' de Sanzves*), Ravenna (*Ca' de Vèn*), and Rimini (*Chésa de Vein*). Wine routes lead to vineyards of Sangiovese, Albana, and Trebbiano. In Emilia, the scenic Colli Bolognesi and Colli Piacentini offer many little-known good wines: the *enoteca* at Castell' Arquato displays the Piacentini wines. Lambrusco's admirers can slake their thirst in the lush plains around Modena and Reggio, specifically at the *enoteca* in the castle at Levizzano Rangone near Castelvetro. The Enoteca Regionale Emilia-Romagna is housed in the Rocca Sforzesca, a medieval castle at Dozza in Romagna's hills.

### Recent vintages

White wines and Lambrusco are to drink young, so this guideline applies mainly to red wines of Emilia (Gutturnio, Barbera, Cabernet, and Merlot) and Romagna (Sangiovese, Rosso Armentano, and Barbarossa).

| | |
|---|---|
| 1983 | A plentiful, good harvest, notable in Colli Bolognesi. |
| 1982 | Overall a decent vintage, outstanding in Romagna. |
| 1981 | Fine year for Lambrusco, but disappointing for most others, particularly in Romagna. |
| 1980 | Record harvest; delightful results in Romagna, satisfactory or better in Emilia. |
| 1979 | Limited, but fine wines nearly everywhere. |
| 1978 | Very good in Romagna, spotty elsewhere. |
| 1977 | Vintage of the decade in Romagna, mediocre elsewhere. |

**Albana di Romagna** DOC w. dr. or s/sw. (sp.) ⌜★→★★★⌝  80 82 83
Romagna's preferred white from the time-honored Albana grape grown in a vast hilly zone between Bologna and Rimini. Either dry or *amabile*, it may also be *spumante*, which is increasingly popular. The *secco*, straw to golden yellow, delicately scented, at best cleanly dry, fruity, and smoothly textured with a bitter-almond background, is to drink in a year or two. The *amabile*, with golden highlights, has fruity fragrance and grapy sweetness from better producers; it holds up for 3–5 years from good vintages. Though DOCG has been requested, Albana seems an unlikely candidate, for quality among some 10 million bottles a year is uneven. New techniques, however, should help others to achieve the consistently superior class of Fratelli Vallunga, Fattoria Paradiso, and Ferrucci.

| | |
|---|---|
| Luigi Baldrati | C. Guidi & Figli |
| Ca' Muma | Marabini |
| C.S. Forlì | Pasolini Dall'Onda |
| Carradora | Provit |
| Celli | Fratelli Ravaioli |
| Cesari | Ronchi |
| Colombina | Ronco |
| Comune di Faenza | Ruffo-Bacci |
| Fratelli Conti | Spalletti |
| Corovin | Tenuta Panzacchia |
| Costa-Archi | Tenuta Zerbina |
| Emiliani | Trerè |
| Fattoria Paradiso | Fratelli Vallunga (Moronico) |
| Ferrucci | Fratelli Varoli |
| Guarini Fabri | Vino dell'Olimpo (Saporetti) |
| Guarini Matteucci di Castelfalcino | |

**Barbarossa di Bertinoro** r. dr.  ★★★  77 79 81 82 83
Unique red from vines discovered by Mario Pezzi and propagated within a plot called *Vigna del Dosso* near Bertinoro. Deep garnet and robust, with rich bouquet, it is already good after 2 years, and excellent

from 5 to 10 as it becomes velvety and austere.
Fattoria Paradiso

**Barbera** r. dr. (fz.)   ★  82 83
The dry, tasty, sometimes frothy table wines are made in Emilia's hills.
DOC in Colli Bolognesi it will also become one in Colli Piacentini.

**Bianco della Pusterla** w. s/sw.   ★★  82 83
Lightly sweet, aromatic white from Malvasia, Moscato, Greco and
Ortrugo grown at Vigolo Marchese in the Colli Piacentini. Suave and
seductive, it is best in 1–3 years.
Pusterla

**Bianco di Scandiano** DOC w. dr. s/sw. fz. (sp.)  ★→★★  DYA
Light white from Sauvignon, Malvasia di Candia, and Trebbiano grown
around Scandiano SW of Reggio Emilia. Usually *frizzante*, sometimes
sparkling, the *secco* is soft and round, the *semisecco* aromatic.
Cantina Cooperative           Elle (Conte Re)
  Colli di Scandiano          Riunite
Casali

**Bonarda di Ziano** r. s/sw. (fz.)  ★→★★  80 82 83
Varietal Bonarda (a strain of Croatina) grown around Ziano SW of
Piacenza. Dark red, lightly sweet, often with a prickle, it is good in 3–4
years with fresh fruit. Should soon be part of Colli Piacentini DOC.
Giancarlo Molinelli

**Bosco Eliceo** or **Rosso del Bosco** r. dr.  ★→★★  DYA
Curious violet-garnet table wine from Uva d'Oro (known elsewhere as
Fortana) grown in sandy plains around the Comacchio lagoon between
Ferrara and the Adriatic. Warm, full-bodied, with acidic bite and grapy
fragrance, it can be good young and cool.
C.S. Bosco Eliceo

**Cabernet** r. dr.  ★★  78 79 80 82 83
Cabernet was prominent a century ago in Emilia, especially in the Colli
Piacentini. Some vines survived and more are being planted through the
Apennine foothills, signaling the advent of both varietal Cabernet
Sauvignon and Cabernet Franc, and Bordeaux-style wines with Merlot.
Cabernet Sauvignon has been approved for DOC in the Colli Bolognesi.
Marchese Malaspina

**Cagnina** r. s/sw.  ★★  DYA
Dessert wine of striking violet-pomegranate color that survives as a
vinicultural curio in the hills around Forlì. Made from the rare Cagnina
grape, it has a fruity aroma and mellow, ripe grape flavor – best young
and cool. A similar wine called Canena is made by Trerè.
C.S. Forlì                    Fratelli Ravaioli
Colombina                     Ronco
Fattoria Paradiso

**Calbanesco** r. dr.  ★★→★★★  79 80 81 82 83
A unique table wine from the Calbanesco vine of undetermined origin
grown at Meldola south of Forlì. Of deep garnet color, it has an ample,
berry-like bouquet, dry, warm flavor with a hint of bitter underneath.
Best in 3–6 years.
Cesare Raggi

**Chardonnay** w. dr.  ★★★→★★★★  80 82 83
Chardonnay is not approved for Emilia-Romagna and therefore under
EEC policy cannot be planted. Nonetheless, one of Italy's best white
wines is the Chardonnay of the Terre Rosse estate, SW of Bologna. It has
unmistakable varietal traits (vanilla on the nose, apples on the palate)
but its personality distinguishes it subtly from other Chardonnays.
Terre Rosse (Vallania)

**Colli Bolognesi** DOC
Promising zone in the Apennine foothills SW of Bologna, split into two
subdivisions (Monte San Pietro and Castelli Medioevali), either of
which may appear on labels. Long a source of everyday wines to
Bologna, the zone's potential for quality has only begun to be realized.
DOC covers eight types.

–**Barbera** r. dr.  ★→★★  79 80 82 83
Most popular of the Colli Bolognesi wines, Barbera (which may contain

15% Sangiovese) has rich ruby-violet color and briskly tannic flavor, mellowing with 2–5 years.
Ag. *riserva* 3 yrs.

– **Bianco** w. dr. or s/sw.  ★ DYA
A rather plain, light golden wine from Albana and Trebbiano.

– **Cabernet Sauvignon** r. dr.  ★★→★★★  78 79 80 82 83
Recently added to the DOC list, this is clearly the best red wine of Bologna's hills. Deep in color with a typically herby bouquet and flavor, its natural gentility comes across even when styled to drink young (1–5 years).
Ag. *riserva* 3 yrs.

– **Merlot** r. dr.  ★→ ★★  82 83
Tasty red from at least 85% Merlot: dark ruby, softly dry, fruity and good for 2–4 years.

– **Pignoletto** w. dr. (s/sw.) (fz.)  ★★ DYA
Newly approved as a distinct local clone somewhat resembling Riesling Italico, this makes a lightly aromatic white, pleasantly fruity, usually dry, though *amabile* and *frizzante* versions are permitted.

– **Pinot Bianco** w. dr. (s/sw.) (fz.)  ★→ ★★★  82 83
Light greenish straw, usually dry (though *abboccato* is permitted), this wine can reach admirable levels from certain producers in good years.

– **Riesling Italico** w. dr. (s/sw.) (fz.)  ★→ ★★  DYA
A light straw, delicately scented white of impressively fruity off-dry flavor that comes across best young and chilled.

– **Sauvignon** w. dr.  ★★→★★★  82 83
Best of the Colli Bolognesi DOC whites, it is pale greenish straw, crisply dry, flinty, and elegantly structured. With a year of age, the Sauvignon of Terre Rosse and Bruno Negroni can equal the class of a good Sancerre.
Al Pazz (Fattoria Montebudello)　Bruno Negroni
Cantina Consorziale　Rivabella
　Comprensorio Monte San Pietro　Terre Rosse (Vallania)
Aldo Conti

**Colli di Parma** DOC
New zone in hills S and W of Parma around Salsomaggiore Terme and the Taro River valley. DOC takes in three types, all still to be proven.

– **Malvasia** w. dr. s/sw. fz. (sp.)  ★ DYA
From Malvasia di Candia with Moscato permitted at 15%, whether dry or *amabile*, the typical aroma of Malvasia is heightened by a bit of fizz.

– **Rosso** r. dr. (fz.)  ★ 82 83
From Barbera with some Bonarda and Croatina, this is similar in style to Lombardy's Oltrepò Pavese Rosso – dark ruby-violet, dry, bitter underneath, often with a prickle.

– **Sauvignon** w. dr. (fz.)  ★ DYA
Dry, delicately flinty, this noble variety could make a white of significance here. Sometimes *pétillant.*
Cantine Dall'Asta　Enopolio di Parma

**Colli Piacentini**
Tentatively approved for DOC, this large zone in the Apennine foothills in Piacenza province comprises three current DOCs – Gutturnio dei Colli Piacentini, Monterosso Val d'Arda, Trebbianino Val Trebbia – plus eight others, mainly varietal wines. Though the appellation is yet to be fully defined and developed, the zone shows promise similar to the adjacent Oltrepò Pavese in Lombardy.

– **Barbera** r. dr. (fz.)  ★→ ★★  82 83
Sturdy red wines, sometimes fizzy, usually to drink inside 3 years. Barbera from Ziano is of special note.

– **Bonarda** r. dr. s/sw. fz.  ★→ ★★  82 83
Dark ruby, often lightly sweet and fizzy, to drink in 2–3 years. Ziano's Bonarda is prized by some.

– **Gutturnio dei Colli Piacentini** r. dr. (s/sw.) (fz.)  ★→ ★★★  79 81 82 83
Once *amabile* and *frizzante*, modern Gutturnio is usually dry and still. From Barbera (60%) and Bonarda, it is deep garnet to violet in color, generous and smooth with fine bouquet. Though good young, some bottles show style after 3–4 years.

– **Malvasia** w. dr. s/sw. fz. (sp.)  \*→[**\*\***]  DYA
The established pop wine of these hills: aromatic, fizzy, off-dry.

– **Monterosso Val d'Arda** w. dr. (s/sw.) fz. (sp.)  [**\*\***]  DYA
Pleasant white, often *frizzante*, sometimes lightly *amabile*. Made from
Malvasia, Moscato, Trebbiano and Ortrugo in the Arda valley, it is
pleasantly fragrant, pale and delicate.

– **Ortrugo** w. dr. s/sw. fz.  \*  DYA
This fine local grape variety should make zesty whites of good class.

– **Pinot Grigio** w. dr. (sp.)  \*  DYA
Growingly popular, the variety will be used for still wines and *spumante*.

– **Pinot Nero** r. (w.) (p.) dr. (sp.)  \*  83
As in the Oltrepò Pavese, Pinot Nero will be used for both still red and
white and rosé sparkling wines.

– **Sauvignon** w. dr. (fz.)  \*→[**\*\***]  DYA
Good white wines made in the area indicate a bright future for this
distinctive varietal.

– **Trebbianino Val Trebbia** w. dr. (s/sw.) fz.  \*→[**\*\***]  DYA
Fragile, spritzy white from Ortrugo, Malvasia, Trebbiano, Moscato and
Sauvignon grown in the Trebbia valley. Delicately dry and fragrant as a
rule, it may also be *amabile*.

– **Val Nure** w. dr. (s/sw.) fz.  \*  DYA
This fleeting white is similar to Trebbianino Val Trebbia.

| | |
|---|---|
| Fratelli Bonelli | Giancarlo Molinelli |
| Cascina di Fornello (Kustermann) | Montepascolo (Cardinali) |
| Castello di Luzzano (Fugazza) | Mossi |
| Castello di Prato Ottesola | Podere "Il Cristo" |
| Armando Clementoni | Pusterla |
| Colombo | Fratelli Rizzi |
| Remo Crosignani | Rocchetta |
| Gino Innocenti | Romagnoli |
| La Solitaria | Italo Testa & Figli |
| Valentino Migliorini | Vitivinicola Colombi |

**Gutturnio dei Colli Piacentini**
See Colli Piacentini.

**Labrusca** p. dr. sp.  [**\*\***]  DYA
Rapturous cherry-pink *spumante* from Lambrusco grapes processed by
the *charmat* method at Correggio, near Reggio Emilia.
Oreste Lini & Figli

**Lambrusco** r. p. dr. s/sw. fz.  [**\***]  DYA
Unclassified Lambrusco grown in Emilia's Po flatlands around Reggio
and Modena. The dry is often consumed locally. Much of the *amabile*,
sometimes pink, is exported to the United States. Some could qualify as
DOC, but when it is sealed with plastic or metal caps (and not the corks
required for DOC) it may not be so labeled. Invariably *frizzante*, its
pressure is held under U.S. limits of sparkling wine to avoid excess taxes.
(Producers do not include all bottler and shipper brands, which could
also be dependable.)

| | |
|---|---|
| Cantina Simoni | Giacobazzi |
| Cella | Remigio Medici & Fratelli |
| Corovin | Riunite |

**Lambrusco Bianco** w. dr. sp.  [**\*\***]  DYA
The must from dark Lambrusco grapes separated from skins, vinified
white and made sparkling by *charmat*. Clean and lively, its fine fruit-acid
balance gives it unexpected tone.

| | |
|---|---|
| Cavicchioli | Oreste Lini & Figli |

**Lambrusco di Parma** r. p. dr. (s/sw.) fz.  \*  DYA
Lambrusco table wine from Parma province.
Enopolio di Parma

**Lambrusco di Sorbara** DOC r. dr. (s/sw.) fz.  \*→[**\*\*\***]  DYA
Considered the most qualified DOC Lambrusco, it is made from
Lambrusco di Sorbara grapes at 60% or more in a zone N of Modena
that includes the village of Sorbara. Ruby to garnet with bright pink
froth and well-scented, the *secco* goes with typical rich Emilian cooking,
especially sausages, and the *amabile* (not often seen) with dessert. Like all

DOC Lambrusco, it must be naturally *frizzante*, usually by *charmat*, sometimes by bottle fermentation.

| | |
|---|---|
| Mario Angiolini | CIV |
| Cancarini-Ghisetti | Contessa Matilde |
| Cavicchioli | Fini |
| Centrale del Lambrusco | Giacobazzi |
| Chiarli | |

**Lambrusco Grasparossa di Castelvetro** DOC r. dr. (s/sw.) fz. ★→★★ DYA

Made from Lambrusco Grasparossa grapes in a zone S of Modena that includes Castelfranco Emilia, Spilamberto, and Sassuolo. Usually dry, sometimes *amabile*, but always *frizzante*, it has a ruby-violet color and a notable fragrance.

| | |
|---|---|
| Cavicchioli | Contessa Matilde |
| Centrale del Lambrusco | Giacobazzi |
| Chiarli | Villa Barbieri |
| CIV | |

**Lambrusco Reggiano** DOC r. p. dr. s/sw. fz. ★→★★ DYA

Made from a blend of Lambrusco subvarieties grown around Reggio Emilia, this is the most heavily produced DOC Lambrusco (about 10 million liters a year) and the most exported. Considered the lightest in body and the most refreshing, whether dry or *amabile* its color varies from bright ruby to purple to pink.

| | |
|---|---|
| G. Alberini & Figli | Remigio Medici & Fratelli |
| Adolfo Donelli & Figlio | Moro |
| Oreste Lini & Figli | Riunite |

**Lambrusco Salamino di Santa Croce** DOC. r. dr. (s/sw.) fz. ★→★★ DYA

Made from Lambrusco Salamino grapes in a zone surrounding Modena that includes the village of Santa Croce. Ruby to purple, usually dry (as Modena's typical table wine), it can also be *amabile*.

| | |
|---|---|
| C.S. di Santa Croce | CIV |
| Cavicchioli | Contessa Matilde |
| Centrale del Lambrusco | Nedo Masetti |
| Chiarli | Severi Vini |

**Malvasia** w. am. dr. s/sw. fz. ★→★★★ DYA

Wines from light Malvasia grapes are made in many parts of Emilia's Apennine foothills. Usually spritzy, aromatic and either off-dry or off-sweet, they can also be still and quite sweet, as is the fine Terre Rosse Malvasia from Bologna. Malvasia is DOC in Colli di Parma and will be DOC in Colli Piacentini.

| | |
|---|---|
| Valentino Migliorini | Terre Rosse (Vallania) |

**Merlot** r. dr. ★→★★ 80 82 83

The popular vine is found in several parts of the region, most notably in Colli Bolognesi, where it is DOC, also in the Colli Piacentini and the Po Delta E of Ferrara.

| | |
|---|---|
| C.S. Bosco Eliceo | Marchese Malaspina |

**Monterosso Val d'Arda**

See Colli Piacentini.

**Müller Thurgau** w. dr. ★★ DYA

Crisp whites from the Riesling-Sylvaner cross have been successful at Ziano in the Colli Piacentini as table wines.

| | |
|---|---|
| Giancarlo Molinelli | Mossi |

**Pagadebit** w. dr. (s/sw.) ★★→★★★ DYA

Delicate white from the nearly extinct Pagadebit Gentile vine being revived on a limited scale around Bertinoro. Though sometimes *amabile*, the Pagadebit of Fattoria Paradiso is now usually dry with graceful texture and fruitiness, due to low-temperature fermentation.

| | |
|---|---|
| Fattoria Paradiso | Mossi |
| Guarini Matteucci di Castelfalcino | Fratelli Ravaioli |
| C. Guidi & Figli | Ronco |

**Picòl Ross** r. dr. fz. ★★★ DYA

One of the best of the Lambrusco family, Picòl Ross is grown at Sant'Ilario d'Enza, SE of Reggio. This unclassified wine is dry, fruity,

and well-scented, with good body and a bright ruby color that erupts into evanescent pink foam when poured.
Moro

**Picolit** w. sw.  ★★  82 83
The renowned vine of Friuli is grown experimentally at Bertinoro and Ziano, where it makes admirable dessert wine not regularly for sale.
Fattoria Paradiso                              Giancarlo Molinelli

**Pinot Bianco**
Grown in various parts of the region; DOC only in Colli Bolognesi.

**Pinot Grigio** w. dr.  ★→★★  DYA
Increasingly planted, Pinot Grigio is to become DOC in Colli Piacentini. The table wine of Terre Rosse near Bologna can match Pinot Grigio from more northerly places.
Terre Rosse (Vallania)

**Pinot Nero**
New interest in this vine both for red wines and sparkling whites is being shown in the hills. Pinot Nero will be DOC in Colli Piacentini.

**Pinot Spumante** w. dr. sp.  ★★  DYA
Good sparkling wines are made from Pinot and Chardonnay grapes in several parts of the Apennine foothills, both by the *charmat* and Champagne methods.
Bruno Negroni                              Italo Testa & Figli

**Rèfolo** w. dr. fz.  ★★  DYA
Exhilarating bubbly from Trebbiano, Prosecco and Pinot made in Romagna. Bright straw, cleanly dry, it has a nice mix of bitter and soft on the finish.
Cesari

**Riesling** w. dr. (fz.)  ★→★★  DYA
Some Riesling Renano but more Italico is grown in the region, used for still and *frizzante* whites of zesty tone and soft fragrance. Riesling Italico is DOC in Colli Bolognesi.

**Ronco Casone, Ronco dei Ciliegi, Ronco delle Ginestre** r. dr.  ★★★
80 81 82 83
Three "crus" from Sangiovese Grosso grown at Casale near Modigliana in Romagna's hills. Aged in small barrels of new French oak, they develop elegant tone in deep ruby color, flowery bouquet in dry but rich and complex flavor. With age, potential for ★★★★ seems within reach.
Gian Matteo Baldi (Castelluccio)

**Ronco del Re** w. dr.  81
This Sauvignon from Casale in '81 developed into a singular white of luxuriant tone, extraordinary nuance and depth, but until another vintage is issued it is difficult to evaluate.
Gian Matteo Baldi (Castelluccio)

**Rosso Armentano** r. dr.  ★★★  75 78 79 82 83
Brilliant combination of Sangiovese di Romagna with Cabernet Franc and Pinot Nero orchestrated by Tommaso Vallunga in a red that needs 6–8 years to show the elegance in bouquet and flavor that puts it in a class by itself in Romagna.
Fratelli Vallunga

**Rosso della Bissera** r. dr.  ★★  80 82 83
Robust table wine from Montepulciano grown at Tenuta Bissera SW of Bologna. Dark ruby, rounded, and perfumed, it is good in 3–5 years.
Bruno Negroni

**Rosso della Pusterla** r. dr.  ★★  80 82 83
Pleasant red table wine from Barbera, Bonarda, and Fruttano grown at Vigolo Marchese in the Colli Piacentini. Soft and warm, it has a slight prickle on a bitter background.
Pusterla

**Sangiovese di Romagna** DOC r. dr.  ★→★★★  79 80 82 83
Varietal red from the Romagnan (as distinguished from the Tuscan) strain of Sangiovese grown in a vast zone of Romagna from the outskirts of Bologna to the Adriatic coast S of Rimini. Though produced in quantity (more than 20 million liters in 1979), Sangiovese is not well

known outside Italy. Habitually consumed fairly young, some *riserva superiore* (exemplified by Spalletti Rocca di Ribano) after 4–5 years shows breed well above its price level. Bright ruby tending to garnet, with rich, flowery bouquet, smooth balance and long finish. The *superiore* comes from specified places long noted for quality.
Ag. 5 months; *riserva* 2 yrs.

| | |
|---|---|
| Luigi Baldrati | Marabini |
| Otello Burioli & Figli | Pasolini Dall'Onda |
| Cantina Baldini | Fratelli Picchi |
| Cantina di Villa I Raggi | Plauto (Premiovini) |
| Cantina Produttori | Provit |
| Predappio | Cesare Raggi (Le Calbane) |
| C.S. Riminese | Fratelli Ravaioli |
| Celli | Ronchi |
| Cesari | Ronco |
| Colombina | Spalletti (Rocca di Ribano) |
| Fratelli Conti | Luciano Tamburini |
| Corovin | Tenuta Amalia |
| Fattoria Paradiso | Tenuta Cella |
| Ferrucci (Domus Caia) | Tenuta del Monsignore |
| Carla Foschi Calisese | Tenuta Zerbina |
| Guarini Matteucci di | Arturo Tesini |
| Castelfalcino | Fratelli Vallunga |

**Sauvignon** w. dr. (fz.) ★→★★ DYA
Sauvignon white wines are increasing in the Apennine foothills. The style has been bright and light (sometimes bubbly), yet there is evidence of wines of real class (Terre Rosse, Ronco del Re). DOC in Colli Bolognesi, Colli di Parma and scheduled for Colli Piacentini.
Moro Italo Testa & Figli

**Scorza Amara** r. dr. fz. ★★ DYA
Full-bodied, dark red *frizzante* from Scorza Amara grapes, a relative of Lambrusco, grown at San Polo d'Enza, SW of Reggio.
Remigio Medici & Fratelli Ina Maria Pellerano

**Trabense** w. dr. sp. ★★ DYA
Refreshingly delicate bottle-fermented *spumante* from Trebbiano and Ortrugo grown at Travo in the Colli Piacentini.
Valentino Migliorini

**Trebbianino Val Trebbia**
See Colli Piacentini.

**Trebbiano di Romagna** DOC w. dr. (s/sw.) (sw.) (sp.) ★→★★ DYA
White, usually dry and still, from the Trebbiano di Romagna vine, considered distinct from other Trebbiano vines but, like most, it yields profusely of rather neutral wines. The zone covers much the same territory as Albana and Sangiovese di Romagna but extends farther N to the flat terrain around Lugo. Pale straw yellow, bone dry, with a faint odor of the grape, it has always been a wine to drink young, though new vinification methods have improved its fruit-acid balance and even given it some character. Production approaches 10 million liters annually. The *spumante* (dry, semisweet, or sweet) is not often seen.

| | |
|---|---|
| Antica Fattoria Brocchi | Il Portico |
| Luigi Baldrati | Marabini |
| Bernardi | Pasolini Dall'Onda |
| Braschi | Fratelli Picchi |
| Cantina di Villa i Raggi | Plauto (Premiovini) |
| Cantina Produttori Predappio | Provit |
| C.S. Forlì | Cesare Raggi (Le Calbane) |
| C.S. Riminese | Ravaglia |
| Carradora | Fratelli Ravaioli |
| Cesari | Ronco |
| Colombina | Ronchi |
| Fratelli Conti | Luciano Tamburini |
| Corovin | Tenuta Amalia |
| Fattoria Paradiso | Tenuta del Monsignore |
| Ferrucci | Tenuta Zerbina |
| Guarini Matteucci di | Trerè |
| Castelfalcino | Fratelli Vallunga |
| C. Guidi & Figli | Fratelli Varoli |

Pasta alone elevates Emilia-Romagna's cooking to the divine. The making of *tagliatelle, tortellini, tortelli, anolini, cappelletti, passatelli, lasagne, gnocchi,* and *gnocchetti,* to name a few, is a daily routine performed by the *sfogliatrice,* living testimony to the regional conviction that pasta must be fresh and made by hand. But pasta is just the entrée of a culinary heritage as religiously adhered to as any of France (whose chefs drew more inspiration than they would care to admit from the cooks of Bologna's region). Bologna, with its *mortadella* and *lasagne verdi* and a dozen other delights of its own, is the capital of Italian gastronomy, but some provincial centers – Parma, Modena, and Reggio – can rival its battery of good things to eat. Foremost are Parmigiano-Reggiano cheese (Parmesan) and *prosciutto* di Parma, but Modena weighs in heftily with its pig's feet sausage (*zampone*) and *aceto balsamico,* which is almost too glorious to be considered vinegar. There is so much more to Emilia-Romagna's cornucopia that this list could only whet your appetite.

**Anatra alla romagnola** Duck cooked with bacon, wine, and seasonings in Romagna.
  ★★★ Sangiovese *riserva superiore* or ★★★ Barbarossa.
**Burlenghi** Hot fried pastry flavored with lard, pork crackling, rosemary, garlic, and grated cheese, famous at Vignola near Modena.
  ★★ Lambrusco Grasparossa di Castelvetro.
**Cappelletti in brodo** The hat-shaped pasta with meat filling served in broth.
  ★★★ Albana *secco* or ★★★★ Chardonnay Terre Rosse.
**Culatello** Prized tenderest part of the *prosciutto,* from the Po flatlands.
  ★★ Monterosso Val d'Arda *secco.*
**Grana** Parmigiano-Reggiano, the greatest of grating cheeses, is also eaten in chunks.
  ★★ Gutturnio.
**Lasagne verdi al forno** Green lasagne cooked with layers of meat

*ragù* and béchamel.
  ★★ Lambrusco di Sorbara.
**Pasticcio di tortellini** Small ear-shaped pasta cooked with *ragù* then baked in a pie crust Bologna style.
  ★★★ Cabernet Sauvignon or ★★ Merlot Colli Bolognesi.
**Piadina** Romagnan flat bread eaten with *pecorino* cheese, *prosciutto,* or salame, like a sandwich.
  ★★ Sangiovese di Romagna.
**Prosciutto di Parma con melone** Parma ham with cantaloupe (or fresh figs).
  ★★ Malvasia dei Colli Piacentini.
**Tortelli all'erbetta** Large pasta squares filled with *ricotta* and *erbetta,* a chard-like green, served with melted butter and Parmesan.
  ★★ Monterosso Val d'Arda *secco* or ★★ Sauvignon.
**Zampone** Pig's feet sausage made in Modena, served with lentils or mashed potatoes.
  ★★ Lambrusco Salamino di Santa Croce.

## Restaurants

Emilia-Romagna has fine restaurants nearly everywhere.
Recommended in or near wine zones: **Colli Bolognesi** *Rocca* at Bazzano; *Nuova Roma* near Calderino. **Colli di Parma** *Aquila Romana* at Noceto; *Trattoria Da Eletta* at Sala Braganza; *Al Tartufo* at Salsomaggiore Terme. **Colli Piacentini** *La Coccinella* at Albarola; *Antica Trattoria della Paolina* at Bobbio; *Da Faccini* and *La Rocca* at Castell'Arquato; *Roma* at Pianello Val Tidone. **Lambrusco zones** *La Noce* at Borzano; *Fini* and *Oreste* at Modena; *Arnaldo Aquila d'Oro* at Rubiera; *Moro* at Sant'Ilario d'Enza; *Il Portone* at Scandiano. **Romagna** *Gigiolè* at Brisighella; *La Frasca* at Castrocaro Terme; *Amici Miei* at Faenza; *San Domenico* at Imola; *La Meridiana* at Lugo.

# Friuli-Venezia Giulia

Friuli-Venezia Giulia

Friuli is the realm of the new Italian white wine. The climate of this northeastern corner of Italy, which borders on Austria and Yugoslavia, is determined by the propitious intermingling of alpine and Adriatic air. The DOC zones of Collio Goriziano, Colli Orientali del Friuli and parts of Grave del Friuli boast remarkably even growing seasons for the venerable local Tocai, Verduzzo, Ribolla, Malvasia, and Picolit and an honor roll of outsiders that comprises Sauvignon, Riesling Renano, Traminer, Müller Thurgau, Pinot Grigio, and Pinot Bianco (much of which is Chardonnay).

Tocai, the local favorite, has the makings of an international celebrity, though its name gets confused with the dissimilar Tokays of Hungary and Alsace. The region's most heavily planted white, Tocai can match the class of Sauvignon, Pinot Bianco-Chardonnay, and coppery Pinot Grigio, which reach peaks of splendor in the hills between Gorizia and Udine.

Picolit is Italy's most fabled dessert wine. Some insist on comparing it with Château d'Yquem, though about all the two have in common is that they are white, sweet, and uncommon. Unproductive, due to a congenital weakness known as floral

**Wine Zones**
1 Collio Goriziano
2 Colli Orientali del Friuli
3 Grave del Friuli
4 Carso

abortion, and prohibitively expensive, Picolit has nonetheless managed a rapid comeback which has raised suspicions that most of what is being sold derives from blends or else from grapes of a cross between Picolit and Verduzzo. Still, here and there, a taste of the nearly pure oldtime grandeur might be had by those patient enough to call on producers door to door. But, for my money, Friuli's best dessert wine is Verduzzo di Ramandolo.

Surprisingly, Friuli produces more red than white. Merlot dominates, though Cabernet (more often Franc than Sauvignon), the native Refosco, and some exciting oddities also thrive. Merlot and Cabernet, which are usually light, soft, fruity wines to drink young, are heavily produced in the flats that take in the DOC zones of Aquileia, Isonzo, Latisana, and parts of Grave.

The smallest of the Tre Venezie – the territory of the Venetian Republic which includes the Veneto and Trentino-Alto Adige – Friuli also has the smallest wine production (130 million liters a year), but a third of that is DOC and much of the rest is still very drinkable.

The land of the ancient Friulian people, and an outpost of the Roman Empire, the region is a crossroads of Germanic, Slavic, and Italianate cultures. There is a prominent Slovenian minority in the southeast around Gorizia and the regional capital of Trieste, Italy's second busiest seaport.

A short drive from Venice along the *Autostrada la Serenissima*, Friuli has become a prime attraction to wine buffs. Collio's hills are traversed by wine roads. The *Strada del Merlot* follows the Isonzo River southwest of Gorizia. The well-stocked *Enoteca La Serenissima* at Gradisca di Isonzo was one of Italy's first public wine libraries. Wineries large and small offer exceptional hospitality, as do the cozy country taverns and inns.

## Recent vintages

As a rule, Friulian dry whites are at their flowery best when young, though increasingly Tocai, Sauvignon and Pinot Bianco defy the rule. Even reds are usually styled for early drinking, but some Cabernet and Refosco improves notably with age.

1983　A fine year for reds and whites, though heat caused problems with wines not processed at low temperature.
1982　Abundant crush, though whites often lacked acidity and may be short lived.
1981　Frost, hail and rot took a heavy toll; select grapes made some good wines.
1980　Uneven; late harvest better for whites than reds.
1979　Outstanding, abundant vintage in all zones.
1978　Reduced crop; average for whites, subpar for reds.

**Aquileia** DOC
Flat zone stretching from the Adriatic north past the ancient Roman city of Aquileia to Palmanova and Trivignano. Vines for red wine prevail in the sandy clay soil, though good white wines are also made. Production is centered in the large Cantina Sociale Cooperative del Friuli Orientale at Cervignano, which sells under its own Molin di Ponte label and supplies Valdo. The DOC list has expanded to include 10 varietals and a rosé.
– **Cabernet** or **Cabernet Franc** or **Cabernet Sauvignon**
r. dr.　★→**★★**　81 82 83
The wines may be labeled in three ways. All tend to be bright ruby, rather light, round, fresh and fragrant, best in 2–4 years.
– **Merlot** r. dr.　★→**★★**　81 82 83
Light, tasty, fruity, medium-ruby color, to drink in 1–3 years. The most heavily produced of Aquileia's varietals.
– **Pinot Bianco** w. dr.　★→**★★**　DYA
Straw yellow, soft, perfumed, and smooth with good varietal character.

– **Pinot Grigio** w. dr. ☒ DYA
Though production is limited, this tends to be the best Aquileia white;
smooth, fruity, dry but flowery with light golden-copper color.

– **Refosco** r. dr. ☒ 79 82 83
From Refosco del Peduncolo Rosso grapes, this has a deep garnet-violet
color, a fairly full body and a pleasant fruity flavor with typically bitter
undertone. To drink in 2–5 years, sometimes more.

– **Riesling Renano** w. dr. ★→☒ DYA
Very small production of this light golden, dry wine that does somewhat
better in cooler places.

– **Rosato** p. dr. ★ DYA
Based on Merlot with other varieties permitted, this is light cherry hued,
soft, subtly grapy.

– **Sauvignon** w. dr. ★ DYA
Newly designated, this white wine could prove to be well suited to
Aquileia's coastal climate.

– **Tocai Friulano** w. dr. ★→☒ DYA
More delicate and drier than Tocai from the hills, but a good fish wine.

| | |
|---|---|
| Amministrazione Ciardi | Valdo |
| Giacomelli | Valle |
| Molin di Ponte | |

– **Traminer** w. dr. ★ DYA
New and unproven.

– **Verduzzo Friulano** w. dr. ★ DYA
Newly approved, this should make a light, lemony white.

| | |
|---|---|
| Amministrazione Ciardi | Molin di Ponte |
| Ca' Bolani | Valdo |
| Giacomelli | Valle |

**Cabernet** r. dr. ★→★★★ 79 81 82 83
Most Cabernet is qualified for DOC in six of Friuli's seven zones, though
certain bottlings, such as EnoFriulia's Cabernet Sauvignon delle Venezie
rates high as a table wine.
EnoFriulia

**Carso** DOC
Tentatively approved appellation applies to two reds based on the
Terrano grape (a strain of Refosco) and a white Malvasia grown in the
Carso hills, the narrow strip of land bordering Yugoslavia between
Trieste and Gorizia.

– **Carso** r. dr. ★ DYA
This must contain at least 70% Terrano grapes in a dark ruby, grapy,
fleshy, rather simplistic wine.

– **Terrano del Carso** r. dr. ★→★★★ 83
At least 85% of Terrano grapes, perfumed (of raspberries), dry but round
and fruity, as epitomized by the Terrano di Sagrado of Castelvecchio.

– **Carso Malvasia** w. dr. ★ DYA
Based on Malvasia Istriana, this straw-colored wine is dry, fruitily
aromatic, fairly soft.
Castelvecchio

**Chardonnay** w. dr. ★★→★★★ 82 83
Table wines labeled Chardonnay or Pinot Chardonnay are appearing
increasingly since it was discovered that at least half of what had been
called Pinot Bianco in Friuli is actually Chardonnay. The variety has
been tentatively approved in Grave del Friuli as Italy's first DOC
Chardonnay. But most is still table wine, some of very good quality.

| | |
|---|---|
| Angoris | Francesco Gravner |
| F. Berin | Isola Augusta |
| Ca' Bolani | Jermann |
| Ca' Ronesca | Plozner |
| Cantina Produttori Vini Cormons | Pradio |
| EnoFriulia | Roncada |
| Fantinel | Tenuta S. Anna |
| Giacomelli | |

**Colli Orientali del Friuli** DOC
Adjacent to Collio (p. 47) and more extensive, Colli Orientali continues
N along the Yugoslav border from Corno di Rosazzo to Tarcento at the
foot of the Julian Alps. Its axis is Cividale del Friuli on the site of the
Roman city of Forum Julii. Though wine production is not as

concentrated as in Collio, Colli Orientali has equally favorable conditions and more space in which to develop. The zone has most of the varietals of Collio, plus Verduzzo, Refosco, Cabernet Sauvignon, and Riesling Renano to enhance its possibilities. Picolit is DOC only here.

– **Cabernet** r. dr.   ★★→★★★   78 79 81 82 83

Either Cabernet Sauvignon or Cabernet Franc or both may be used in this red, which at best shows more elegance in body and bouquet than other Friulian Cabernets. Deep ruby with herb-like, tarry flavors typical of the family, the *riserva* shines with 3–7 years.

Ag. *riserva* 2 yrs.

– **Merlot** r. dr.   ★★→★★★   81 82 83

Supple, smooth, and versatile, it is tastiest in 1–3 years, or, if *riserva*, 3–5. In either case, it can rank with Italy's best.

Ag. *riserva* 2 yrs.

– **Picolit** w. s/sw. or sw.   ★★→★★★   78 79 82 83

In Colli Orientali, uniquely, Picolit's authenticity is controlled. Yet, among some 40,000 bottles issued annually from an estimated 50–60 producers, quality is rarely up to price. Permitted yields are 4000 kilograms of grapes per hectare (about 1500 standard bottles from an acre), the lowest for any DOC wine anywhere. Most growers say they get less. Up to 10% of other varieties may be included under DOC, which prescribes wine of at least 15% alcohol of deep straw color, with lightly perfumed aroma and warm, harmonious, delicate flavor, whether *amabile* or *dolce*. The best examples surpass that description.

Ag. *riserva* 2 yrs.

– **Pinot Bianco** w. dr.   ★★→★★★★   82 83

Some of Italy's finest Pinot Bianco originates here: fragrant, fruity, with remarkable harmony and structure to improve over 2–5 years.

– **Pinot Grigio** w. dr.   ★★→★★★   DYA

The best of Colli Orientali can equal any Pinot Grigio in both the light and *ramàto* (coppery) styles.

– **Pinot Nero** r. dr.   ★→★★   78 82 83

Red Burgundy's grape rarely achieves grandeur here, though it tends to show more stuff than in Collio and can take a little more aging.

Ag. *riserva* 2 yrs.

– **Refosco** r. dr.   ★★→★★★   78 79 80 81 82 83

Wine from this native variety can rival the French imports in class and age somewhat longer. Deep violet tending to garnet with age, its warm, full, lightly tannic flavor comes into its own in 4–7 years.

Ag. *riserva* 2 yrs.

– **Ribolla** w. dr.   ★→★★   DYA

The very little Ribolla made is similar to Collio's.

– **Riesling Renano** w. dr.   ★★→★★★   DYA

Not enough has been done with this true Riesling, which is clearly superior to Riesling Italico. Pale golden yellow with blossomy bouquet and fruity freshness in a basically dry, smooth flavor.

– **Sauvignon** w. dr.   ★★→★★★   DYA

Similar to Collio Sauvignon if not yet quite equal to the best.

– **Tocai** w. dr.   ★★→★★★★   82 83

From certain producers – Abbazia di Rosazzo, for instance – this can rival the best of Collio, holding impressively for 2–3 years.

– **Verduzzo (Ramandolo)** w. dr. or s/sw.   ★★→★★★★   78 79 80 81

Wine from this antique, indigenous vine may be either dry or sweet or, better yet, in between. The dry version is bright greenish gold, nicely fruity with flowery bouquet, and of light body – good v en young with summer dishes. The *amabile*, from slightly dried grapes, has more of everything – color, aroma, and smoothness – its ripe fruit sweetness offset by a sensational dry finish (Abbazia di Rosazzo and Ronchi di Fornaz make outstanding Verduzzo *amabile*). The Verduzzo *amabile* from a sector of the community of Nimis may be called Ramandolo (G.B. Comelli and Giovanni Dri excel).

Angoris

Fratelli Antonutti

Bandut

Bosco Romagno (Arzenton)

Bosco Romagno (Zambotto)

Mario Budini

Livio Olivo Buiatti

Valentino Butussi

Campeglio

Cantarutti Alfieri

Cantoni

Casa di Legno (Lesizza)

E. Collavini

Colli di Novacuzzo

Colli di Spessa

G.B. Comelli

| | |
|---|---|
| Gianfranco d'Attimis Maniago | Rocca Bernarda |
| Di Ipplis | Paolo Rodaro |
| E. Domenis & Figli | Ronchi di Cialla |
| Girolamo Dorigo | Ronchi di Fornaz |
| Giovanni Dri | Ronchi di Manzano |
| Marino Ermarcora | Ronco del Gnemiz |
| Livio Felluga | Dante Sara |
| I Moros (Tavagnacco) | Selva |
| Francesco Lui | Cisiro Snidero & Figli |
| Giovanni Monai | Tenuta Maseri Florio |
| V. Nascig | Isidoro Tilatti |
| G. & E. Panizzo | Valle |
| G. Franco Pascolini | Vigne dal Leon |
| Giuseppe Picogna | Villa Belvedere |
| Pitotti | Villa Rubini |
| Fratelli Pozzo | Volpe Pasini |

**Collio Goriziano** or **Collio** DOC
A strip of hills against the Yugoslav border running from near Gorizia W and N past Cormons, reputed to have one of Europe's most privileged microclimates for white wines. The wines of numerous small-scale growers have improved steadily as expert assistance has become available. Besides 12 DOC types, Chardonnay, Cabernet Sauvignon, Müller Thurgau and Riesling Renano make impressive table wines. Though whites dominate, reds are notable for supple, youthful style.

– **Cabernet Franc** r. dr. ★★ 82 83
Light and bright, with understated varietal character, pleasant to drink in 1–4 years, rarely more.

– **Collio** w. dr. ★→ ★★ DYA
The only non-varietal among the region's DOCs, Collio comes from Ribolla, Malvasia, and Tocai, a delicate dry white wine, sometimes a touch *pétillant*, to drink very young.

– **Malvasia** w. dr. ★→★★ DYA
Zippy white with subtle Malvasia aroma, very dry, good with fish.

– **Merlot** r. dr. ★★→★★★★ 79 81 82 83
Usually light in body and color, soft, nicely scented with herb-like traits of the grape, but Merlot can be bigger. Borgo Conventi's limited bottling of Merlot '79 aged in new wood may be the finest example to date of this varietal in Italy.

– **Pinot Bianco** w. dr. ★★→★★★★ 82 83
Sometimes light and fruity, occasionally luxuriant, enhanced by the unannounced presence of Chardonnay and, from a few producers, a little barrel seasoning. Younger Pinot Bianco tends to have a light straw color, crisp acidity, and flowery fragrance. With a year or more of age, the better examples tend to golden with ample bouquet hinting of vanilla and almonds, and the buttery texture of white Burgundy.

– **Pinot Grigio** w. dr. ★★→★★★ 82 83
Some vinify for light yellow wine, fruity and crisp when young. Others leave the fermenting wine in contact with the skins to achieve a pale smoky gold *ramato* (coppery) style, fuller in body, flavor, and aroma – a fine aperitif with a year or more of bottle age.

– **Pinot Nero** r. dr. ★→★★ 82 83
Pleasant red from the temperamental variety that even in better years shows only a vague resemblance to red Burgundy. Ruby and rotund, it can be fragrant, fleshy, and smooth in 1–4 years, but never dramatic.

– **Ribolla** w. dr. ★★ DYA
Recently added to the Collio collection, this white from the ancient, indigenous Ribolla Gialla vine has a lemon-yellow color, delicate grapy aroma and a fairly full, distinctive flavor.

– **Riesling Italico** w. dr. ★→★★ DYA
Good, lively, dry to off-dry white with fruity flavor and aroma and pale gold color; however, the non-DOC Riesling Renano does better.

– **Sauvignon** w. dr. ★★→★★★★ 82 83
Not enough of this noble Bordelaise is planted, but some of what is yields results to compare with the finest Sauvignons of France and California. Pale straw with golden-green highlights, elegant fruit-acid balance and flowery, flinty nose, it is smooth and long, full of Sauvignon personality.

– **Tocai Friulano** w. dr. ★★→★★★★ 82 83
Even workaday Tocai is good in Collio, where it is drunk as a versatile meal wine. In the hands of a few, it reaches heights unequalled elsewhere. Pale straw with lemon-yellow reflections, its scent is of wild

flowers and its flavor, dry but ample, is full of nuances, most markedly ripe fruit and almond, with velvety texture and length.

– **Traminer** w. dr.  ★★→★★★  DYA
Produced in minuscule quantity, this native of Alto Adige has probably not realized its full potential, though Mario Schiopetto, for one, has raised it to significant levels from some vintages. Medium golden yellow, its usually spicy aroma is somewhat subdued here, but the inherent richness comes through in the otherwise dry flavor.

| | |
|---|---|
| Al Cret (Butelli) | Marcello & Marino Humar |
| Fratelli Antonutti | Jermann |
| Attems | Alessio Komjanc |
| F. Berin | Fratelli Pighin |
| E. Collavini | Silvestro Primosic |
| Borgo Conventi | Doro Princic |
| Mario Burdin | Radikon |
| Fratelli Buzzinelli | Roncada |
| Paolo Caccese | Ronco Blanchis |
| Campagnis (Zampar) | Ronco della Chiesa |
| Cantina Produttori Vini Cormons | Russiz Superiore |
| Ca' Ronesca | Russolo |
| Carlo Drufovka | Mario Schiopetto |
| Colli di Novacuzzo | Giovanni Scolaris |
| Conti Formentini | Subida di Monte |
| EnoFriulia | Tenuta Catemario |
| Livio Felluga | Villa Russiz |
| Marco Felluga | Villa San Giovanni |
| Giulio Furlani | P. Zorutti (Comis) |
| Gradimir Gradnik | Luigi Zorzon |
| Francesco Gravner | |

**Dragarska** r. dr.  ★★★  79 82 83
Merlot and Cabernet grown at Oslavia in Collio and mixed with more aplomb than most Friulian varietals of either type.

**Engelwhite**
See Pinot Nero.

**Franconia** r. dr.  ★★→★★★  79 81 82 83
An oddball that can be excellent. Made from a grape known variously as Franconia, Limberger, Blaufränkisch, and Bleufrancs, believed to have come from Croatia. Bright ruby red, it has a generous bouquet, good body and a clean, dry flavor against a background of raspberry-like sweetness. Reaches prime in 3–6 years.

| | |
|---|---|
| Cantina Produttori Vini Cormons | Roncada |
| Il Castello (Fantinel) | Ronchi di Manzano |
| Francesco Lui | Giuseppe Toti |
| V. Nascig | Valle |

**Grave del Friuli** DOC
This zone, which dwarfs all others, accounts for about half the region's DOC wine. Grave covers low hills and plains from the border of Veneto eastwards past Udine. More than half of Grave's output is in Merlot, which thrives in gravelly lowlands similar to parts of Bordeaux. Grave is also a major producer of Tocai and Cabernet and has no shortage either of Refosco or of the white Pinots. Several of Friuli's largest wineries, both cooperative and private, are here. Recently expanded, the appellation takes in 13 types, including three styles of Cabernet and the first DOC Chardonnay in Italy. Though much of the wine is of sound, everyday quality, some is superb, for Grave has microclimates similar to those of Collio and Colli Orientali. Within its confines is the world's largest vine nursery, the *Vivai Cooperativi Rauscedo*, which prepares 30 million shoots a year for Italy and other nations.

– **Cabernet** or **Cabernet Franc** or **Cabernet Sauvignon**
r. dr.  ★→ ★★★  79 81 82 83
Cabernet Sauvignon exists, but Cabernet Franc is favored for its quicker maturation and *gout de terroir*, the earthy, herby taste that inspires its admirers. Most is to drink young, but some holds up for 5 years or more.

– **Chardonnay** w. dr.  ★→ ★★★  83
Italy's first DOC Chardonnay, this can show good balance and varietal character here, as exemplified for years by Plozner.

– **Merlot** r. dr. ★→★★★ 81 82 83
Grave is Italy's capital of Merlot, with some 10 million liters a year, some of it solid enough to improve over 3–5 years. Even the everyday stuff is good – supple, fruity and fragrant.
– **Pinot Bianco** w. dr. ★→ ★★★ 82 83
Quality ranges from pedestrian to very good in wine of solid class and character.
– **Pinot Grigio** w. dr. ★→ ★★★ DYA
Whether light or coppery, Pinot Grigio at its best concedes nothing to its neighbors in Collio and Colli Orientali.
– **Pinot Nero** r. dr. ★→★★ 83
Just approved, this should in some cases compare with Pinot Nero of Colli Orientali.
– **Refosco** r. dr. ★→ ★★★ 78 79 81 82 83
This seductive red, popular locally, from better producers ranks with the region's finest. Ages 4–7 years or more.
– **Riesling Renano** w. dr. ★ DYA
Though new and unproven, this could be admirable from the cool heights of Grave.
– **Rosato** p. dr. ★ DYA
Just introduced, this will make light use of dark varieties.
– **Sauvignon** w. dr. ★ DYA
Another newcomer, this could be the most promising white in this gravelly zone.
– **Tocai** w. dr. ★→ ★★★ 82 83
Grave makes more Tocai than Collio and Colli Orientali combined; choice bottles stand with the region's elite.
– **Traminer Aromatico** w. dr. ★ DYA
A new and still questionable entry.
– **Verduzzo** w. dr. ★→ ★★ DYA
The dry is preferred here in a golden-yellow wine with greenish tints, best young when its fruity freshness is offset by an almost salty dryness.

| | |
|---|---|
| Fratelli Antonutti | La Delizia (C.S. Casarsa) |
| Duca Badoglio | Molino delle Streghe |
| Cantina del Friuli Centrale-Bertiolo | Morassutti |
| Cantine Bidoli | Morelli De Rossi |
| Cantoni | Fratelli Pighin |
| Castello di Porcia | Fratelli Pistoni |
| E. Collavini | A. Pittau |
| Germano Filiputti | Plozner |
| Antonio Furchir | Pradio |
| Giacomelli | Santa Margherita |
| Il Castello (Fantinel) | Tenuta Catemario |
| Paolo De Lorenzi | Vigneti Pittaro |
| Kechler | Villa Ronche |

**Isonzo** DOC
Small zone along the Isonzo River reaching from the coastal plain near Monfalcone to gentle rises around Gradisca d'Isonzo, Cormons, and Gorizia. Isonzo's terrain and microclimate favor Cabernet and Merlot, which, among its ten types, most consistently rate with Friuli's finest.
– **Cabernet** r. dr. ★★→★★★ 79 82 83
From either Cabernet Sauvignon or Cabernet Franc, a soft, smooth, buoyantly fragrant wine, light but remarkably drinkable in 2–6 years.
– **Malvasia Istriana** w. dr. ★ DYA
From the native Istrian strain of Malvasia, a light, fragile, pale fish wine.
– **Merlot** r. dr. ★★→★★★ 82 83
The most heavily produced Isonzo wine, Merlot tends to show more consistent class here than in any other zone. Light in color and body, brilliantly fresh in bouquet and flavor, it hits peaks in 1–4 years.
– **Pinot Bianco** w. dr. ★→★★ DYA
Pleasantly brisk when young, Pinot Bianco does better in high places.
– **Pinot Grigio** w. dr. ★→★★ DYA
Usually made in the light, pale style here.
– **Riesling Renano** w. dr. ★★ DYA
The small amount made shows more class than might be expected. Pale, greenish yellow, and fragrant, it is best very young.

– **Sauvignon** w. dr. ★★ DYA
Isonzo's climate favors consistent if unspectacular quality in this variety.

– **Tocai** w. dr. ★★ DYA
The favorite white is solid and good, if never up to Collio's top echelon.

– **Traminer Aromatico** w. dr. ★ DYA
Very little of this cold-climate vine is planted. Maybe just as well.

– **Verduzzo Friulano** w. dr. ★ DYA
Simple, tasty, of limited production; Verduzzo's heights are reached elsewhere.

| | |
|---|---|
| Angoris | Luisa Eddi |
| Bader | Eredi Dott. Gino Cosolo |
| Fratelli Brotto | Conti Prandi d'Ulmhort |
| Antonio Burdin | Stelio Gallo |
| Cantina Produttori Vini Cormons | S. Elena |
| Cappelletti | Tenuta Villanova |

**Latisana** DOC
This zone in the coastal plains follows the Tagliamento River N from the Adriatic past the town of Latisana. Similar in geography to Aquileia and Isonzo, Latisana's seven types are dominated by Merlot, Cabernet, and Tocai.

– **Cabernet** r. dr. ★→★★ 82 83
Cabernet Sauvignon and/or Franc make soft, light, scented wine to drink in 2–4 years.

– **Merlot** r. dr. ★→★★ 82 83
Popular everyday wine, its easygoing nature is appreciable in 1–3 years.

– **Pinot Bianco** w. dr. ★★ DYA
Made in limited quantity, finely scented, smooth, with varietal tone.

– **Pinot Grigio** w. dr. ★→★★ DYA
The light style prevails here in very limited quantities.

– **Refosco** r. dr. ★★ 79 82 83
Though overwhelmed in numbers by the other reds, Refosco is more robust and durable and can show distinctive style.

– **Tocai** w. dr. ★→★★★ DYA
The favored white is more consistently impressive in Latisana than other low-lying zones; some can rival the good Tocai of the hills.

– **Verduzzo** w. dr. ★ DYA
Common here.

| | |
|---|---|
| Fattoria Fratelli Ferrari | Tenuta San Francesco della Vigna |
| Isola Augusta | Volderie (Dal Ferro Galvan) |
| Sergio Pevere | A. Zaglia |
| Fratelli Rabbiosi | |

**Malbec** or **Malbeck** r. dr. ★★ 79 82 83
The Bordeaux vine, usually secondary in composites with Cabernet and Merlot, makes a good varietal in W Friuli around Pordenone.
Castello di Porcia

**Malvasia** or **Malvasia Istriana** w. dr. ★ DYA
DOC in Carso, Collio and Isonzo. It makes ordinary table wines elsewhere.

**Merlot** r. p. dr. ★→★★ 82 83
Table wines, usually red, occasionally rosé, from Friuli's most popular grape variety may carry the varietal name and a place when not qualified for DOC. Merlot is DOC in six of the seven zones.

**Montsclapade** r. dr. ★★★ 82 83
A classic Bordeaux blend of Cabernets, Merlot and Malbec aged in small, new oak barrels, this promises to evolve into a red of notable class with 5–6 years of aging.
Girolamo Dorigo

**Müller Thurgau** w. dr. ★★→★★★★ 82 83
The Riesling-Sylvaner cross has been gaining favor in Friuli, especially in Collio, where it can make extraordinary wine. Pale in color, subtly but distinctively perfumed, it tends to be bone dry and crisply fruity when young, becoming smooth, almost voluptuous, with bottle age.

| | |
|---|---|
| Fratelli Buzzinelli | Ronco del Gnemiz |
| Cantoni | Tenuta Maseri Florio |
| EnoFriulia | Mario Schiopetto |

**Picolit** w. s/sw. or sw. **→*** 78 79 82 83
DOC in Colli Orientali, Picolit is also made in other parts of Friuli. Its
quality can be comparable even if authenticity isn't controlled.

| | |
|---|---|
| Abbazia di Rosazzo | Gradnik |
| Campeglio | Jermann |
| Cantina Zardetto | Komjanc |
| Cappelletti | Livon |
| Conte di Maniago | Ronchi di Fornaz |
| Girolamo Dorigo (Montsclapade) | Villa Russiz |
| Antonio Furchir | Vittorio Nalon |
| Fratelli Furlàn | |

**Pignolo**
Recently rescued from extinction, this ancient vine now makes
authorized table wine in E Friuli, though little is in commerce.

**Pinot Bianco** w. dr. *→*** 82 83
DOC in six of the seven zones. As table wine its quality ranges from
decent to very good.
EnoFriulia

**Pinot Grigio** w. dr. *→*** 82 83
DOC in six of the seven zones. Much wine from this overtaxed vine is
loosely identified as Pinot Grigio delle Venezie and the like. Excessively
popular – much more "Pinot Grigio" is sold than grapes could possibly
provide – some is nonetheless very good.
EnoFriulia

**Pinot Nero** r. p. (w.) (sp.) *→*** 79 82 83
DOC in Collio, Colli Orientali and Grave, Pinot Nero also makes table
wines, usually red or rosé. Grapes are used increasingly for *brut spumante*,
but it can make a fine, still white: EnoFriulia's Pinot Nero in Bianco and
Jermann's Engelwhite.

| | |
|---|---|
| EnoFriulia | Jermann |

**Pinot Spumante** w. p. dr. sp. **→*** DYA
Pinot and sometimes Chardonnay and even Prosecco grapes are the basis
of new sparkling wines in Friuli, both by *charmat* and *champenoise*. Early
examples include Angoris with Modolet and Rebùla; Collavini with Il
Grigio and Nature; Duca Badoglio with Il Blanc-Blanc; Livon with
Princeps Brut and Mandi Spumante Classico. Others are entering the
market.

| | |
|---|---|
| Angoris | Livon |
| E. Collavini | Mandi |
| Duca Badoglio | |

**Ramandolo**
DOC as a subdenomination under Colli Orientali del Friuli Verduzzo.

**Refosco** r. dr. *→*** 78 79 80 81 82 83
Friuli's preferred native red is DOC in all zones but Collio and Isonzo.
The best known clone is Refosco del Peduncolo Rosso, though there is
also Refosco Nostrano and, in the Carso area, it is known as Terrano.
Table wine from the grape can also be very good.

| | |
|---|---|
| Cantina Produttori Vini Cormons | Marco Felluga |
| Conti di Maniago | Giovanni Monai |
| Paolo De Lorenzi | Villa San Giovanni |
| Luisa Eddi | Volderie |

**Ribolla** or **Ribolla Gialla** w. dr. *→** DYA
Approved as DOC in Colli Orientali, Ribolla was delayed in Collio
where producers were still issuing their wines as *vino da tavola*.

**Riesling Italico** w. dr. * DYA
DOC only in Collio; occasionally used for table wine elsewhere.

**Riesling Renano** w. dr. *→*** DYA
DOC in Aquileia, Colli Orientali, Grave and Isonzo, some table wine
from Collio and other places can upstage the classified bottles.

| | |
|---|---|
| Valentino Butussi | Mario Schiopetto |
| EnoFriulia | |

**Ronco Acacie** w. dr. *** 82 83
Impressive blend of Tocai, Pinot Grigio and Ribolla grown at Rosazzo

in a white of remarkable delicacy and finesse after a youthful explosion of flowers and fruit.
Abbazia di Rosazzo

**Ronco dei Roseti** r. dr. ★★★ 82 83
Bizarre blend of local curiosities – Franconia, Tazzelenghe, Refosco – with Cabernet and Merlot seasoned in new oak by Walter Filiputti. Though rather wild at first, with bottle age the elements come together in a red of singular personality.
Abbazia di Rosazzo

**Runk** w. dr. ★★★ 82 83
Pinot Bianco with a flattering 20% of Tocai in a convincing table wine made at Oslavia in Collio.
Carlo Drufovka

**Sauvignon** w. dr. ★→★★★ DYA
This most promising variety is DOC in Collio, Colli Orientali, Grave and Isonzo. Vague as its origins are, EnoFriulia's Sauvignon delle Venezie is exemplary.

| | |
|---|---|
| Castello di Porcia | Luisa Eddi |
| Conti di Maniago | EnoFriulia |

**Schioppettino** r. dr. ★★→★★★ 77 78 79 82 83
A cult has grown around this esoteric red from the indigenous Ribolla Nera or Schioppettino vine, which makes it home only at Albana di Prepotto in the heart of the Colli Orientali. Schioppettino rates superlatives for its singular rustic breed, marked by bright ruby color, fragrance of ripe berries, and marked acidity that only seems to enhance its depth and length of flavors.

| | |
|---|---|
| Conte Antonio di Trento | Giuseppe Toti |
| Rieppi | Fratelli Zorzettig |
| Ronchi di Cialla | |

**Tazzelenghe** or **Tacelenghe** r. dr. ★★ 77 78 79 82 83
The name, dialect for *tazzalingua*, alludes to its tannic sharpness on the tongue, though this dark ruby-violet table wine has a way of being gratifyingly smooth with 3–6 years of age.

| | |
|---|---|
| Brava | Tenuta Maseri Florio |
| Girolamo Dorigo | Vigne dal Leon |
| (Ronc di Juri) | |

**Terrano del Carso**
See Carso.

**Terre Alte** w. dr. ★★★ DYA
From Tocai, Pinot Bianco and Sauvignon grown in the Oleis vineyards in Colli Orientali, this is a soft, flowery white whose youthful tone might belie its keeping capacities.
Livio Felluga

**Tocai Friulano** w. dr. ★→ ★★ DYA
Friuli's favorite white is DOC in six of seven zones. A few non-DOC table wines are also made.

**Traminer** or **Gewürztraminer** or **Traminer Aromatico**
w. dr. ★→★★★ DYA
Though technical differences between Traminer and the superior Gewürztraminer exist, they are often ignored in Italy where wines are usually labeled Traminer or Traminer Aromatico. DOC in Collio, Grave and Isonzo, it makes table wine elsewhere. EnoFriulia's Traminer delle Venezie, wherever it comes from, stands out.

| | |
|---|---|
| Antonutti | Giacomelli |
| Budini | Isola Augusta |
| Cantarutti Alfieri | Plozner |
| Cantina del Friuli Centrale | Rocca Bernarda |
| Castelvecchio | Selva |
| EnoFriulia | |

**Verduzzo** w. dr. (s/sw.) ★ DYA
DOC in Colli Orientali, Grave, Isonzo, and Latisana, Verduzzo is also used for table wines, often dry.

**Vintage Tunina** w. dr. ★★★→★★★★ 80 81 82 83
Special white from Pinot Bianco, Chardonnay, and Sauvignon with a
hint of Picolit selected by Anna and Sylvio Jermann in their Tunina plot
at Villanova di Farra in Collio. When right, it may be Italy's closest rival
to a great white Burgundy in texture, bouquet, nuance of flavors, and
breed. Yet it is entirely original; almost uniquely among Italian whites it
undergoes a malolactic fermentation which gives it greater body and
structure.
Jermann

**Zuc di Volpe** r. dr. ★★★ 81 82 83
An unlikely mix of Pinot Nero at 70% with Cabernet Sauvignon and
Merlot grown in the Colli Orientali. Though young, the '81 and '82 had
fine bouquet and fascinating flavor that should reach harmony in 4–6
years after the harvest.
Volpe Pasini

## Wine & Food

In Friuli, East meets West around the *fogolar*, the cozy open
hearth with a conical chimney that expresses the region's warm
hospitality in nearly every dining room. A melting pot of
European cookery, Friuli-Venezia Giulia gives its own touch to
*gulasch, knödel*, Viennese pastries, cabbage soups, and strudel. But
the tangs of Slovenia, Croatia, Bohemia, Austria, and Hungary
are merely a bonus added to Friuli's own tasty peasant heritage
of pork, beans, mutton, sausages, soups, blood puddings,
polenta, turnips, game, and cheese. Venezia Giulia, the coastal
strip, contributes fish to the menu with soups, chowders, and
refined risottos with prawns, squid, or scallops that reflect the
influence of Venice. From the hill town of San Daniele comes a
*prosciutto* which some consider to be the most exquisite made.

**Boreto alla gradese** Fish (turbot
is ideal) cooked in oil, vinegar,
garlic, and water, a speciality of
the isle of Grado.
  ★ Malvasia Istriana
  or ★ Verduzzo *secco*.
**Brovada** Turnips marinated in
fresh wine pressings, then cut into
strips and cooked with *muset*, a pork
sausage.
  ★★ Merlot or ★★ Cabernet.
**Capriolo in salmi** Venison in a
rich wine sauce.
  ★★★ Refosco
  or ★★★ Schioppettino.
**Frico** Cheese, both fresh and aged,
fried with onions in butter until
crunchy.
  ★★★ Sauvignon.
**Granzevola alla triestina**
Tender spider crab meat baked
with breadcrumbs, garlic, and
seasonings.
  ★★★→★★★★ Tocai
  or ★★★→★★★★ Pinot Bianco.
**Gulasch** or **gulyas** Beef cooked
with tomato, onions, paprika.
  ★ Terrano del Carso or beer.
**Jota** Nourishing and tasty soup of
pork, beans, cabbage, cornmeal.
  ★★ Cabernet Franc.
**Paparot** Cream soup that includes
spinach and corn flour.
  ★★→★★★ Pinot Grigio.
**Prosciutto di San Daniele** Paper
thin slices of air-cured ham.
  ★★★ Tocai.
**Strucolo** Friuli's answer to
strudel, made with *ricotta* or apples
or other fruit.
  ★★★→★★★★ Verduzzo
Ramandolo.

## Restaurants
Recommended in or near wine zones: **Carso** *Skabar* at Monrupino.
**Collio** *Al Cacciatore Sirk*, *Felcaro* and *Il Giardinetto* at Cormons; *Trattoria
Blanch* at Mossa; *Parco Formentini* at San Floriano. **Colli Orientali**
*Locanda al Castello* and *Zorutti* at Cividale del Friuli; *Boschetti* at Tricesimo.
**Grave** *Del Doge* in the Villa Marin at Passariano del Codroipo; *Antica
Trattoria La Primula* at San Quirino; *Alla Buona Vite* at Udine. **Isonzo** *Al
Ponte* and *Al Commercio* at Gradisca d'Isonzo; *Da Bruno* and *Hannibal* at
Monfalcone. **Latisana** *Da Toni* at Gradiscutta; *La Bella Venezia* at
Latisana.

# Latium

Lazio

Rome calls to mind wines of golden hue, which is not to suggest that their memories are always golden. Frascati and Est! Est!! Est!!!, the legends on Latium's wine list, are white, as are more than 90% of the region's DOCs and most of the table wines, too. Frascati is prima donna of the Castelli Romani, the green-clad clump of spent volcanoes southeast of Rome that harbors six of Latium's 16 DOC zones and lies within view of seven others. Est! Est!! Est!!!, whose vineyards surround the yawning crater of Lake Bolsena north of Rome, is primogenitor of that species of wine (like Liebfraumilch and California Burgundy) that lurks behind a trumped-up name.

Every noteworthy white of Latium is based on Malvasia or Trebbiano or, most often, combinations of the two. Both make wines highly prone to oxidation, which explains why they were habitually drunk up quickly and close to home. Hot bottling and other contrivances have stopped premature browning and enabled them to be sold worldwide, but their most sincere admirers still prefer them close to home.

Latium's finest wines are red, though the evidence is not easy to find. Some consist of the native Cesanese, or else Montepulciano and Sangiovese or, most remarkably, Cabernet and Merlot. Three alone – Torre Ercolana, Fiorano *rosso*, and Colle Picchioni

– could advance Latium's case for eminence, if only a few bottles remained after local fans take their quotas.

Latium is central Italy's most prolific wine region, with some half-a-billion liters a year. Not all the good wines appear in the A–Z listing, for the simple reason that they are rarely available in labeled bottles. All through the hills on either side of the Tiber north of Rome vines flourish, still often mixed with other crops, rendering personable wines to be sampled at the *cantina* or, perhaps, at the nearest *frasca*, a simple locale advertised by a laurel branch above the door. For the adventurous, the modern versions of the old Roman roads – the Aurelia, Cassia, Flaminia, and Salaria – can lead to pleasant surprises. Some wines carry recognized names, such as Baccanale, Bolsena *rosso*, Colli Cimini, Colli Etruschi, Colli Rufeno, Colli Sabini, Feronia, Greghetto di Gradoli, Mentana-Monterotondo, Morlupo, Quintaluna, and Ronciglione, though that doesn't mean they'll be easy to find.

The most enchanting wine trip from Rome is a circuit of the Castelli Romani, taking in Frascati, Marino, Colli Albani, Colli Lanuvini, Montecompatri Colonna, and Velletri. An extended trip includes Zagarolo, Cori, Aprilia and the three Cesanese DOC zones in the ruggedly pretty Ciociaria hills toward Frosinone.

Among several shops with good choices of regional and national wines are the *Enoteca Trimani*, *Enoteca Cavour* and *Enoteca Palombi* in Rome.

### Recent vintages

For red wines and the few whites that may be kept more than a couple of years, recommended vintages appear with each entry.

**Aleatico di Gradoli** DOC r. sw. ⟦**★★**⟧ 78 79 80 81 82 83
Little of this fragrant dessert wine from the antique Aleatico grape is made in the hills W of Lake Bolsena. The basic version is violet-red, lightly alcoholic, and aromatic, best in early years with fruit, especially cantaloupe. The *liquoroso* of 17.5% is for after dinner, like Port. It can last 5–10 years or more.
C.S. di Gradoli

**Aprilia** DOC
Three outside varieties grown in the plains around Aprilia S of Rome are prolific, the wines usually pedestrian.
– **Merlot** r. dr. ★→⟦**★★**⟧ 82 83
Soft, balanced, tasty with 1–3 years of age, this tends to be the best of the Aprilia trio.
– **Sangiovese** r. or p. dr. ★ DYA
Whether pale red or dark pink, this rates little interest.
– **Trebbiano** w. dr. ★ DYA
This neutral white is plentiful and widely distributed. Its chief attributes seem to be that it is cheap and inoffensive.

| | |
|---|---|
| Bolla | Enotria (C.S. di Aprilia) |
| Colli del Cavaliere | Villa dei Priori |

**Bianco Capena** DOC w. dr. or s/sw. ★→⟦**★★**⟧ DYA
From Malvasia and Trebbiano grown around Capena and Morlupo, N of Rome, the *superiore* (of 12%) can rival the best Castelli Romani whites.
C.S. Feronia

**Castel San Giorgio** r. w. dr. ⟦**★★→★★★**⟧ 78 79 80 81 82 83
Table wines from the Maccarese flatlands N of Rome's Fiumicino airport. The *rosso*, from Merlot, Montepulciano, and Pinot Nero, is generous, smooth, and distinguished from better vintages after aging 5–8 years. The *bianco*, above average for a Roman white, contains some Sémillon and Sauvignon with the regular varieties.
Maccarese S.p.A.

**Castelli Romani** r. p. w. (s/sw.) ★ DYA
Recognized table wines from various grape varieties grown in the

Castelli Romani SE of Rome. The *bianco*, usually dry, occasionally
*abboccato*, is similar to the several DOC whites (Frascati, Marino, etc.) of
the hills. Unclassified red and rosé wines also often carry the Castelli
Romani name. They are based on Sangiovese, Montepulciano, and
Cesanese, and are good young.

Gotto d'Oro (C.S. Marino)           Fontana di Papa (C.S. Colli
                                     Albani)

**Cecubo** r. dr.  ★★  78 79 80 81 82 83
Contemporary red from Abbuoto, Negroamaro, and other grapes grown
where the ancient Roman Caecubum originated along the S Latium
coast near Gaeta. Deep ruby, perfumed, dry, and robust, it ages well for
3–8 years, sometimes more.
Cantine Cenatiempo

**Cerveteri** DOC r. w. dr. s/sw.  ★→★★  81 82 83
Large zone along the coast NW of Rome around Cerveteri and
Civitavecchia. The *rosso*, from Sangiovese and Montepulciano, is
balanced ruby red wine of good body that holds up well for 1–4 years.
The *bianco*, from Trebbiano and Malvasia, dry or *abboccato*, is mellow
with a light bitter undertone. Drink young.
Cantina Cooperativa di Cerveteri

**Cesanese del Piglio** DOC r. dr. (s/sw.) (sw.) (fz.) (sp.)  ★★  80 81 82 83
Good basic red from Cesanese grapes grown in the Ciociaria hills SE of
Rome around villages of Piglio, Anagni, and Paliano. Though made in a
confusing range of types – *secco, asciutto, amabile, dolce, frizzante,* and
*spumante* – the dry versions are the most convincing. Garnet red, well-
scented, tannic, and warm, dry Cesanese is good in 2–6 years. The
semisweet and sweet wines have local admirers.
C.S. Cesanese del Piglio             Ruffo di Calabria

**Cesanese di Affile** DOC r. dr. (s/sw.) (sw.) (fz.) (sp.)  ★★  80 81 82 83
Virtually the same as neighboring Cesanesé del Piglio, the zone
surrounds the town of Affile. Some consider this the best Cesanese, but it
is hard to find.

**Cesanese di Olevano Romano** DOC r. dr. (s/sw.) (sw.) (fz.) (sp.)  ★★
80 81 82 83
Grown around Olevano Romano, this Cesanese is nearly identical to its
neighbors in character and types.
C.S. Vini Tipici Cesanese

**Colle Picchioni** r. dr.  ★★★  78 79 80 81 82 83
Though unclassified, this might be the best wine from the Castelli
Romani in commerce, proof that the volcanic soil of the hills suits reds at
least as well as whites. From Merlot and Cesanese with some Sangiovese
and Montepulciano, this robust, dark ruby wine develops warmth, poise,
and winning bouquet with 4–6 years, sometimes more. The wine from
the tiny Vigna del Vassallo is the estate's special "cru".
Paola Di Mauro

**Colli Albani** DOC w. dr. (s/sw.) (sp.)  ★  DYA
White from various Malvasia and Trebbiano subvarieties grown in the
Castelli Romani around Lago Albano and Castelgandolfo. Soft, straw
yellow to golden, it is usually dry but may be *amabile* and *spumante*. Colli
Albani *superiore* must have 12.5% alcohol.
Fontana di Papa (C.S. Colli
   Albani)

**Colli Lanuvini** DOC w. dr. (s/sw.)  ★→★★  DYA
Scarcely known, this can be among the better Castelli Romani whites.
Grown between Lago di Nemi and Aprilia around the town of Lanuvio,
it is soft, usually dry, convincingly fresh, and fragrant.
Colle Rubro                          Monte Giove
Colle San Gennaro                    Valle Vermiglia

**Cori** DOC r. w. (s/sw.) (sw.)  ★  82 83
Obscure zone adjacent to the Castelli Romani around the town of Cori.
The *rosso*, from Montepulciano, Nero Buono di Cori, and Cesanese, can
be interesting. The *bianco*, from the usual mélange of Castelli grapes, has
little to say, whether dry, *amabile*, or *dolce*.

**Est! Est!! Est!!! di Montefiascone** DOC w. dr. (s/sw.)  ★→★★  DYA
The wine was once as ludicrous as the name, a hangover from a 12th-
century legend about a tippling bishop's servant whose antics suggest he
was a victim of *delirium tremens*. Legends aside, this white from Trebbiano
and Malvasia grown beside Lake Bolsena is getting better from certain
producers. Usually dry, lightly fruity, almondy, and, lately, crisper than
most other Latium whites. Annual production is about 1 million liters.
C.S. di Montefiascone                          Italo Mazziotti
Marchesi Antinori

**Falerno** or **Falernum** r. w. dr.  ★→★★  78 79 80 81
Table wines from S. Latium where Falernum, the Roman favorite, once
thrived. The *rosso*, from Aglianico and Barbera grown around Formia,
Gaeta, and Fondi, is rich and full, improving with 4–6 years, sometimes
more. The white, from Falanghina, has golden tones and goes well with
fish when young. With age it turns amber and flat.
Cantine Cenatiempo

**Fiorano** r. w. dr. s/sw.  ★★★→★★★★  70 74 75 77 78 79 80 81
Extraordinary table wines made along the ancient Appian Way just
outside Rome. The *rosso*, from Merlot and Cabernet Sauvignon, is a
leading Italian example of a Bordeaux composite, with the breed to
improve over a decade or more. Deep ruby tending to garnet-amber, it is
austere, rich in extract, taking on bouquet and nuance of flavor with age.
The golden Fiorano *bianco* comes from Malvasia di Candia, worthiest of
local light grapes. Barrel age gives it more elegance and depth than any
of the Roman DOCs. It can take several years of age. Fiorano Sémillon,
from the Sauternes *cépage*, is a refined rarity, delicately off-dry with pale
crystalline color and light, flowery aroma.
Boncompagni Ludovisi, Principe
    di Venosa

**Frascati** DOC w. dr. s/sw. (sw.) (sp.)  ★→★★  DYA
Latium's most famous wine. Historically often *cannellino* (rather sweet as
a result of raisining grapes), it was sold from the vat in Frascati or in
cooled containers in Rome's *trattorie*. Today it is usually dry and bottled.
Made from a blend of Malvasia, Trebbiano, and other light grapes
grown around the towns of Frascati, Grottaferrata, and Monteporzio
Catone, the wine is soft, smooth, and dry or off-dry, with plenty of
Malvasia aroma and a straw-golden color. Romans drink it with
everything from *fettuccine* to fish to fruit. Crisper, cleaner, and paler than
before, the wine's fragility is often combated with flash pasteurization. Of
more than 15 million liters a year, much is exported. *Cannellino* and
*amabile* are sometimes seen, *spumante* rarely. *Superiore*, of which Fontana
Candida's Vigneti Santa Teresa stands out (★★★), must have 12%
alcohol. (Producers do not include bottler and shipper brands, which
could also be dependable.)
C.S. di Monteporzio Catone              A. De Sanctis & Figli
Casa Vinicola Pavan                          Fontana Candida
Castel De' Paolis (Lepanto)              Gotto d'Oro (C.S. di Marino)
Colli di Catone                                 Fratelli Mennuni
Colli di Tuscolo (C.S. di Frascati)     San Matteo
Conte Zandotti                                 Villa Beatrice

**La Selva** r. dr.  ★★  78 79 80 81 82 83
Good red from Cesanese and Barbera grown at the estate of La Selva
near Paliano in SE Latium. Dark, dry, and robust, with deep bouquet, it
improves for 4–7 years after seasoning in chestnut barrels.
Ruffo di Calabria

**Maccarese** r. w. dr.  ★  DYA
Tasty everyday wines from the flatlands N of Rome's Fiumicino airport,
the *rosso* from Montepulciano, Cesanese, and Merlot, the *bianco* from
Malvasia and Trebbiano. See also Castel San Giorgio.
Maccarese S.p.A.

**Marino** DOC w. dr. s/sw. (sp.)  ★→★★  DYA
Marino is second to Frascati in volume and prestige among Castelli
Romani whites, though some Romans prefer it, for it tends to be a shade
stronger, deeper in color and aroma, with a marked almondy finish in its
soft, grapy flavor. Best young in the simple *osterie* of Marino, much is now
pasteurized and shipped by the huge cooperative. Made from a similar

combination of grapes in a zone adjacent to Frascati NW of Lake Albano. Marino is sometimes fermented briefly with the skins and aged in barrels to give it old-fashioned character. *Spumante* is rare. *Superiore* must have 12.5%. Paola Di Mauro's special bottling called "Oro" from '83 was as precious as its name, promising at least ★★★.

Paola Di Mauro                          Gotto d'Oro (C.S. di Marino)
Due Santi (Lepanto)                     Principe Pallavicini

**Montecompatri Colonna** DOC w. dr. s/sw.  ★  DYA
White from the NE corner of the Castelli Romani, made from the usual mélange of grapes. Labels may carry the full denomination or the name of either town – if, indeed, any is sold with labels.

**Orvieto**
Part of the DOC zone centered in Umbria extends S into Latium. See description under Umbria.

**Santa Giulia del Poderaccio** r. dr.  ★★  74 77 78 79 81 83
Austere red from what is described as "Bordeaux" grapes grown at Castiglione in Teverina in N Latium. Strong, dry, capable of a decade or more of aging.
Conte Vaselli

**Torre Ercolana** r. dr.  ★★→★★★★  75 77 78 79 80 81 83
Table wine from nearly equal parts of Cesanese, Cabernet, and Merlot, grown at Anagni in SE Latium. Only 1,000 to 1,500 bottles are made from good vintages, enough to have convinced a fortunate few in Italy of its magnificence while remaining a secret from the rest of the world. Different each year, because of the way each variety responds to the season, from outstanding vintages (1970, 1978) it is singular, opulently perfumed with an authoritative concentration of flavors that explode on the palate and linger there. Suited to roast beef and game, it's also worth contemplating all alone – if you can find a bottle.
Cantina Colacicchi

**Torre in Pietra** r. dr.  ★★  80 81 83
Sturdy table wine from Sangiovese, Montepulciano and others grown near Torre in Pietra along the Via Aurelia NW of Rome. Dry, limber, and rotund, it can hold up for several years.
Castello di Torre in Pietra

**Velletri** DOC r. w. dr. (s/sw.)  ★★  82 83
The lone DOC red of the Castelli Romani and a stereotypical but better-than-average white originate around the town of Velletri S towards Cisterna. The *rosso*, from Cesanese, Montepulciano, and Sangiovese, is fresh and fruity, best on the young side. The *bianco*, whether *secco* or *amabile*, is more delicate and fragrant than most Castelli whites.
Cantina Viticoltori Velletri              Colle Piombo (Gabrielli)
Casa Vinicola Pavan                       Consorzio Produttori Vini Velletri

**Zagarolo** DOC w. dr. s/sw.  ★  DYA
Only a few thousand liters of this white are made annually in a zone E of the Castelli Romani from the same sort of grapes. Mellow and grapy, whether dry or *amabile*, it is best on the spot. *Superiore* must have 12.5%.

Contemporary Roman cooking is a monument to hodge podge, the foundations of which – the recipes of the ancient Romans and the bourgeoisie of ensuing epochs – have all but crumbled away. What remains has been patched together by the poor and propped up by what could be borrowed or stolen from other places. Yet, for all the salt cod and salt pork, tripe, brains, entrails, feet, tails, dried beans, mussels, anchovies, chickpeas, and salty *pecorino romano*, Rome lays one of the most pungently tasty and vividly colored tables of Italy. A rare extravagance is *abbacchio*, sucking lamb so tender that even poor people can't resist it. But what really enriches the Roman diet are the vegetables that arrive fresh daily from the region's truck gardens. Many dishes of Rome (and Latium) don't seem to go with wine. The Roman answer is to quaff carafe whites from the beloved Castelli Romani – sometimes mercifully diluted with effervescent mineral water.

**Abbacchio alla cacciatora** Baby lamb cooked with rosemary, garlic, anchovies, and vinegar.
  ★★★→★★★★  Torre Ercolana
  or ★★★→★★★★  Fiorano *rosso*.
**Bucatini alla matriciana** Long, narrow pasta tubes with a sauce of *guanciale* (salt pork from the pig's jowl), red peppers (sometimes tomatoes), and grated *pecorino*.
  ★  Castelli Romani *rosato*
  or  ★  Colli Albani.
**Carciofi alla giudia** Tender artichokes flattened flower-like and deep-fried, a speciality of Rome's Jewish quarter. *Carciofi alla romana* are artichokes sautéed in oil, garlic, and mint.
  ★  Trebbiano di Aprilia or mineral water.
**Coda alla vaccinara** Oxtail stewed with onion, tomatoes, lots of celery, and wine.

  ★★  Castel San Giorgio
  or ★★  Cesanese *secco*.
**Cozze alla marinara** Mussels cooked in their juice with parsley, garlic, and sometimes tomato.
  ★★  Marino *superiore secco*.
**Fettuccine al burro** Feather-light egg noodles with lashings of butter, cream, and Parmesan.
  ★★  Frascati *superiore secco*.
**Penne all'arrabbiata** Pasta tubes with raging hot pepper sauce.
  ★  Any carafe white.
**Saltimbocca alla romana** Veal filets with *prosciutto* and sage sautéed in butter.
  ★★★  Colle Picchioni.
**Spaghetti alla carbonara** The hot pasta is plunged into a mix of *guanciale*, grated Parmesan, *pecorino*, hot peppers, and raw eggs, which curdle and adhere to the strands.
  ★★  Colli Lanuvini.

## Restaurants

Recommended in or near wine zones: **Castelli Romani** *D'Artagnan* at Frascati; *Al Fico*, *Da Gastone* and *Tuscolo* at Grottaferrata; *Antonio al Vigneto* near Marino; *Lo Specchio di Diana* at Nemi. **Cesanese zones** *Del Gallo* at Anagni; *Sora Maria e Arcangelo* at Olevano Romano.
**Est! Est!! Est!!!** *Dante* at Montefiascone.

# Liguria

Liguria

Wine is an almost irrelevant item in the economy of the Italian Riviera which flanks Italy's busiest seaport of Genoa. Still, on the verdant hillsides of this slender crescent arching along the Ligurian Sea from France to Tuscany grow more than 100 types of vines. This remarkable testimony to self-reliance in the region with the next to the lowest volume of production (Valle d'Aosta trails) is also a factor behind the obscurity of Liguria's myriad local wines.

A conspicuous exception is Cinqueterre, whose reputation was built more on past achievements than present. Other wines merit greater esteem, especially Rossese di Dolceacqua, the only other DOC, and the white Pigato and Vermentino, which do so well around Albenga that official recognition can't be denied much longer.

There's a definite fascination in tracking down local wines. Most are white and go well with fish or even *pesto* (basil and garlic sauce) and can seem divine when sipped on a terrace at Rapallo or Portovenere (what they'd taste like back home probably doesn't matter). Local wines to look for are Coronata and Polcevera on the outskirts of Genoa; the whites and reds of Piematone (near Bordighera); and the red Granaccia of Quiliano near Savona. Most others are called simply *nostrano* (ours) – but proudly.

Visitors may find the rusticity of the Dolceacqua zone against the French border a relaxing counterpoint to the crowded playgrounds of nearby San Remo and Monte Carlo. The vineyards of Cinqueterre northwest of La Spezia are also out-of-the-way and posed dramatically on cliffs above the sea. In Genoa, the annual *Bibe* in November is one of Italy's major wine fairs, with bottles displayed from all regions. The *Enoteca Sola* in Genoa provides an intelligent selection of Ligurian wines with the best from other places. Also recommended are the *Enoteca Mantelli* in Genoa and the *Enoteca Baroni* at Lerici.

## Recent vintages

Recommended vintages appear with each entry for the few Ligurian wines for aging.

**Barbera di Linero** r. dr. **★★→★★★** 78 79 81 82 83
One of the better Barberas made outside Piedmont, it improves with 5–7 years, more from exceptional vintages. Garnet red, balanced, its bouquet is extraordinary. The estate also produces good Linero *rosso* and *bianco* from vineyards in the Colli di Luni near La Spezia.
Cantina G. Tognoni

**Buzzetto di Quiliano** w. dr. **★→★★** DYA
Local wine from the Buzzetto grape grown at Quiliano above Savona. Bright straw yellow, fragile (10% or so), zestfully acidic, its underripe freshness makes it right for *pesto*. Growers issue bottles with a uniform label. Still, a taste might entail a trip, and while there try the red Granaccia.

**Cinqueterre** DOC w. dr. **★** DYA
Praised and poeticized through the ages, Cinqueterre's romantic history alone is worthy of respect, but, sadly, the modern wine rarely lives up to past notices. From Bosco grapes with some Albarola and Vermentino grown on steep seaside slopes of the "Five Lands" – the villages of

Monterosso, Vernazza, Corniglia, Manarola, and Riomaggiore – the
wine is (ideally) straw green, dry, fresh, and delicately scented.
– **Sciacchetrà** am. s/sw. sw. ★★ 79 82 83
The dessert version of Cinqueterre from the same grapes semidried. Of at
least 17% alcohol, it is golden amber, smooth, sometimes dry enough for
aperitif, and it keeps for years. Very rare.
Ag. 1 yr.

| | |
|---|---|
| Agricoltura di Cinqueterre | Liana Rolandi |
| Silvano Cozzani | |

**Lumassina** w. dr. ★ DYA
Lumassina, probably the same as the Buzzetto grape of Quiliano, makes
this simple white, noted near Pietra Ligure as the perfect match for *pesto*.

| | |
|---|---|
| Giuseppe Maffei | Zanobbio |

**Pigato di Albenga** or **Pigato Ligure** w. dr. (s/sw.) ★★→★★★ DYA
Several of Liguria's better whites are made from this variety grown only
along the Riviera di Ponente, notably in the hills above Albenga. Pale
straw to sunny yellow, it has remarkable aroma, ample structure and
velvety texture, with dry but mouth-filling flavor (occasionally
*abboccato*), accented by alcohol of 13–14%. Parodi's Cascina Fèipu dei
Massaretti stands out.

| | |
|---|---|
| Cascina Fèipu dei Massaretti | Fratelli Pozzo |
| Bruna Donato Francesco | Salea (Cantine Calleri) |
| Eno Val D'Arroscia (Lupi) | Vairo |
| Vincenzo Mariano | |

**Pornassio Ormeasco** r. dr. ★★→★★★ 78 79 81 83
From Pornassio, this ruby-cherry colored wine can match any
Piedmontese Dolcetto for longevity and finesse. After 5–8 years it is
velvety and superbly balanced, with a rich bouquet of berries and spice.
Eno Val d'Arroscia (Lupi)

**Rosa di Albenga** p. dr. ★★ DYA
The best-known of several rosés from the native Barbarossa grape
prominent around Albenga. Cherry pink, dry, convincing.
Cantine Calleri

**Rossese di Albenga** or **Rossese Ligure** r. dr. ★★→★★★ 82 83
Two styles of table wine from Rossese, Liguria's outstanding dark grape
grown around Albenga and Finale Ligure: one light in color and body,
flowery, fluent, and tasty when young; the other of deeper ruby color,
more polished, good for 2–5 years.

| | |
|---|---|
| Anfossi | Salea (Cantine Calleri) |
| Cascina Fèipu dei Massaretti | Vairo |

**Rossese di Dolceacqua** or **Dolceacqua** DOC r. dr. ★★→★★★ 79 80
82 83
The inherent beauty of this red was appreciated by Napoleon, but its
glamor still isn't fully expressed. Yet, even when rustic, it's seductive.
From Rossese grown on hills behind Ventimiglia, Bordighera, and San
Remo, centered in the town of Dolceacqua, it is bright ruby to deep
violet, as flowery on the nose as it is fruity on the palate, with warmth
and plushness after 2–5 years, sometimes more. The trend is toward
youthfully soft wines similar in style to some Beaujolais *crus*.
Ag. *superiore* 1 yr.

| | |
|---|---|
| Silvio Anfosso (Roquin) | Rubino Balestra & Tornatore |
| Crespi | Solamito & Garoscio |
| Enzo Guglielmi | Tenuta Giuncheo (Diamonti) |
| Michele Guglielmi | Pippo Viale |
| Nano | Vigneti d'Arcagna |
| Antonio Orrigo | Vigneto Curli (Croesi) |

**Terizzo** r. dr. ★★→★★★ 82 83
Stylish ruby-garnet wine from Sangiovese and Cabernet grown at
Castelnuovo Magra. Aged in chestnut casks, it is full-bodied with a
lovely bouquet and an opulence that lasts at least 3–4 years.
La Colombiera (Ferro)

**Vermentino** w. dr. ★→★★★ DYA
Liguria's preponderant white grape stands out in table wines on the
Riviera Ponente between Imperia and Pietra Ligure, though it has also
shown exceedingly well in eastern Liguria in the Colli di Luni above La

Spezia. Pale straw green to yellow, it is finely scented and can be either light and crisp or smooth and textured. In both cases it is best young.

| | |
|---|---|
| Cantine Calleri | Romano Ramoino |
| Crespi | Robaudi del Belluomo |
| Eno Val d'Arroscia (Lupi) | Lino N. Spotorno |
| La Colombiera (Ferro) | Tenuta Giuncheo (Diamonti) |
| Lambruschi | Vairo |

# Wine & Food

As seafaring people, Ligurians rely on fish prepared in artistic and savory ways. There are tiny white *bianchetti* (whitebait), *datteri* (sea dates), *tartufi del mare* (oyster-like sea truffles), shrimp, squid, octopus, mullet, seabass, and dozens of others, many of which appear in the fish soups known as *buridda* or *ciuppin*. But fish isn't all. Cramped for space between the sea and the precipitous Apennines, Ligurians resourcefully work magic with nearly anything edible their terraced gardens, orchards and herb-scented hillsides provide. Basil is revered, the base of the glorious *pesto* among many uses. Nuts, herbs, mushrooms, and spices are features of the exotic sauces and dressings for pasta and other dishes, so deftly delicious that they're called *tocchi* (touches). Meat is secondary, though rabbit braised with olives is adored along the western Riviera. Another exquisite speciality of that region is dried tomatoes under oil. Though day-to-day dining is simple enough, Ligurians like the elaborate on special occasions, expressed in *cima alla genovese*, *torta pasqualina*, and, the epitome of indulgence, *cappon magro*.

**Branzino in tegame** Sumptuous Mediterranean seabass cooked with white wine, tomato, and seasonings.
   *** Vermentino.

**Cappon magro** At least a dozen types of fish are piled pyramid-style on a base of sea biscuits and topped with oysters and lobsters.
*Capponada* is a simpler version that contains preserved fish.
   *** Vermentino.

**Castagnaccio** Crunchy chestnut cake with raisins and pine nuts.
   ** Cinqueterre Sciacchetrà.

**Cima alla genovese** Veal breast rolled with vegetables, nuts, herbs, spices, eggs, and cheese.
   ** Rossese d'Albenga, young.

**Coniglio al Rossese** Rabbit braised in Rossese with tomato, garlic, rosemary, and olives.
   **→*** Rossese di Dolceacqua.

**Farinata** Irresistible snack of chickpea paste cooked in oil and served in crisp slabs like pizza; known as *panissa* when onions are included.
   ** Rosa di Albenga.

**Pansôti** Type of ravioli filled with *ricotta* and chard and topped with a walnut cream sauce.
   *** Pigato.

**Torta pasqualina** Monumental Easter tart, its multitude of ingredients spread through 33 layers.
   *** Pigato.

**Trenette al pesto** Slender ribbon noodles (sometimes with boiled potatoes included) topped with Genoa's sauce of basil, cheese, nuts, oil, and garlic.
   * Lumassina.

**Troffie al pesto** Slender pasta and potato spikes with the famous sauce.
   *→** Buzzetto di Quiliano.

## Restaurants

Recommended in or near wine zones: **Cinqueterre** *Aristide* at Manarola; *Da Claudio* at Monterosso; *Gianni Franzi* at Vernazza; **Colli di Luni** *Paracucchi-Locanda dell'Angelo* at Ameglia; *La Lucerna* at Bocca di Magra; *La Luna* at Campiglia; *Le Due Corone* at Lerici; **Rossese-Pigato zones** *Palma* at Alassio; *La Capanna* at Apricale; *L'Uliveto* at Castellaro; *Nannina* at Imperia; *Gino* at Piani di Camporosso.

# Lombardy

## Lombardia

Lombardians, perhaps uniquely among Italians, prefer other wines to their own. The nation's most populous and prosperous region has three outstanding wine areas: the Valtellina in the north, the Oltrepò Pavese in the southwest and the province of Brescia (with seven DOC zones) in the east. And yet, in Milan, the commercial capital of Italian wine, it's harder to find a bottle from the home region than a white from Friuli or Trentino, a red from Piedmont, or one of the omnipresent triumvirate from Verona. Though Lombardy grows more Pinot for *spumante* than does any other region, well-heeled Milanese habitually celebrate with Champagne at double the cost.

This cosmopolitanism may be admirable in some ways, but when it comes to wine, Lombardians don't seem to know what they're missing. True, the Oltrepò Pavese, which shares neighboring Piedmont's aptitude for quality, hasn't lived up to its

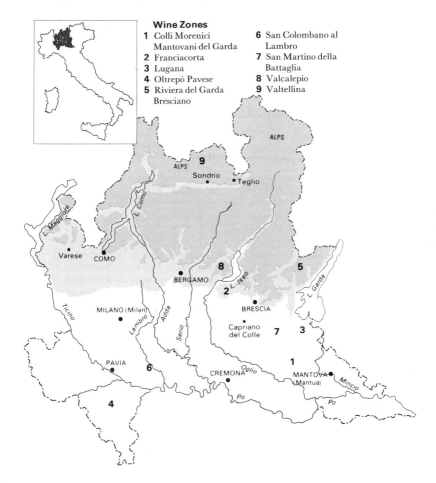

**Wine Zones**

1 Colli Morenici Mantovani del Garda
2 Franciacorta
3 Lugana
4 Oltrepò Pavese
5 Riviera del Garda Bresciano
6 San Colombano al Lambro
7 San Martino della Battaglia
8 Valcalepio
9 Valtellina

promise – yet. Growers still sell their best Pinot grapes to outsiders, who rarely mention the origins on labels.

The Valtellina produces more DOC wine from Nebbiolo grapes than any other (Barolo follows), but its reputation is better abroad than at home. Brescia's wines have only recently begun to rise from obscurity. Franciacorta Pinot *spumante* leads the way, but the reds of Franciacorta, Botticino, and Cellatica, the white Lugana and Tocai di San Martino della Battaglia, and the *rosso* and *chiaretto* of Riviera del Garda Bresciano have winning personalities, too.

Visitors to the Lombardian lake country can take in Lugana and the Riviera del Garda on the shores of Lake Garda, and Franciacorta, which touches on pretty Lake Iseo. The Valtellina is a gorgeous valley in the Alps. The Oltrepò Pavese lies in rustically scenic hills south of Pavia. Oltrepò wines are screened for display and tasting at the *enoteca* in Certosa di Pavia.

Milan has some of the nation's best supplied wine shops – *Enoteca Solci*, *Enoteca Cotti*, *N'Ombra de Vin* and *Provera* among many – as well as restaurants with impressive cellars. Also in the provinces are outstanding collections, such as *Enoteca Italo Castelletti* at Ponte San Pietro near Bergamo, *Enoteca Rocco Lettieri* at Cantù near Como and *L'Enotenca* at Isola Dovarese near Cremona.

## Recent vintages

Lombardy's longest-lived wines are the reds of Oltrepò Pavese and Valtellina, which may improve for a decade or more. In Brescia and other zones, most reds are drunk inside 6–7 years.

1983    Another fine year in the Oltrepò Pavese; good to very good in the northeast.

1982    Outstanding harvest everywhere, one of the best in memory in Oltrepò Pavese.

1981    Sharply reduced, especially in Oltrepò Pavese; quality was generally acceptable, but subpar in Valtellina.

1980    Late harvest with whites better than reds in Oltrepò and Brescia; fine, durable wines in Valtellina.

1979    Very good, abundant crop in Oltrepò; good to excellent in Valtellina and Brescia.

1978    Though reduced in volume, quality was good to excellent in long-lived reds.

1977    Uneven; satisfactory in Oltrepò and Brescia, poor in Valtellina.

1976    Spotty; some fine whites in Oltrepò and Brescia, but reds average at best.

1975    Middling quality in Oltrepò and Brescia, good in Valtellina.

1974    Fine harvest in Oltrepò and Brescia, only fair in Valtellina.

1973    Average everywhere.

1972    A year to forget.

1971    Fine harvest for Oltrepò and Valtellina.

**Barbacarlo**
See Oltrepò Pavese.

**Barbera**
Probably the most heavily planted vine of Lombardy. DOC in Oltrepò Pavese.

**Bonarda**
Strain of Croatina popular in SW Lombardy. DOC in Oltrepò Pavese.

**Botticino** DOC r. dr.   ★★→★★★   80 82 83
Bright garnet-red wine from Barbera, Marzemino, Schiava, and Sangiovese grown in limited quantity E of Brescia. Warm, fairly robust, and lightly tannic, it develops bouquet and touches of elegance in 3–4 years.

Contessa Cazzago              Giacomo Giossi
Emilio Franzoni               Tenuta Bettina (Bracchi)

**Buttafuoco**
See Oltrepò Pavese.

**Canneto** r. dr. ☐**★★**☐ 80 82 83
Table wine from Barbera, Croatina and others grown at Canneto Pavese in the Oltrepò. Bright ruby, dry, vinous, its marked bitter undertone explains why it is often called Canneto Amaro.
Angelo Bazzini & Figli              Fratelli Giorgi
Pietro & Carlo Faravelli          Francesco Quaquarini

**Capriano del Colle** DOC r. w.   ★ 82 83
Little-known recent DOC from the town of Capriano del Colle S of Brescia. The *rosso*, from Sangiovese and Marzemino, is supposedly bright and lively when young. The Trebbiano is pale straw green and tart.

**Cellatica** DOC r. dr. ☐**★★**☐ 82 83
From Schiava Gentile, Barbera, and Marzemino grapes grown at Cellatica, N of Brescia, this tasty, scented, ruby-red is popular locally in 2–4 years.
Cooperativa Vitivinicola          Bernardo Corti
   Cellatica-Gussago             Tenuta Santella (Tonoli)

**Clastidio** r. p. w. ★★ 79 82 83
Table wines from Casteggio. The *rosso* is similar to Oltrepò Pavese DOC and the *rosato* comes from the same Barbera, Croatina, and Uva Rara grapes. The *bianco* is from Riesling and Pinot.
Angelo Ballabio

**Clastidium** w. dr. ★★★→★★★★ 78 82
Extraordinary white from Pinot Nero and Pinot Grigio grown at Broni in Oltrepò Pavese and vinified at Casteggio (the Roman Clastidium) under a secret method that involves several years' aging in oak casks. Dry but mouth-filling and silky, it maintains light color, gorgeous fruity flavor, and flowery bouquet for 8–10 years or more. Made in extremely limited quantity.
Angelo Ballabio

**Colle del Calvario** r. w. dr.   ★→★★★ 78 80 81 82 83
Table wines from the town of Grumello between Bergamo and Lake Iseo. The *rosso*, from Merlot, Cabernet Sauvignon, and Marzemino, illustrates potential for Bordeaux-style reds in these alpine foothills. It ages well with 6–8 years. The *bianco*, from Pinot Bianco and Grigio, is fruity and fresh, good young.
Tenuta Castello

**Colli Morenici Mantovani del Garda** DOC r. p. w.   ★ DYA
Unproven DOC between Mantua and Lake Garda. The *rosso*, from Rondinella, Merlot, and Rossanella, is lightweight and dry; it may be called *rubino*. The *rosato*, from the same grapes, pale cherry in color and delicate, may be called *chiaretto*. The *bianco*, from Garganega and Trebbiano, bears a vague family resemblance to Soave.
C.S. Colli Morenici Alto
   Mantovano

**Cortese**
See Oltrepò Pavese.

**Franciacorta** DOC
Zone NW of Brescia centered in the town of Cortefranca and fronting on Lake Iseo, noted for two distinctive categories of wine.
– **Pinot** w. (p.) dr. sp.   ★★→★★★★
Both still white (Pinot Bianco di Franciacorta, based on Pinot Bianco grapes) and sparkling white and rosé (Pinot di Franciacorta *spumante*, which may include Pinot Nero and Grigio, as well as Chardonnay grapes) are covered by this category. The still wine is pale yellow with hints of green, smooth, fruity and balanced – best within 2–3 years. The *spumanti* may be either non-vintage *charmat* or vintage *méthode champenoise brut*, which includes the *pas dosé* or *nature*. The Guido Berlucchi firm is widely known. Others are coming admirably close to fine Champagne in class, notably Monte Rossa, Aziendo Vinicola Montorfano with Bellavista and Ca' del Bosco, a model estate, with its Dosage Zero, Crémant, and vintage Brut.
– **Rosso** r. dr. ☐**★★→★★★**☐ 80 81 82 83
Bright ruby red from a unique combination of Cabernet Franc, Barbera,

Nebbiolo, and Merlot. Fragrant, smooth, and dry, with a round, mellow flavor, it is versatile and impressive in 2–5 years.

| | |
|---|---|
| Bellavista (Azienda Vinicola Montorfano) | Longhi-De Carli |
| | Monte Rossa |
| Fratelli Berlucchi | Barone Monti della Corte |
| Guido Berlucchi | Montorfano (Faccoli) |
| Bersi Serlini | Nobili Barboglio de' Gaioncelli |
| Ca' del Bosco | G. Ragnoli |
| Cattarich-Ducco | Ricci Curbastro |
| Cavalleri | Uberti |
| Cornaleto | |

**Frecciarossa**
Estate near Casteggio with wines once known internationally as Grand Cru, St George (both red), and La Vigne Blanche (white), now under Oltrepò Pavese DOC without these designations.

**Gaggiarone**
See Oltrepò Pavese Bonarda.

**Groppello** r. dr.  ★★→★★★   81 82 83
Fine table wine from the Valtenesi on SW shore of Lake Garda. Based on Groppello, it has a lively ruby color, medium body, and a dry, fresh, fruity flavor with an almondy finish. Good in 2–4 years, sometimes more.

| | |
|---|---|
| Angelo Baldo | Fulvio Leali |
| G. Battista & G. Franco Comincioli | Giuseppe Leali |
| | Redaelli de Zinis |

**Grumello**
See Valtellina Superiore.

**Inferno**
See Valtellina Superiore.

**Lambrusco Mantovano** r. dr. fz.  ★  DYA
Lambrusco from the province of Mantova, similar to Emilian types.

| | |
|---|---|
| Alberini | C.S. Cooperativa di Revere |

**Lugana** DOC w. dr. (sp.)  ★★→★★★   DYA
Fine white from Trebbiano di Lugana grown S of Lake Garda in a zone reaching into the Veneto at Peschiera. Straw green to sunny yellow, delicately flowery, its considerable grace and personality make it one of the most consistently good whites of the Garda-Verona area (including Soave). Good young, some Lugana develops depth with a year or more in bottle. A passable *spumante* is made, usually by *charmat*.

| | |
|---|---|
| Ambrosi | Podere Co' de Fer |
| Aziende Agricole del Lugana | Prandell |
| Pietro Bordignon & Figlio | Provenza |
| Ca' Furia | Salvalai |
| Pietro Dal Cero | San Grato (Premiovini) |
| Fratelli Fraccaroli | Scamperle |
| Giovanni Franzoni | Vigneti Venturelli |
| Lamberti | Visconti |
| Marangona | Zenato |
| Andrea Pasini & Figli | Zenegaglia |
| Conti Pellizzari di San Girolamo | |

**Merlot** r. (p.) dr.  ★→★★   82 83
Varietal table wines of good quality are made in Oltrepò Pavese, San Colombano al Lambro, Bergamo, and Brescia, among other places. They are usually to drink in 1–4 years. The rare rosé is to drink young.

| | |
|---|---|
| C.S. Colli Morenici Alto Mantovano | Pietro Dal Cero |
| | Montelio (Mazza Sesia) |
| C.S. della Bergamasca | |

**Montevecchia** r. w. dr.  ★→★★   82 83
Montevecchia in the Brianza hills makes what is sometimes called Milan's "local" wine because the town's vineyards are supposedly closest to the city. The *rosso*, from Barbera, Nebbiolo, and Merlot, is sturdy enough to take 3–4 years' aging. The *bianco*, from a blend including Trebbiano, Riesling, and Pinot, is light and fragile.
Conte Titta Gilberti

**Moscato**
See Oltrepò Pavese.

**Moscato di Scanzo** r.–am. sw. ★★★ 74 78 80 82
From the Merera clone of dark Moscato grown at Scanzo in the province
of Bergamo, this ruby-amber dessert wine has exquisite Muscat
fragrance and refined sweetness. Extremely rare, the few bottles
produced are considered priceless.

**Müller Thurgau** w. dr. ★★→★★★ 82 83
Table wines from the Riesling-Sylvaner cross, grown in the Oltrepò
Pavese, can do as well as DOC whites in class. Fine, fragrant and smooth,
they are often good young but can take on persuasive nuances with 2–3
years in bottle.

| | |
|---|---|
| Italo Contardi | Membretti-Balestreri |
| Fratelli Faravelli | Montelio (Mazza Sesia) |
| Giovanni Ferrari & Fratelli | Fratelli Padroggi |
| Isimbarda | |

**Narbusto** r. dr. ★★★ 71 74
Though made from the usual Oltrepò red grapes, this is kept apart as an
unusually long-lived table wine aged at least 8 years in casks, 2 in bottle,
and capable of lasting another decade beyond. Rich bouquet of berries
and tar, deep ruby color, the flavor is austere with lingering warmth.
Angelo Ballabio

**Oltrepò Pavese** DOC
A large zone in hills S across the Po from the city of Pavia in SW
Lombardy. Despite outstanding capacity (100 million liters a year, 17%
DOC) and a tradition of millennia, Oltrepò Pavese remains a potential
giant of Italian wine groping for an identity. Italy's leading source of
Pinot for *spumante* (usually made in Piedmont), the zone also produces
fine Barbera, Bonarda, Riesling, Moscato, and Müller Thurgau grapes.
Still, the few wines with widespread reputations (Frecciarossa, Ballabio,
and Monsupello, for example) rely on individual identities. The DOC
covers ten general types: six varietal names (though Pinot and Riesling
apply to more than one variety); a *rosso* (of Barbera, Croatina, Uva
Rara, and Ughetta); and three special denominations (Barbacarlo,
Buttafuoco, and Sangue di Giuda, all based on grapes for the red). To
confuse things, some wine that could qualify as DOC isn't sold as such.
Still, an active consortium is making progress in this major zone.
– **Barbacarlo** r. dr. s/sw. fz. ★★→★★★ 75 78 79 81 82 83
Restricted zone near Broni named after Barbacarlo estate of Maga Lino,
which continues to make the best wine among several producers. Deep
ruby, robust, and dry (though an *amabile* is permitted), it has the
almondy bitter background typical of Oltrepò reds. Among the longest-
lived, most expensive and best of Italy's *frizzante* reds.
– **Barbera** r. dr. ★→ ★★★ 79 81 82 83
Whether drunk young, when its tannic robustness is inviting, or after
5–10 years, when it develops bouquet and composed character, this can
rank with the finest wines of the name.
– **Bonarda** r. dr. ★→★★★ 81 82 83
Dark, thick, grapy, bitter, Bonarda epitomizes the rustic goodness of
Oltrepò reds. Usually good in 3–4 years, it can age to garnet red and
austere, as epitomized by the Gaggiarone of Giacomo Agnes.
– **Buttafuoco** r. dr. (fz.) ★★→★★★ 79 81 82 83
Colorfully named (sparks like fire), this inky, generous, dry, often bubbly
wine has distinctive personality from Bianchina Alberici. Good after 3–4
years, from special vintages it can last longer.
– **Cortese** w. dr. ★ DYA
The tiny amount of wine from Piedmont's prime white grape is light,
crisp and unremarkable.
– **Moscato** w. s/sw. sw. sp. ★★ DYA
Dessert wines, nearly always sparkling, can match all but the very finest
Moscatos of Piedmont.
– **Pinot** r. p. w. dr. sp. ★→ ★★★ 81 82 83
The name applies to Pinot Grigio and Pinot Nero in still wines (either
white, coppery, rosé, or red) and *spumanti* (white or rosé made by either
*charmat* or Champagne methods). Some still red and rosé are very good,
though there's little of them. Pinot Grigio alone can compare with almost
any other of NE Italy, but most Pinot grapes of the Oltrepò go into
sparkling wines, sometimes excellent, only a few of which are DOC
(see Oltrepò Pavese Pinot Spumante).

– **Riesling** w. dr. (sp.)  ★★→★★★  82 83
The name applies to Riesling Renano or Riesling Italico, or both, in still
or sparkling wines. Both thrive in the Oltrepò in pale straw-green,
delicately perfumed, dry wines of real character.

– **Rosso** r. dr.  ★→ ★★★  79 81 82 83
Made by many in somewhat different styles and under many different
names. Some are common, but quite a few are good to excellent. Dark
ruby turning to garnet, the best versions are ample in body, nicely tannic
and lightly bitter, with smoothness and bouquet after 3–4 years.

– **Sangue di Giuda** r. dr. fz.  ★→★★  79 81
Usually the fizziest of the Oltrepò reds, "Judas's Blood" is let in limited
quantities from a restricted zone near Broni. Lively, soft, sometimes with
a hint of sweetness, it is dominated by Croatina. Best inside 3 years.

| | |
|---|---|
| Pietro Achilli | Le Fracce (Mairano) |
| Giacomo Agnes | Madonna Isabella (Venco) |
| Bianchina Alberici | Maga Lino |
| Badalucca (Zuffada) | Maggi |
| Fratelli Bagnasco | Malpaga (Pontiroli) |
| Marco Bellani | Martini & Rossi |
| Bersano | Membretti-Balestreri |
| Dante Bianchi | Mombrione (Cavazzana) |
| Boffalora | Monsupello (Boatti) |
| Ca' Longa (Brega) | Francesco Montagna |
| Ca' Montebello (Scarani) | Monteceresino |
| C.S. Casteggio | Montelio (Mazza Sesia) |
| C.S. Intercomunale di Broni | Montenato Groppallo |
| C.S. Retorbido | Nazzano |
| C.S. Santa Maria della Versa | Enrico Orlandi & Figli |
| Casa Ré | Fratelli Padroggi |
| Castello di Luzzano | Pezzolo |
| Cella di Montalto | Poggiopelato (Agnes) |
| Cinzano | Francesco Quaquarini |
| Italo Contardi | 4 Castagni |
| Conte Dal Pozzo | Giuseppe Riccardi & Figli |
| Giuseppe Dagradi | Tenuta di Oliva |
| Fratelli Faravelli | Tenuta Pegazzera |
| Frecciarossa (Odero) | Dino Torti |
| Fratelli Gancia | Travaglino |
| Fratelli Giorgi | Edmondo Tronconi |
| Il Casale (Denari) | Luigi Valenti |
| Il Frater (Bellani) | Vigna al Castello (Dezza) |
| Isimbarda | Vilide |
| La Costaiola | Villa Bellaria |
| La Marzuola | Vitivinicola Doria |

## Oltrepò Pavese Pinot Spumante DOC/non-DOC

w. (p.) dr. sp.  ★★→★★★★
Many Italian sparkling wines are based on grapes from Oltrepò (mainly
Pinot Nero, but also Pinot Grigio, Pinot Bianco and Chardonnay),
though the source is not always clear on labels and few wines are DOC.
Often they are made outside Lombardy and blended with wines from
other places, notably Trentino-Alto Adige. They can be of superior
quality and value, especially when made by the *méthode champenoise*,
marked (m.c.).

– **Ballabio Brut (m.c.), Ballabio Rosé (m.c.)**
Angelo Ballabio

– **Bosca Riserva del Nonno (m.c.), Record Brut**
Luigi Bosca & Figli (Piedmont)

– **Carlo Gancia Brut (m.c.), Gancia Il Brut, Pinot di Pinot,
Riserva Brut di Pinot**
Fratelli Gancia (Piedmont)

– **Cinzano Brut (m.c.), Principe di Piemonte Blanc de Blancs**
Cinzano (Piedmont)

– **Conti della Cremosina Brut (m.c.)**
Bersano (Piedmont)

– **Contratto Bacco d'Oro (m.c.), Contratto Brut (m.c.), Imperial
Riserva Sabauda (m.c.), Reserve for England (m.c.)**
Contratto (Piedmont)

– **Cora Brut, Pinot del Poggio, Royal Ambassador Brut Blanc de Blancs (m.c.)**
G. & L. Fratelli Cora (Piedmont)
– **Cristal Pinot Brut (m.c.), Fontanahiara Brut (m.c.), Fontanhiara Pinot (m.c.)**
Maggi
– **Gilardino Brut (m.c.)**
Gilardino (Piedmont)
– **Giorgi Gran Spumante (m.c.)**
Fratelli Giorgi
– **Gran Duca Brut (m.c.)**
Duca d'Asti (Piedmont)
– **La Versa Brut (m.c.)**
C.S. La Versa
– **Malpaga Brut (m.c.)**
Malpaga
– **Pegazzera Brut (m.c.)**
Tenuta Pegazzera
– **Pinot Brut, Realbrut (m.c.)**
Calissano (Piedmont)
– **President Brut Riserva Privata (m.c.), President Reserve Crystal Extra Secco, President Reserve Rosé**
Ottavio Riccadonna (Piedmont)
– **Riserva Montelera (m.c.)**
Martini & Rossi (Piedmont)
– **Santa Maria Brut**
Pietro Achilli
– **Scarani Brut (m.c.)**
Ca' Montebello
– **Valdo Brut (m.c.)**
Valdo (Veneto)
– **Valentino Brut (m.c.)**
Valentino Migliorini (Piedmont)
– **Vilide Brut Gran Riserva (m.c.)**
Vilide

**Pinot**
Lombardy is Italy's leading producer of Pinot, both light and dark varieties, for use in still wines and, most notably, sparkling. See Franciacorta Pinot, Oltrepò Pavese Pinot and Oltrepò Pavese Pinot Spumante DOC/non-DOC.

**Prandell Brut, Prandell Rosé** w. p. sp. ★★ DYA
Two *méthode champenoise spumanti* from dark and light Pinot grapes and Chardonnay grown S of Lake Garda.
Prandell

**Riesling**
Both Riesling Renano and Riesling Italico are grown in Lombardy, notably in Oltrepò Pavese as DOC wines.

**Riviera del Garda Bresciano** DOC r. p. dr. ★→ ★★★ 82 83
A large zone W and SW of Lake Garda in Brescia province. Both the *rosso* and *chiaretto* are from Groppello, Sangiovese, Barbera, and Marzemino – bright, clean, tasty, dry wines that can match the more famous reds from across the lake (Valpolicella and Bardolino). The *rosso* gets a little barrel age, but its light, fruity qualities make it best inside 3 years. The *chiaretto*, light and delicate, is refreshing very young.
Ag. *superiore* 1 yr (*rosso*).

| | |
|---|---|
| Nevio Baruffolo | Giuseppe Giovanelli |
| Bertanzi | Lamberti |
| Cascina La Torretta Spia d'Italia | Andrea Pasini & Figli |
| Castello di Drugolo | Conti Pellizzari di San Girolamo |
| Fabio Bottarelli & Figlio | Prandell |
| Franco & Valerio Bottarelli | Redaelli di Zinis |
| Domenico Chiappini & Figli | Giovanni Robazzi |
| Colombaro (Pinna Berchet) | San Grato (Premiovini) |
| Fattoria Saleri | Vigneti Venturelli |
| Giuseppe Fontanella | Visconti |
| Girolamo Frassine | Zenato |

**Ronco di Mompiano** r. dr.   ★★  80 82 83
Bright red table wine from Marzemino and Merlot grown at Mompiano
on the edge of Brescia. Dry, smooth, and scented, it is good in 3–4 years.
M. Pasolini

**Rosso di Bellagio** r. dr.   ★  82 83
From Cabernet, Merlot, Malbec, and Pinot Nero grown at Bellagio on
Lake Como, this ruby-garnet wine can develop impressive bouquet and
flavor over 3–5 years, though most is drunk locally as table wine.

**San Colombano al Lambro** r. p. w. dr. (fz.)   ★→★★  81 82 83
Increasingly noticed zone around San Colombano SE of Milan, where
the *rosso* of Barbera and Bonarda is a DOC candidate. Current table
wines show character: the reds – from Barbera, Bonarda, Merlot,
Cabernet, and Malbec – are hearty, lively, usually dry, sometimes
*frizzante*, good for 2–4 years, sometimes more; the whites – from Verdea,
Riesling, Tocai, and Pinot Grigio – are to drink young.

Banino (Panigada)                          Podere Costa Regina (Pietrasanta)
Nettare dei Santi (Riccardi)

**Sangue di Giuda**
See Oltrepò Pavese.

**Sassella**
See Valtellina Superiore.

**Sfursat** (or **Sfurzat, Sforzato**)
See Valtellina.

**Tocai di San Martino della Battaglia** DOC w. dr.   ★★→★★★  DYA
Fine white from Tocai Friulano grown S of Lake Garda around San
Martino della Battaglia. Bright lemon yellow, flowery, with dry, lightly
bitter almond flavor, it is good very young.

Cascina La Torretta Spia d'Italia      Giovanni Robazzi
Conti Pellizzari di San Girolamo       Ercole Romano
A. & G. Pergreffi                      Vigneti Venturelli
Prandell                               Zenato

**Valcalepio** DOC r. w. dr.   ★→★★  79 80 82 83
DOC zone between Bergamo and Lake Iseo. The *rosso*, from Merlot and
Cabernet Sauvignon, is dark ruby with dry, robust flavor and herb-like
bouquet after 2–4 years. *Bianco*, from Pinot Bianco and Grigio, is straw
yellow, delicate, dry, and light, good young.
Ag. 2 yrs (*rosso*).

C.S. Bergamasca                        Tenuta Castello
Fuzier a Negrone                       Tenuta La Cornasella
Le Corne                               Villa di Serio (Casselle Alte)
Bortolo Locatelli & Figli

**Valgella**
See Valtellina Superiore.

**Valtellina** DOC
Zone along the Adda River around Sondrio near the Swiss border, with
terraced vineyards split into minuscule plots. Praised since Roman times,
the Valtellina is one of the few places outside Piedmont where Nebbiolo
(here called Chiavennasca) thrives. In fact, it is the most prolific of all
Nebbiolo zones with about 9.5 million bottles a year, of which less than
half is Valtellina Superiore (see opposite). Much of the production is
controlled by foreign capital for consumption in Switzerland.

– **Rosso** r. dr.   ★→★★  79 82
The basic Valtellina red can be made throughout the DOC zone from at
least 70% Nebbiolo with other dark varieties permitted. It has lively red
color, delicate scent, and somewhat tannic flavor. Good in 3–5 years.
Ag. 1 yr.

– **Sfursat** (or **Sfurzat, Sforzato**) r. dr.   ★★→★★★  75 78 79 82
The names are dialect versions of the vinification process that depends on
semidried grapes (same as for basic Valtellina) to bring alcohol to the
required 14.5%. Ample in body, with rich ruby-orange color, it becomes
warm and perfumed after 4–5 years and can age for a decade or more.
Some consider this to be the Valtellina's best.
Ag. 1 yr.
(See producers under Valtellina Superiore.)

**Valtellina Superiore** DOC r. dr. ★★→★★★ 75 78 79 82 83
Name applied to four subdenominations, each named for a delimited
area within the Valtellina zone. All wines must consist of at least 95%
Nebbiolo. Though subtle variations exist, basic traits are similar: ruby-
red color, tending to garnet with age as bouquet becomes ethereal and
the dry, lightly tannic flavor becomes smoother and more austere over
6–7 years (longer from outstanding vintages). Bottles often appear with
individualistic names – Antica Rhaetia, Castel Chiuro, Fracia, Paradiso,
Perla Villa, Sassorosso, Signorie, and Villa – in addition to the formal
appellation. Ultimately, winemaking skill is often more important than a
precise place of origin.
Ag. 2 yrs. (1 in barrel); *riserva* 4 yrs.
– **Grumello**
The vineyards take the name of a 13th-century castle between Sondrio
and Montagna in Valtellina.
– **Inferno**
The zone is adjacent to Grumello to the E around Poggiridenti. Best
plots are known as Inferno and Paradiso.
– **Sassella**
Most often considered the best of the four, the zone lies W of Sondrio
toward Castione Andevenno.
– **Valgella**
Between the towns of Chiuro and Teglio, this is the most heavily
produced of the four.

| | |
|---|---|
| Franco Balgera | Nera |
| Fratelli Bettini | Nino Negri |
| Cantina Cooperativa Villa-Bianzone | A. Pelizzatti |
| Enologica Valtellinese | Rainoldi |
| La Castellina (Fondazione Fojanini) | San Carlo |
| | Tona (G. Bonisolo) |
| | Fratelli Triacca |

*Wine & Food*

Natural opulence is reflected in Lombardy's multifarious diet.
Milan, unavoidably, instigates food forms called "fast," "international," "*nouvelle*," but the city also has more fine "Italian"
restaurants than any other. Milanese gourmets still relish their
*ossobuco, costoletta* and *risotto alla milanese*. The outlying seven
provinces have so clung to tradition that Lombardian cooking is
more accurately described as provincial than regional. Still,
everybody eats veal, beef, pork (though cuts and cooking differ),
and cheese (besides blue-veined *gorgonzola* there are *grana padano*
to rival Parmesan, *stracchino, taleggio, robiola,* and *bitto*). Risotto
reigns in the flatlands, polenta and pasta in the hills, though
there is plenty of crossover. In Pavia, they eat frogs and snails, in
Bergamo small birds, in Mantua pasta with pumpkin, and in
Cremona candied fruit laced with mustard (*mostarda*). Perhaps
the leading preserve of provincial cooking is the Valtellina
around Sondrio where, among other nutritious eccentricities,
buckwheat is used for pasta and polenta.

**Bresaola** Beef cured much as
*prosciutto* and served in paper-thin
slices.
    ★★ Inferno.
**Busecca** Richly flavored Milanese
tripe soup.
    ★★ Franciacorta *rosso*
or ★★ Oltrepò Pavese *rosso.*
**Casonsei** Ravioli of Brescia filled
with sausage, cheese, and bread.
    ★★ Riviera del Garda *chiaretto.*
**Cassoeula** Various cuts of pork
cooked with cabbage, celery, and
carrots and often served with
polenta.
    ★★★ Oltrepò Pavese Barbacarlo
or ★★ San Colombano al
Lambro *rosso.*
**Costoletta alla milanese**
Breaded veal cutlet with mashed
potatoes.
    ★★★ Oltrepò Pavese Pinot Nero.
**Ossobuco e risotto alla
milanese** Braised veal shank with
saffron risotto, the pride of Milan.
    ★★★ Oltrepò Pavese Barbera.

**Panettone** Milan's dome-shaped Christmas cake.
**★★** Oltrepò Pavese Moscato *spumante*.

**Pizzoccheri** Rustic buckwheat noodles served with boiled potatoes, cabbage, and melted cheese in the Valtellina.
**★★** Valtellina, fairly young.

**Polenta e osei alla bergamasca** Polenta with small game birds cooked with butter and sage, a speciality of Bergamo.
**★★★** Colle del Calvario *rosso* or **★★** Valcalepio *rosso*.

**Risotto alla certosina** Elaborate risotto with freshwater prawns, frogs, perch, and vegetables, cooked in white wine.
**★★★** Oltrepò Pavese Riesling or **★★★** Müller Thurgau.

**Sciatt** Fritters of buckwheat and white flour, *bitto* cheese, and grappa.
**★★** Sfursat.

**Tortelli di zucca** Pasta envelopes filled with pumpkin paste flavored with *amaretto* and nutmeg, served with butter and grated *grana*.
**★★★** Lugana.

**Vitello tonnato** Veal filet dressed with a tuna-flavored cream sauce.
**★★★** Pinot *spumante méthode champenoise*.

## Restaurants

Recommended in or near wine zones: **Brescia, Garda**, and **Colli Morenici** *Miramonti* at Caino; *La Capra* at Cavriana; *Tre Corone* at Desenzano; *Tortuga* at Gargnano del Garda; *Il Bersagliere* at Goito; *Vecchia Lugana* at Lugana di Sirmione; *Trattoria alle Piante* at Manerba del Garda. **Oltrepò Pavese** *Locanda La Buta* at Bosnasco; *Castello di San Gaudenzio* at Cervesina; *Chalet della Certosa* at Certosa di Pavia; *Hostaria Il Casale* at Sante Maria della Versa; *Il Gallo* at Stradella; *Reale d'Italia* at Voghera. **Valtellina** *Baita da Mario* at Ciuk di Bormio; *Sassella* at Grosio; *San Fedele* at Poggiridenti; *Cerere* at Ponte in Valtellina.

# Marches

Marche

If Verdicchio is the only wine of the Marches with an international reputation, much credit is due to its instantly recognizable green amphora bottle. Not to detract from the wine's basic worth: even the French concede that with fish it rivals Muscadet. In the United States, it ranks second to Soave in sales of DOC white wines. But the exported Verdicchio is often a standardized, non-vintage product that does not express the maximum that this temperamental vine can do in the chalky-clay soil of the Marches.

A well-kept secret is that Rosso Piceno is the region's leading DOC – in quantity and, some would contend, in quality. More than 10 million liters of this attractive red from Sangiovese and Montepulciano are made each year, but, oddly, only a fraction leaves the Marches. Another ruby-colored gem is Rosso Cònero, based on Montepulciano grown on the Cònero massif near Ancona, the ancient Greek seaport that is now the region's capital. Most of the other wines are meant to go with regional food, fish in particular, which is always fresh and usually modestly priced at the many good restaurants.

Most people come to the Marches to bask on Adriatic beaches, but those who wander off into the interior in search of wine will also find eye-pleasing scenery in the hills – topped with castles, monasteries, and walled towns – that roll down in green waves from the Apennines to the Adriatic. Urbino is an art center, Loreto a religious shrine, and Ascoli Piceno is one of many well-preserved medieval towns.

**Wine Zones**

1 Bianchello del Metauro
2 Bianco dei Colli Maceratesi
3 Falerio dei Colli Ascolani
4 Rosso Cònero

5 Rosso Piceno
6 Sangiovese dei Colli Pesaresi
7 Verdicchio dei Castelli di Jesi
8 Verdicchio di Matelica

*Recent vintages*

Most white wine is to drink young, so the chart applies mainly to Rosso Piceno and Rosso Cònero, neither of which usually benefits from more than 4–8 years of aging.

1983   A good year for Verdicchio and red wines, though heat left results spotty in places.
1982   Generally fine year, though drought cut the size.
1981   Small, uneven harvest; some good wines, many mediocre.
1980   Normal crop of mostly average wines.
1979   Fine, abundant, exceptional for Rosso Cònero.
1978   Small crop of fair to very good wines.
1977   Excellent nearly everywhere.

**Bianchello del Metauro** DOC w. dr.   ★→ **★★**   DYA
A snappily acidic little white noted for its affinity with seafood. From Bianchello grapes grown along the Metauro River valley.
Anzilotti-Solazzi                           Umani Ronchi
COVIM

**Bianco dei Colli Maceratesi** DOC w. dr.   ★→ **★★**   DYA
The zone is large, stretching from the Adriatic inland past Macerata toward the Apennines, but little of this light white from Trebbiano Toscano and Maceratino is made. Delicate in odor, scent, and flavor.
Attilio Fabrini                              Villamagna (Compagnucci-
La Torraccia (Costantini)                    Compagnoni)

**Falerio dei Colli Asolani** DOC w. dr.   ★→ **★★**   DYA
White based on Trebbiano Toscano grown in hills N of the Tronto River between Ascoli Piceno and the Adriatic. Straw green and rather neutral with an acidic vein, it should be drunk young with fish.
Boccabianca                                  Picenum
Cantina Sant' Angelo                         Tattà
Fratelli Cocci Grifoni                       Vallone
Costadoro                                    Villa Pigna (Rozzi)

**Fontanelle** w. dr.   ★★★   82 83
Fine white from Verdicchio grown at Cossignano near Ascoli Piceno. Bright golden, dry, perfumed, and smoothly textured with fine fruit-acid balance, it rounds into form in 2 years.
Tattà

**Gallia Togata** am. sw.   ★★★   73
Sweet golden Malvasia aged by Massimo Schiavi for 7 years and gaining from bottle age. Deep golden color, hints of nuts and tobacco on the nose, rich, long, warming flavor. Rare and expensive.
Fattoria di Montesecco

**Montepulciano delle Marche** r. dr.   ★→ **★★★**   81 82 83
Though usually blended with Sangiovese (as in Rosso Cònero and Rosso Piceno), Montepulciano also makes a varietal table wine. Villa Pigna's aptly named Vellutato rivals the Abruzzi's best.
C.S. Val di Nevola                           Villa Pigna (Rozzi)
Tattà

**Moscato Nobile del Cònero** w. dr.   ★★★   82 83
Moscato made at Sappanico at the edge of Ancona by a winemaker priest. Golden with typical aroma, it is surprisingly dry and crisp.
Vigna del Curato (Marinoni)                                    •

**Rosato delle Marche** p. dr.   ★→ **★★**   DYA
The predominant Sangiovese and Montepulciano of the Marches adapt well to rosé, table wine popular with summer tourists.

**Rosato di Montanello** p. dr.   ★★★   DYA
Fine rosé from Sangiovese and Montepulciano grown outside Macerata. Pale roseate, flowery on the nose, it is light, dry, and fruity.
Villamagna (Compagnucci-Compagnoni)

**Rosso Cònero** DOC r. dr.   **★★→★★★**   79 81 82 83
Distinguished red from the Monte Cònero massif overlooking the Adriatic S of Ancona. From Montepulciano (though it may include 15%

Sangiovese), it is deep ruby, robust, and rather austere, with fine bouquet and plenty of depth in its warm, somewhat tannic flavor, which mellows over 3–6 years, sometimes more.

| | |
|---|---|
| Castelfiora | Cesare Serenelli |
| Fazi-Battaglia | Fratelli Torelli |
| Fattoria Le Terrazze | Umani Ronchi |
| Federici & Gagliardini | Vigna del Curato (Marinoni) |
| Garofoli | |

**Rosso di Corinaldo** r. dr. ★★→★★★ 79 81 82 83
Can be one of Italy's better Merlots, from a special vineyard at Corinaldo in hills inland from Senigallia. Dark ruby red, rich, and silky smooth, with hints of tar and herbs, it peaks in 3–6 years.
C.S. Val di Nevola

**Rosso Piceno** DOC r. dr. ★★→★★★ 79 81 82 83
Elegant red from Sangiovese at 60% and Montepulciano at 40%, made in quantity in a zone covering much of the E Marches between Ascoli Piceno and Senigallia. Two years in oak casks (not required by DOC) and another year or two in bottle bring out the natural finesse that make it one of central Italy's most promising red wines. Ruby red tending to garnet, in 3–7 years it becomes smooth, composed, with bouquet and charm. *Superiore* covers a restricted area between Ascoli Piceno and San Benedetto del Tronto.

| | |
|---|---|
| Boccabianca | Picenum |
| C.S. di Cupramontana | Tattà |
| C.S. Val di Nevola | Umani Ronchi |
| Fratelli Cocci Grifoni | Vallone |
| Costadoro | Villamagna (Compagnucci- |
| Fazi-Battaglia | Compagnoni) |
| La Torraccia (Costantini) | Villa Pigna (Rozzi) |
| Giuseppe Pennesi | |

**Sangiovese dei Colli Pesaresi** r. dr. ★→★★ 81 82 83
Made in the N around Pesaro and Urbino from the Romagnan strain of Sangiovese, this rare, light red can be tasty young.

| | |
|---|---|
| Anzilotti-Solazzi | COVIM |
| C.S. dei Colli Pesaresi | Fattoria di San Cristoforo |
| Ciardiello/Evalli | |

**Sangiovese delle Marche** r. dr. ★→★★ 82 83
Table wines from Sangiovese are made in many parts of the Marches, usually for drinking young and close to home.

**Tristo di Montesecco** w. dr. ★★→★★★ 81 82 83
Table wine of singular personality from Trebbiano Toscano, Malvasia di Candia, Riesling Italico, and Pinot Grigio grown at Montesecco near Pergola in N Marches. Pale brassy yellow with fruity aroma, it is soft but complex with a pleasant bitter background after 2–3 years, including a spell in wood conducted by enologist-owner Massimo Schiavi.
Fattoria di Montesecco

**Vellutato**
See Montepulciano delle Marche.

**Verdicchio dei Castelli di Jesi** DOC w. dr. (sp.) ★→★★★ DYA
The best-known Verdicchio zone covers inland hills drained by the Esino, Misa, and Musone rivers adjacent to the town of Jesi. *Classico* takes in all but the NW portion. This Verdicchio can be excellent from a skilled artisan like Brunori, but the wine's fragility has prompted exporters to flash pasteurize and blend vintages while including the permitted 20% of Trebbiano and Malvasia. Trends to low-temperature fermentation and sterile filtration should help restore its natural goodness. Pale straw with green tints, it has a fine scent and, at best, taut dryness and good fruit-acid balance underlined by a hint of bitter almond. Verdicchio also makes a fine bubbly wine, especially by *méthode champenoise*, as exemplified by Garofoli. Average output is nearing 10 million liters a year. A trend by prominent producers toward special bottlings by vineyard is resulting in superior wines: Garofoli with Macrina, Umani Ronchi with Casal di Serra and Monte Schiavo with Colle del Sole, Coste del Molino, and the remarkable late-harvested Il Pallio. (Bottler and shipper brands could also be dependable.) ▶

| | |
|---|---|
| M. Brunori & Figlio | Garofoli |
| C.S. Val di Nevola | Monte Schiavo |
| Castelfiora | Tombolini |
| Castellucci | Fratelli Torelli |
| Colonnara (C.S. di | Umani Ronchi |
| Cupramontana) | Vigna del Curato (Marinoni) |
| Fazi-Battaglia | Vinimar |
| Federici & Gagliardini | |

**Verdicchio di Matelica** DOC w. dr.  ★★→★★★  DYA
Insiders contend that the best DOC Verdicchio comes from this zone in
W Marches between Fabriano and Camerino. But evidence is scarce.
Though similar to Castelli di Jesi, Verdicchio di Matelica tends to be
stronger and drier with somewhat more structure.

| | |
|---|---|
| La Monacesca | Villa Pigna |
| Italo Mattei | Vinimar |

**Verdicchio di Montanello** w. dr.  ★★★  DYA
Table wine made at Montanello near Macerata. With its fragrance and
smooth balance, it compares favorably with any still Verdicchio.
Villamagna (Compagnucci-Compagnoni)

**Verdicchio Pian delle Mura** w. dr. sp.  ★★→★★★  DYA
The still version is good, the *brut nature spumante* superior, with
Verdicchio's best traits enhanced by the persistent *perlage* and delicately
yeasty scent of a skillfully made *méthode champenoise*.
Attilio Fabrini

**Vernaccia di Serrapetrona** DOC r. dr. s/sw. sw. sp.  ★→★★★  DYA
Curious sparkling red based on Vernaccia di Serrapetrona grapes grown
around Serrapetrona W of Macerata. Deep garnet-purple, grapy, and
fragrant with mouth-cleansing bitterness on the finish, it can be dry,
*amabile*, or *dolce*. Most producers have replaced the traditional special
process of bottle fermentation with *charmat*, but Attilio Fabrini insists on
the *méthode champenoise*, which gives clearly superior results.

| | |
|---|---|
| Attilio Fabrini | Raffaele Quacquarini |
| Umberto Francioni | |

## Wine & Food

The food of the Marches, immediately likeable – like the wine or,
for that matter, the people – never lets you down. Cooks draw
from land and sea and, without too much fuss, put the best of
both on the table, often together. Roast pig (*porchetta*) is cooked
with wild fennel, rosemary, garlic, and pepper, as are duck,
rabbit, and even shellfish. Both fowl and fish may be cooked *in
potacchio*, with tomato, rosemary, garlic, onion, and white wine.

**Anatra in porchetta** Duck
cooked with wild fennel, garlic,
ham, and bacon. *Coniglio* (rabbit)
may be done the same way.
   ★★★  Rosso Piceno.
**Brodetto** Among many fish soups
of the name, Ancona's version is
most famous, maybe because it
includes at least 13 types of fish.
   ★★  Verdicchio dei Castelli di Jesi.
**Faraona in potacchio** Guinea
fowl cooked with onion, garlic,
rosemary, and tomato in wine.
   ★★★  Rosso Cònero.

**Olive all'ascolana** Hollowed
giant green olives of Ascoli with a
meat stuffing, fried in olive oil.
   ★  Falerio dei Colli Ascolani.
**Piccione ripieno** Squab stuffed
with chestnut-butter purée and
baked.
   ★★★  Vernaccia di Serrapetrona
   *secco*.
**Vincisgrassi** An elaborate
lasagne which includes butter,
cream, *prosciutto*, and black truffles.
   ★★★  Verdicchio *spumante méthode
   champenoise*.

### Restaurants
Recommended in or near wine zones (which take in all but the
mountainous areas): *Alle Terrazze* at Arcevia; *Posta Vecchia* at Calcinelli;
*Villa Amalia* at Falconara Marittima; *La Quinta* at Fano; *Boschetto* at
Filetto di Senigallia; *Da Secondo* at Macerata; *Rivazzurra* at Marotta; *La
Cantinetta del Cònero* at Osimo Scalo; *La Cantinella* at Ostra; *La Ginestra* at
Passo del Furlo; *Da Carlo al Mare* and *Lo Scudiero* at Pesaro; *Emilia* and
*Giacchetti* at Portonovo.

# Molise

After years of deprivation as the only region without a DOC, Molise has just emerged with two new appellations. Neither Biferno nor Pentro has been widely tested, so they remain to be proven. And it might just be that their promotion was more an act of charity than recognition of inherent class.

However, Molise already had some good wines. Examples are the Montepulciano del Molise and Ramitello *rosso* from Masseria Di Majo Norante near the Adriatic. The wines of Serra Meccaglia from Gambatesa, east of the region's capital of Campobasso, aren't bad either. Conceivably. Molise's neglected hillsides may one day make wine of real worth. The climate is right and those rocky inclines aren't suitable for much else.

Perhaps the most inviting thing about Molise is that few people go there, possibly because few people know where it is. It has a narrow strip of Adriatic coast (at Termoli) and extensive uplands to explore, while enjoying the rustically tasty wine and food at true bargain prices.

## Recent vintages

Data has not been recorded long in Molise. Recommended vintages are given with red wines, which rarely last more than 4 years.

**Bianco del Molise** w. dr.  ★ DYA
From Trebbiano Toscano and/or Bombino Bianco grown in various parts of Molise, this is straw yellow, dry, neutral in scent and flavor.
Cantina Valbiferno        Colle Sereno

**Biferno** DOC r. p. w.  ★ 83
From the Biferno River valley E of Campobasso, the *rosso* and *rosato* are based on Montepulciano and the *bianco* on Trebbiano Toscano. The red might prove interesting.
Ag. *superiore* 3 yrs.
Cantina Valbiferno

**Montepulciano del Molise** r. dr.  ★→ ★★★ 80 81 82 83
Table wine from Montepulciano grapes grown in several parts of the region. Ruby to brick red, it is robust and dry, acquiring smoothness and style with 3–4 years.
Masseria Di Majo Norante       Serra Meccaglia

**Moscato** w. s/sw. (fz.) (sp.)  ★ DYA
Dessert wines, both still and bubbly, are made from light Moscato grapes in various places. Sometimes good, rarely memorable.
Tenuta San Marco

**Pentro** or **Pentro di Isernia** DOC r. p. w. dr.  ★
A new name in Isernia province for *rosso* and *rosato* from nearly equal parts of Montepulciano and Sangiovese and *bianco* from Trebbiano Toscano with some Bombino Bianco. The first DOC wines were expected in 1984.

**Ramitello** r. w. (fz.)  ★★→★★★ 81 82 83
Wines from the Ramitello vineyards near Campomarino. The *rosso*, from Sangiovese and Montepulciano, is deep ruby and smooth with a light bitter aftertaste, good in 3–4 years. The *bianco*, from Trebbiano and Malvasia, is aged a little to develop a golden color and some aroma. *Frizzante* wines are made too, a light red from Sangiovese and a white from Trebbiano, both to drink young and cool.
Masseria Di Majo Norante

**Rosato del Molise** p. dr.  ★ DYA
Table wines from Montepulciano and Sanglovese vinified as rosé are
made in several places.
Masseria Di Majo Norante

**Rosso del Molise** r. dr.  ★  82 83
Montepulciano, Sangiovese and other both dark and light grapes go into
these ruby, rather soft table wines, best to drink in 1–3 years.
Rocca del Falco (Serra Meccaglia)

**Sangiovese** r. dr.  ★  81 82 83
Table wines from Sangiovese are made in various places. Light ruby and
dry, they become smooth over 2–3 years.
Serra Meccaglia

**Tifernum** r. p. dr.  ★→★★  81 82 83
Table wines from Montepulciano, Sangiovese, and Aglianico grown at
Petrella Tifernina. The *rosso* is deep red and scented, with good body and
balance over 3–4 years. The *rosato* is tasty when young.
Colle Sereno

**Trebbiano di Serra Meccaglia** w. dr.  ★ DYA
Delicate, straw-yellow wine from Trebbiano grown at Gambatesa.
Serra Meccaglia

**Vernaccia di Serra Meccaglia** w. dr.  ★★  DYA
Simple but satisfying white from Vernaccia di San Gimignano grapes
grown at Gambatesa.
Serra Meccaglia

Molise doesn't have a *cucina* all its own, but instead shares recipes
with the Abruzzi, while picking up an occasional idea from
neighboring Apulia, Campania, and Latium. The cooking is
rustic and authentically good. Lamb and kid are stalwarts in the
hill country, where *pecorino* cheese is eaten in chunks or grated
over pasta, and pork is preserved in *prosciutto* and salame.
Mountain streams provide trout and crayfish. Along the coast,
the usual range of Adriatic fish is consumed.

**Calcioni di ricotta** Circular
pasta shells folded over a paste of
*ricotta, provolone, prosciutto,* and eggs,
then deep-fried in oil.
　★  Bianco del Molise.

**Fiadone** Easter tart filled with
beaten eggs, mild *pecorino*, sugar,
cinnamon, and lemon rind.
　★  Moscato *amabile* or *dolce*.

**Gamberi d'acqua dolce ai ferri**
Freshwater crayfish grilled over
coals.
　★★  Vernaccia di Serra
　Meccaglia.

**Mazzarelle d'agnello** Lamb's
lung and intestines wrapped in
beet greens and cooked in oil and
white wine.
　★→★★  Montepulciano del
　Molise.

**Tacconi** Quadrangular pasta
often served with meat sauce.
　★  Sangiovese.

**Trota alle brace** Fresh brook
trout grilled over coals.
　★  Ramitello *bianco*.

**Zuppa di ortiche** Soup of nettle
sprouts, tomato, bacon, and onion.
　★  Rosato del Molise.

### Restaurants
Recommended near wine areas: *Da Emilio* at Ferrazzano; *Piccolo Hotel de
Ida* at Pesche; *Il Drago* and *Torre Sinarca* at Termoli; *Vittoria* at Venafro.

# Piedmont

## Piemonte

Techniques may be reforming at a faster clip elsewhere, but Piedmont provides lasting proof that Italy produces wines of the highest order. A visit to the Langhe hills around Alba where Barolo and Barbaresco are grown ought to convince any doubter. There is something reminiscent of Burgundy there: in the manicured vineyards fragmented into single-owner plots on every south-facing slope; in the trim villages, where the lusty odor of fermenting grapes perfumes the autumn air; in the self-assured way the *vignaiolo* hands you a glass of his best. In the Langhe, as in the Côte d'Or, wine is a way of life.

But, without doubt, Piedmont and its wines stand alone, so alone that they demand concentration to truly comprehend. Every important Piedmontese wine derives from a native vine. Most are from single varieties, though not all carry varietal names. The noblest vine is Nebbiolo, the source of Barolo and Barbaresco, Italy's most distinguished DOCG wines, as well as Gattinara, Ghemme, Carema, Lessona, Nebbiolo d'Alba, and other jewels.

Piedmontese consume far more red wine than white. Nearly half the red is Barbera, much of which is for everyday, some of which is remarkable. Dolcetto is even more attractive, smooth and supple with an almondy finish and too good to escape international acclaim much longer. Grignolino and Freisa, though declining because of meager yields, remain much more than local curiosities.

Among whites, Asti Spumante, from the Moscato di Canelli grape, is the world's second most lauded sparkling wine after Champagne. Cortese, at its best from Gavi, is a rising star among dry whites.

Though Piedmont ranks only sixth among Italian regions in volume of production, its quality wines are the most thoroughly categorized; it has 35 DOC zones, the most of any region. Viticulture is most intense in the Langhe and Monferrato hills around Asti and Alessandria, where thousands of growers work vineyards that are often little larger than a hectare. Many sell grapes to industrial wineries centered in Canelli, Asti, and Turin, firms which often base their economies on vermouth, Asti and other sparkling wines. Lately, there has been a trend to make wine from individual vineyards, either directly by the grower or by small-scale winemakers. This practice may soon lead to a *cru*-style classification of vineyards, starting with Barolo and Barbaresco.

Piedmont's other outstanding wine district is in the alpine foothills between Valle d'Aosta and Lake Maggiore in the provinces of Vercelli and Novara. There Nebbiolo prevails in Gattinara, Ghemme, Lessona, and other fine wines.

Piedmont is by far the best organized Italian region for wine tourism. Focal points for travelers are the Langhe and Monferrato hills and the towns of Alba and Asti, reachable by car in just over two hours from Milan and in even less time from Turin and Genoa. Well-marked wine roads cover a score of production zones. Signs from Alba lead to vineyards and cellars of Barolo, Barbaresco, Dolcetto d'Alba, Barbera d'Alba, Nebbiolo d'Alba,

**Wine Zones**
1 Barbaresco
2 Barolo
3 Boca
4 Bramaterra
5 Carema
6 Cortese dell'Alto Monferrato
7 Fara
8 Lessona
9 Malvasia di Casorzo d'Asti
10 Rubino di Cantavenna
11 Sizzano

and Moscato d'Asti. Public *enoteche* provide places to buy and drink the wines. Not to be missed are the castles of Grinzane Cavour (Alba wines), Costigliole d'Asti (Asti and Monferrato wines), and Vignale Monferrato (Monferrato Casalese wines), all with good restaurants serving local specialities. The villages of Barolo and Barbaresco also have official *enoteche* to show off their production. Interesting wine museums include *Abbazia dell'Annunziata* near La Morra, *Bersano* at Nizza Monferrato, and *Martini & Rossi* at Pessione. Most wineries large and small welcome visitors.

### *Recent vintages*

#### Barolo and Barbaresco

As a rule, Barbaresco from an average-to-good harvest rounds into form at 4–6 years and Barolo at 5–8, after which they hold well for several more years. From the best vintages, a couple of years more are needed. In both cases, *riserva* and *riserva speciale* are designated for longer aging, often well over a decade.

1983    Fine fall weather made this a good to very good year for Nebbiolo wines and Barbera, though Dolcetto was spotty.

1982   Hailed as one of the greatest years this century; time will tell with
       these big, well-balanced wines.
1981   Disappointing after a promising start, but select wines were
       satisfactory or better.
1980   Record quantity despite curious weather that forced the latest
       harvest in memory. Middling-to-very-good wines.
1979   Nearly equal to '80 in size, generally superior in quality. Early
       maturing, charming wines to enjoy from the mid-1980s onwards.
1978   Near disaster from early damp and cold turned to an unexpected
       glorious vintage. A small amount of luxuriant, very expensive
       wines for long aging.
1977   Weak, small crop. What remains should be drunk soon.
1976   Average harvest of uneven quality with some conspicuous bright
       spots. Drink soon.
1975   Only fair, though some delightful wines were made. Drink now.
1974   An excellent, abundant crop, similar to '79, '70. Some wines will
       last to 1990.
1973   Fair, but with some attractive wines, which should be mostly
       gone by now.
1972   A disaster. Both Barolo and Barbaresco were declassified as DOC.
1971   Great year which produced some splendid wines, though not all
       have aged as well as expected.
1970   Excellent and ample; overshadowed by '71, but some wines show
       nearly as much class and endurance.
Earlier fine vintages: '67, '65 (especially Barolo), '64 (especially
Barbaresco), '62, '61, '58, '57, '52, '51, and '47.

## Novara-Vercelli hills and Carema

Though Nebbiolo is often mixed with Bonarda and Vespaiola in
these alpine foothills, some wines can equal Barolo in longevity.
Gattinara, Carema, Lessona, Ghemme, Caramino, and choice
Spanna need 4–6 years to be drinkable and sometimes more than
a decade to reach prime. Wines containing less Nebbiolo – Boca,
Fara, Sizzano, and Bramaterra – usually mature sooner.

1983   A fine year but it lacked consistency.
1982   A great year almost everywhere; balanced wines should age very
       well.
1981   Mediocre. Select wines may be good but short lived.
1980   Extraordinarily late harvest resulted in average quantity with
       some fine, promising wine from select grapes.
1979   Big year in both volume and quality in well-structured wines with
       better-than-average life expectancy.
1978   Miracle vintage, thanks to a warm, dry autumn after a miserable
       spring and early summer reduced size. Great in Carema, near
       great elsewhere in wines which will be ready in the late 1980s.
1977   Poor; only select wines were worth bottling.
1976   Fine harvest in Novara-Vercelli, with excellent Gattinara.
       Average at best for Carema. Sturdy wines to drink soon.
1975   Normal crop with some sound wines to drink now.
1974   Grand year with big wines for keeping in Novara-Vercelli,
       slightly less spectacular but solid in Carema.
1973   Uneven; excellent in Ghemme, average in Carema, subpar in
       Gattinara.
1972   Limited production of fair-to-good but short-lived wines.
1971   Excellent for most, though Gattinara was disappointing.
1970   Superb year all around; most wines should be at prime.
Earlier fine vintages: '69, '64, '61, and '52.

**Arneis dei Roeri** w. dr. \*\*→\*\*\* DYA
An ancient vine of the Roeri hills N of Alba, Arneis is enjoying a revival,
though production is still limited. Soft but richly textured, it can range
from moderately interesting to elegant, complex and fascinating.

| | |
|---|---|
| G. Battista Arduino | Perdaudin (Negro) |
| Castello di Neive | Produttori Montaldesi Associati |
| Cornarea | Renato Rabezzana |
| Bruno Giacosa | Vietti |
| La Brenta d'Oro | Voerzio |
| Malvira (Damonte) | |

**Asti Spumante** or **Asti**
See Moscato d'Asti.

**Barbaresco** DOC-DOCG r. dr.   ★★★→★★★★   71 74 78 79 80 82 83
One of Italy's great red wines. Made from Nebbiolo grown around the villages of Barbaresco, Neive, and Treiso, adjacent to Alba, Barbaresco production is about 3 million bottles a year. With its neighbor Barolo it shares the robust, austere, dramatic elegance of well-aged Nebbiolo. Though Barbaresco rarely equals the sheer power of the biggest Barolo and requires less maturing in barrel and bottle to develop bouquet (4–8 years), it is sometimes credited with more finesse and more consistent quality from year to year. DOCG took effect with the '81 vintage issued in 1984 and could be applied retroactively to '80 and '79. (See also Nebbiolo delle Langhe.)
Ag. 2 yrs (1 in barrel); *riserva* 3 yrs; *riserva speciale* 4 yrs.

Accademia Torregiorgi
Fratelli Barale
Bersano
Aldo Bianco
Fratelli L. & M. Bianco
Luigi Bianco & Figli
Carlo Boffa & Figli
Franco Bordino
Cantina del Glicine
Cantina della Porta Rossa
Cantina Vignaioli Elvio
  Pertinace
Castello di Neive (Santo
  Stefano)
Ceretto (Asili, Bricco Asili)
Fratelli Cigliuti
Confratelli di San Michele
Giuseppe Cortese
Paolo De Forville
Fontanafredda
Franco-Fiorina
Gaja (Costa Russi, Sorì San
  Lorenzo, Sorì Tildin)
Gemma
Bruno Giacosa (Santo Stefano)
Giovanni Giordano & Figli

La Spinona
Marchesi di Gresy (Camp
  Gros, La Martinenga)
Giuseppe Mascarello & Figli
  (Bernardotti)
Enrico Giovanni Moresco
Fratelli Oddero
Parroco di Neive
Secondo Pasquero-Elia
Luigi Pelissero
Pio Cesare
Produttori del Barbaresco
  (Moccagatta, Ovello, Rabajà)
Alfredo Prunotto (Montestefano)
Francesco Rinaldi & Figli
Rizzi
Roagna-I Paglieri (Crichët
  Pajé)
Dario Rocca & Figli
Giuseppe Rocca & Figlio
Pierino Rocca
Scarpa (I Tetti di Neive,
  Payoré Barberis)
Vietti (Masseria)
Voerzio

**Barbera** r. (p.) (w.) dr. (sw.) (sp.)   ★→★★★   79 80 82 83
Generic name for many unclassified wines from Barbera, source of about half of Piedmont's reds. Light ruby to inky in color, sharply acidic at times, most Barbera is rustic and inexpensive, but some is unexpectedly refined, capable of approaching fine Nebbiolo wines in class. There are also sweet and sparkling Barberas, rosé and even Barbera *bianca*, which is designed to use up excess grapes. (Producers do not include bottler and shipper brands, which could also be dependable.)

Braida (Vigneto la Monella)
Bronda
Cappellano
Mario Capuzzo
Giorgio Carnevale
Cascina Spagarino
Aldo Cassina

Ceretto
Luigi Dessilani & Figli
Francesco Destefanis & Figlio
Luigi Einaudi
Armando Piazzo
Antonio Vallana & Figlio

**Barbera d'Alba** DOC r. dr.   ★★→★★★   78 79 80 82 83
Rich in color and body, smooth in scent and flavor, somewhat tannic, this is often the longest-lived Barbera. Some producers vinify for drinking within a year, others in 2–3 years, others for longer aging. Quality has improved steadily.
Ag. 1 yr; *superiore* 2 yrs.

Accademia Torregiorgi
Fratelli Barale
Bera
Fratelli Brovia
Brezza
Cantina del Glicine
Cappellano
Castello di Nieve

Luciano Aquino Cavaletto
Cavallotto
Ceretto (Vigneto Piana-Brunate)
Fratelli Cigliuti
Cogno-Marcarini
Confratelli di San Michele
Aldo Conterno
Giacomo Conterno

Gemma
Angelo Germano & Figli
Bruno Giacosa
Marchesi di Barolo
Giuseppe Mascarello & Figlio
Fratelli Oddero
Dogliani 7 Cascine
Redento Dogliotti & Figli
Dosio
Riccardo Fenocchio
Fontanafredda
Franco-Fiorina
Gaja (Vignarey)
Podere Rocche dei Manzoni-
  Valentino

Parroco di Neive
Luigi Pelissero
Romano Penna
Pio Cesare
Alfredo Prunotto
Renato Ratti
Mario Savigliano & Figlio
Alfredo Scavino
Paolo Scavino & Figli
Enrico Serafino
Terre del Barolo
G. D. Vajra
Sergio Vezza & Figli
Vietti (Rocche)
Voerzio

**Barbera d'Asti** DOC r. dr. [★→★★★] 78 79 80 82 83
Robust and full-bodied, it tends to be less acidic and somewhat fruitier
and softer than Barbera d'Alba and, at its best (exemplified by Scarpa),
hard to beat. Most Barbera d'Asti is to drink fairly young, though in this
vast zone of heavy production it is hard to define a style.
Ag. 1 yr; *superiore* 2 yrs.

Anforio (Premiovini)
Antica Contea di Castelvero
Antonio Benso
Bersano
Podere Borlotto
C.S. Antiche Terre dei Galleani
C.S. di Canelli
C.S. di Cassine
C.S. di Castelnuovo Calcea
C.S. di Maranzana
C.S. Stazione Calamandrana
Cantine Bava
Giorgio Carnevale
Cascina Canova (Barbero)
Cascina Castlèt
Cascina Croce (Brema)
Cascina La Spinetta (Rivetti)
Ca' Tesi della Pianca
Castello di Gabiano
Contratto
R. Cortese

Duca d'Asti
Fassio
Marchesi Spinola
Moncucchetto (Biletta)
Montetusa (Bertelli)
Livio Pavese
Luigi Pia
Pinbologna
Poderi Bricco Mondalino (Gaudio)
Pracalliano (Gremmo)
Renato Rabezzana
Giuseppe Ratti
A.B. Ravetto
Ronco
Giovanni Rosso
Scarpa
Fratelli Spagarino
Tenuta dei Re
Tenuta Tenaglia (Quattrocolo)
G.L. Viarengo & Figlio
Vignaioli Piemontesi

**Barbera del Monferrato** DOC r. dr. (fz.) [★→★★★] 81 82 83
This Barbera from Monferrato hills N and S of Asti and Alessandria may
include up to 15% of Freisa, Grignolino, or Dolcetto, which tend to
make it lighter and suppler than Barberas of Asti and Alba. Often
*frizzante*, it is best in 1–4 years.
Ag. *superiore* 2 yrs.

Antica Contea di Castelvero
Balestrino & Vivalda
Bersano
Carlo Brema
Lorenzo Bertolo
Pietro Calvo
Renzo Campagnola
C.S. del Monferrato
C.S. Mombercelli
C.S. San Giorgio
Cantine Bava
Castello di Gabiano
Castello di Salabue (Cassinis)
Castel Taglioloi
Duca d'Asti

Amilcare Gaudio
Enrico Imarisio
Ermenegildo Leporati
Dante Montiglio
Nuova Cappelletta
Livio Pavese
Podere Soria di Calosso
Giuseppe Ratti
Ronco
Tenuta Cannona
Tre Castelli
Tenuta Tenaglia (Quattrocolo)
Valmosè
Zavanone di Mirabello

**Bardonè** r. dr. ★★ DYA
A mix of Barbera, Dolcetto and Nebbiolo vinified to be fresh, fruity and
youthfully light (11%) to drink within a year.
Fontanafredda

**Barolo** DOC–DOCG r. dr.   ★★★→★★★★   70 71 74 78 79 80 82 83
"King of wine and wine of kings," as the Piedmontese define it, Barolo is indeed a regal wine, deservedly the most esteemed red of Italy. Made in the Langhe hills SE of Alba, it takes the name of the village of Barolo. It needs time to lose its initial tannic hardness (8 years or more from such vintages as '71, '78 and '82) and it takes an experienced palate to master its complex grandeur. Barolo's austere robustness and intense concentration of fruit and extract can remain largely intact for well over a decade as color evolves from deep ruby garnet toward brick red, and bouquet becomes increasingly refined and ethereal. Production of just over seven million bottles a year is centered in the villages of Castiglione Falletto, Monforte d'Alba, and Serralunga d'Alba (where the biggest wines are made), and Barolo and La Morra (from where the most graceful wines come). Regularly twinned with Barbaresco, Barolo can surpass it in size and longevity, if not in finesse and overall class. DOCG took effect with the '80 vintage issued in 1984 and could be applied retroactively to '79, '78 and '77. (See also Nebbiolo delle Langhe.)
Ag. 3 yrs (2 in barrel); *riserva* 4 yrs; *riserva speciale* 5 yrs.

Accademia Torregiorgi
Giovanni Accomasso & Figlio
    (Vigneto Rocchette)
Elio Altare
Fratelli Anselma
Fratelli Barale (Castellero)
Bersano
Giacomo Borgogno & Figli
Serio & Battista Borgogno
Gianfranco Bovio
Brezza
Fratelli Brovia (Rocche)
Cantina della Porta Rossa
Cantina Mascarello
Cappellano
Giorgio Carnevale
Castello di Verduno
Cavallotto
Ceretto (Bricco Rocche, Prepò,
    Vigneto Zonchetta 1a)
Aldo Conterno (Bussia Soprana,
    Colonello di Bricco Bussia)
Giacomo Conterno (Casina
    Francia, Monfortino)
Contratto
Paolo Cordero di Montezemolo
    (Enrico VI, Monfalletto)
Lorenzo Denegri
Dogliani 7 Cascine
Dosio
Luigi Einaudi
Riccardo Fenocchio (Pianpolvere
    Soprano)
Michele Fontana
Saverio Fontana
Fontanafredda
Franco-Fiorina
Maurizio Fracassi Ratti Mentone

Gemma
Angelo Germano & Figli
Bruno Giacosa (Rionda di
    Serralunga, Rocche)
Marcarini (Brunate, La Serra)
Marchesi di Barolo
Giuseppe Mascarello & Figlio
    (Monprivato, Villero, Vigna
    Rionda)
Fratelli Oberto
Fratelli Oddero
Pio Cesare
E. Pira & Figli
Podere Rocche dei Manzoni-
    Valentino
Ponte Rocca-Pittatore
Giovanni Pozzetti & Figlio
Teobaldo Prandi & Figlio
Alfredo Prunotto (Bussia,
    Cannubi)
Renato Ratti (Marcenasco)
Giuseppe Rinaldi
Gigi Rosso
Luciano Sandrone
Scarpa (Boscaretti di Serralunga,
    I Tetti di La Morra)
Alfonso Scavino
Paolo Scavino (Bric dël Fiase)
Renzo Seghesio
Filippo Sobrero & Figli
Tenuta Montanello
Terre del Barolo
G. D. Vajra
Vietti (Briacca, Bricco Colonello,
    Rocche)
U. Vignolo-Lutati & Figli
Voerzio
Basilio Zunino (Sorì di Baudana)

**Barolo Chinato** r. dr.   ★★★   NV
Barolo DOC permits production of a tonic made by steeping *china* (quinine, the bark of the chinchona tree) in the wine until it takes on the flavor. This fine *amaro* is found only in winemakers' homes.

**Bianco dei Roeri** w. dr.   ★★   DYA
An unusual blend of light Arneis and dark Nebbiolo vinified off the skins in a crisp, well-structured white.
Tenuta Carretta

**Boca** DOC r. dr.   ★★→★★★   78 79 80 82 83
Fine red from Nebbiolo (Spanna) at 45–70% with Vespolina and Bonarda grown in the Novara hills near Boca. Robust and aggressive when young, it grows smooth with 4–5 years, taking on a violet scent.   ▶

Ag. 3 yrs (2 in barrel).

| | |
|---|---|
| Lorenzo Bertolo | Guido Ponti |
| Ermanno Conti | Antonio Vallana & Figlio |
| Podere ai Valloni | |

**Brachetto** r. s/sw. sw. (dr.) fz. sp.   ★→★★★   DYA
The Brachetto grape usually makes pleasant, strawberry colored, sweet bubbly wines in the Monferrato hills, sometimes not DOC. An exception is Scarpa's Brachetto di Moirano, dry, still, ruby-violet and enticingly drinkable in its youth.

| | |
|---|---|
| Contratto | Scarpa |
| Franco-Fiorina | Tenuta Carretta |
| Pio Cesare | |

**Brachetto d'Acqui** DOC r. s/sw. sw. fz. sp.   ★★→★★★   DYA
Light red, either *frizzante* or sparkling, made from Brachetto grapes in the Acqui Terme area. With delicate Muscat-like aroma and some sweetness, it is served cool with pastry, fruit, and even sausages.

| | |
|---|---|
| Antica Contea di Castelvero | Giorgio Carnevale |
| Bersano | Marchesi Spinola |
| Braida | Valmosè |
| C.S. di Cassine | Villa Banfi |
| C.S. di Maranzana | |

**Bramaterra** DOC r. dr.   ★★   76 78 79 80 82 83
Recent DOC of Nebbiolo (Spanna) at 50–70% with Croatina, Bonarda, and Vespolina, grown in Vercelli hills at village of Bramaterra. Full-bodied and sturdy, it gains harmony and grace with 4–8 years.
Ag. 3 yrs (2 in barrel).

| | |
|---|---|
| Luigi Perazzi | Sella Bramaterra |

**Bricco del Drago** r. dr.   ★★★   78 79 80 82 83
Distinctive blend of Dolcetto with Nebbiolo grown near Alba in a rich, ruby-violet wine, soft and attractive with its own sort of authority in 4–6 years, sometimes more.
Cascina Drago (De Giacomi)

**Bricco Manzoni** r. dr.   ★★★→★★★★   78 79 80 82 83
An ingenious mix of Nebbiolo and Barbera grown in the Barolo zone at Monfortex in a stylish red that matures sooner than Barolo but shows similar depth and class.
Podere Rocche dei Manzoni-Valentino

**Briona** r. dr.   ★★★   78 82 83
Nebbiolo with Bonarda grown in the Novara hills, this is a well structured, elegantly dry but full-flavored wine of attractive bouquet, to drink in 4–8 years or more.
Antoniolo

**Cabernet Sauvignon**
Recent plantings of the Bordeaux vine in a region where it once thrived are expected to result in wines of real interest later in the decade.

**Caluso Passito**
See Erbaluce di Caluso.

**Campo Romano** r. dr. fz.   ★★   DYA
Delightful table wine made near Alba from Freisa with about 30% Pinot Nero. Deep in color but light and fruity in flavor, it is clean and balanced with a refreshing prickle.
Cascina Drago (De Giacomi)

**Caramino** r. dr.   ★★→★★★   74 78 79 80 82 83
Elegant red based on Nebbiolo from vineyards around the Caramino castle at Fara in the Novara hills. Similar to Gattinara, it can develop extraordinary depth of flavor and bouquet with 8–10 years of age.

| | |
|---|---|
| C.S. dei Colli Novaresi | Luigi Dessilani & Figli |

**Carema** DOC r. dr.   ★★→★★★★   71 74 78 79 82 83
Tiny, mountainous zone next to Valle d'Aosta in which vines are trained over trellises on rocky terraces. Made from Nebbiolo (here called Picutener or Pugnet), Carema is garnet-hued with somewhat less body and durability than other Nebbiolo wines, but cold climate and stony terrain account for unique refinement in bouquet and flavor developed through long barrel- and bottle-aging. Needs 5–6 years or more.
Ag. 4 yrs (2 in barrel).   ▶

Lorenzo Bertolo                      Enoteca Eporediese
Cantina Produttori Nebbiolo di       Luigi Ferrando
   Carema

**Chardonnay** w. dr.
Recent plantings of this noble vine should give a new and welcome
dimension to Piedmontese whites. In the Alba area, Gaja, Marchesi di
Gresy and Pio Cesare were expected to issue their first vintages soon.

**Colli Tortonesi** DOC
Zone near the town of Tortona in SE Piedmont with two varietal wines.
– **Barbera** r. dr.  ★→★★  79 80 82 83
Lively, robust red from at least 85% Barbera. The *superiore* improves
with 3–5 years.
Ag. *superiore* 2 yrs.

– **Cortese** w. dr. (fz.) (sp.)  ★→★★  DYA
Pale, delicate, bone-dry, rather acidic white from Cortese. Good with
seafood, it is sometimes bubbly.
Sergio Borasi                        Cantine Volpi
C.S. di Tortona                      Torricella (Bergaglio)

**Contessa Rosa Brut Nature** w. dr. sp.  ★★★  DYA
Vintage *spumante* made by *méthode champenoise* from Pinot grapes grown at
Serralunga d'Alba. Processed without the *dosage*, it is crisp and clean
with fine *perlage*, one of Italy's most elegant sparkling wines. The firm
also makes a good *charmat* called Noble Sec.
Fontanafredda

**Cortese dell'Alto Monferrato** DOC w. dr. (fz.) (sp.)  ★→★★  DYA
Crisp, pale, straw-green wine of at least 85% Cortese grown in a large
area of the Alto Monferrato hills. Sometimes *frizzante* or sparkling.
C.S. di Cassine                      Oberto Pinelli Gentile
Contratto                            Tre Castelli
Cossetti                             Vignaioli Piemontesi

**Cortese di Gavi** or **Gavi** DOC w. dr. (fz.) (sp.)  ★★→★★★  DYA
The most prestigious wines from the Cortese grape come from the hills
around Gavi in SE Piedmont. One of N Italy's most fashionable whites,
it is noted for acute dryness and fresh, flinty acidity, which make it good
with fish. Occasionally *frizzante* or sparkling (see also Gavi dei Gavi).
Balestrino & Vivalda                 La Battistina
Nicola Bergaglio & Figlio            La Chiara
Bersano                              La Giustiniana
Broglia (La Meirana)                 La Piacentina
Cantina Produttori del Gavi          La Raia
Giorgio Carnevale                    La Scolca
Cascina Pessenti (Barile)            Pio Cesare
Castel di Serra                      Principessa Gavia (Villa Banfi)
Castello di Tassarolo                Raggio d'Azeglio
Contratto                            Tenuta San Pietro
R. Cortese                           Valmosè
Luigi Gemme (La Merlina)             Villa Costa
Granduca (Duca d'Asti)               Villa Sparina

**Dolcetto** r. dr. (fz.)  ★→★★★  82 83
Generic name for many unclassified wines from Dolcetto grown
throughout S Piedmont. Styles vary from zone to zone, from thick, deep
purple and somewhat tannic to fairly light, bright ruby and fruity.
Always dry with a pleasant bitter-almond background, Dolcetto's soft,
grapy qualities make it a wine to drink in a year or two, though some
insist on aging it. Sometimes *frizzante*, rarely rosé.
Bronda                               Mirella Luzi Donadei
F. Bruni                             Alessandro Odore
Giorgio Carnevale                    Scarpa
Fratelli Carosso

**Dolcetto d'Acqui** DOC r. dr.  ★→★★  82 83
Among the softest and lightest of Dolcettos, from Acqui Terme.
Ag. *superiore* 1 yr.
Argusto (Villa Banfi)                Il Cascinone di Castel Rocchero
C.S. di Cassine                      Francesco Poncini & Figlio
Castello d'Orsara                    Marchesi Spinola
Castel Tagliolo                      Vignaioli Piemontesi

**Dolcetto d'Alba** DOC r. dr. ★★→★★★   82 83
Steady improvements in technique have enabled producers in the Alba
zone to achieve Dolcetto of unequalled appeal; balanced, smooth,
gracefully grapy, mouth-filling wine to drink within 1–3 years.
Ag. *superiore* 1 yr.

| | |
|---|---|
| Accademia Torregiorgi | Drago (De Giacomi) |
| Giovanni Accomasso & Figlio | Riccardo Fenocchio |
| Fratelli Barale | Franco-Fiorina |
| Bera | Gaja (Vignabajla) |
| Bersano | Bruno Giacosa |
| Carlo Boffa & Figli | I Paglieri-Roagna |
| Borgà d'Arion | La Spinona |
| Fratelli Brovia | Marchesi di Barolo |
| Cantina della Porta Rossa | Marchesi di Gresy |
| Cantina del Glicine | Giuseppe Mascarello & Figlio |
| Cantina Mascarello | Fratelli Oddero |
| Cantina Vignaioli Elvio | Parroco di Neive |
| Pertinace | Luigi Pelissero |
| Cappellano | Pio Cesare |
| Castello di Neive | Podere Rocche dei Manzoni- |
| Cavallotto | Valentino |
| Ceretto | Alfredo Prunotto |
| Fratelli Cigliuti | Renato Ratti |
| Elvio Cogno | Rizzi |
| Confratelli di San Michele | Gigi Rosso |
| Aldo Conterno | Luciano Sandrone |
| Giacomo Conterno | Alfonso Scavino |
| Paolo Cordero di Montezemolo | Paolo Scavino |
| Giuseppe Cortese | Terre del Barolo |
| R. Cortese | Traversa |
| De Forville | G.D. Vajra |
| Francesco Destefanis & | Sergio Vezza & Figlio |
| Figlio | Vietti |
| Dogliani 7 Cascine | U. Vignolo-Lutati & Figlio |
| Redento Dogliotti & Figli | Voerzio |
| Dosio | Basilio Zunino |

**Dolcetto d'Asti** DOC r. dr.  ★→★★   82 83
From the Monferrato hills in the province of Asti, an easy-drinking but
lightweight Dolcetto is made in limited quantity.
Ag. *superiore* 1 yr.

| | |
|---|---|
| Antica Contea di Castelvero | Giorgio Carnevale |
| Balestrino & Vivalda | Cossetti |
| Bersano | La Gosa |
| Carlo Brema & Figlio | Vincenzo Ronco & Figli |
| C.S. di Canelli | Vignaioli Piemontesi |
| C.S. di Maranzana | |

**Dolcetto delle Langhe Monregalesi** DOC r. dr.  ★★   82
Made in minute quantities in the Langhe between Dogliani and
Mondovi. Though lighter than others, it is noted for special bouquet.
Not often seen in commerce.
Ag. *superiore* 1 yr.
Cascina La Meridiana

**Dolcetto di Diano d'Alba** DOC r. dr.  ★★→★★★   82 83
The Dolcetto from Diano is among the best, noted for its deep purple
color, smooth texture and grapy fragrance and flavor.
Ag. *superiore* 1 yr.

| | |
|---|---|
| Anforio (Premiovini) | Mario Savigliano |
| Sergio Casavecchia | Terre del Barolo |
| Coluè | Giovanni Veglio & Figlio |
| Fontanafredda | |

**Dolcetto di Dogliani** DOC r. dr.  ★★   82 83
The Dolcetto vine reputedly originated at Dogliani, where it makes wine
of firm tone and some depth.
Ag. *superiore* 1 yr.

| | |
|---|---|
| Lorenzo Bertolo | Luigi Einaudi |
| Francesco Boschis | Adalberto Schellino |
| Cappellano | |

**Dolcetto di Ovada** DOC r. dr.  ★★ →★★★   78 79 80 82 83
Dolcetto from hills around Ovada in SE Piedmont rivals the best of Alba

in class. Sturdy structure favors aging; some big vintages last a decade.
Ag. *superiore* 1 yr.

| | |
|---|---|
| C.S. Stazione Calamandrana | Tenuta Cannona |
| Duca d'Asti | Tenuta di Savoia |
| Giuseppe Poggio (Trionzo) | Terre del Dolcetto |
| Giuseppe Luigi Ratto | Tre Castelli |
| Giuseppe Scazzola | Valmosè |

**Erbaluce di Caluso** DOC
The appellation covers two basic types of white wine from the Erbaluce
grape grown around Caluso and Ivrea NE of Turin.
–**Bianco** w. dr.  ★→★★  DYA
Light, dry, rather acidic, this pale, straw-colored wine is to drink young.
New methods of vinification promise more significant style, possibly on
the order of Cortese di Gavi.
–**Caluso Passito** am. sw.  ★★→★★★   74 76 78 79 80 82 83
Made from semidried Erbaluce grapes, Caluso Passito is sweet and
rather strong (13.5% minimum), golden to amber and velvety with a
few years of age. The fortified Caluso Passito *liquoroso* is sweeter,
smoother, stronger (16%), and capable of great age. Both sweet versions
go well with strong cheese.
Ag. 5 yrs.

| | |
|---|---|
| Lorenzo Bertolo | Istituto Professionale di Stato per |
| Vittorio Boratto | l'Agricoltura Carlo Ubertini |
| C.S. della Serra | Macellio (Bianco) |
| Luigi Ferrando | Orsolani |
| Corrado Gnavi | Mattia Thione-Bosio |
| Filiberto Gnavi | |

**Fara** DOC r. dr.  ★★   78 79 80 82 83
Red of noteworthy character from Nebbiolo, Vespolina, and Bonarda
grown in the Novara hills. Robust and nicely scented, it improves over
4–8 years, sometimes longer.
Ag. 3 yrs (2 in barrel).

| | |
|---|---|
| C.S. dei Colli Novaresi | Luigi Ferrando |
| Luigi Dessilani & Figli | |

**Favorita** w. dr.  ★→★★  DYA
New interest in this pale, acidic white wine from the once-forgotten
Favorita grown in the Roeri and Langhe hills has led to a modest
comeback. Bone dry and light, when well made it is not as simplistic as it
may seem on first sip.

| | |
|---|---|
| C.S. del Nebbiolo | Angelo Negro & Figli |
| Cavallotto | Renato Rabezzana |
| Franco-Fiorina | Voerzio |
| Monticelli-Oliveri (La Corte) | |

**Freisa** r. dr. (s/sw.) fz. sp.  ★★→★★★   82 83
Once popular in central Piedmont as a rustic bubbly wine with unique
sweet-acidic flavor (something like lightly salted raspberries), Freisa has
lost ground. But lately some producers, especially around Alba, have
resumed making dry Freisa of good balance, whether *frizzante*, *spumante*,
or still. With enticing ruby-cherry color and raspberry-like aroma, they
show enough class to herald a revival.

| | |
|---|---|
| Cantina Sant'Uffizio | Fratelli Oddero |
| Fratelli Cigliuti | Pio Cesare |
| Aldo Conterno | Alfredo Prunotto |
| Giacomo Conterno | Scarpa |
| Redento Dogliotti & Figli | Tenuta Carretta |
| Drago (De Giacomi) | Terre del Barolo |
| Franco-Fiorina | Vietti |
| Gaja | Voerzio |
| Bruno Giacosa | |

**Freisa d'Asti** DOC r. dr. or s/sw. fz. sp.  ★→★★  DYA
Though DOC, Freisa d'Asti rarely equals the select unclassified Freisa of
Alba. Dry or *amabile*, still, *frizzante*, or sparkling, it has lively acidic flavor
with a berry-like undertone and bright cherry-garnet color.

| | |
|---|---|
| Antica Contea di Castelvero | Contratto |
| Bersano | Moncucchetto (Biletta) |
| C.S. di Canelli | Vignaioli Piemontesi |
| Giorgio Carnevale | |

**Freisa di Chieri** DOC r. (dr.) s/sw. fz. sp. ☒ 82 83
Limited production from this zone at the doorstep of Turin is mostly
consumed in the area. The *amabile* is preferred.
Balbiano                                    Lorenzo Bertolo

**Furmentin** or **Fromentin** w. dr.  ★★  DYA
Rare white believed to come from Furmint, the vine of Hungarian
Tokay. Grown SE of Alba, it is pale straw yellow with green highlights
and has a grassy scent and a hint of sweetness in its dry, smooth flavor.
C.S. Dolcetto & Moscato                     Renato Rabezzana

**Gabiano** DOC r. dr.  ★★  74 78 79 80 82 83
Newly approved DOC based on Barbera from the village of Gabiano in
the Monferato Casalese hills. Very limited, it is noted for extraordinary
longevity.
Castello di Gabiano

**Gattinara** DOC r. dr.  ★★→★★★  70 74 76 78 79 82 83
Wine of ancient renown, Gattinara is capable of greatness, though it
rarely lives up to its name. At best, this red from Nebbiolo (Spanna)
grown in the Vercelli hills can rival Barolo in dimensions, durability,
style, and depth. But Nebbiolo, which may be mixed with 10% Bonarda,
develops distinct nuances in the glacial moraine N of the town of
Gattinara. There is a hint more of violets and tar on the nose, that
slightly softer texture and sense of bitter almond at the finish that set it
apart. Recent self-discipline has improved quality, but more consistency
is needed in Gattinara's production of some 400,000 bottles a year.
Ag. 4 yrs (2 in barrel).
Pasquale Albertini                          Luigi Dessilani & Figli
Antoniolo (Vigneto Osso San                 Luigi Ferrando
  Grato)                                     Umberto Fiore
Guido Barra & Figlio                        Luigi & Italo Nervi
Lorenzo Bertolo                             Giancarlo Travaglini
Agostino Brugo

**Gavi**
Alternate name for Cortese di Gavi.

**Gavi dei Gavi** w. dr.  ★★★→★★★★  82 83
Though this wine from the estate of La Scolca is officially a Cortese di
Gavi DOC, it stands in a class by itself as the grandest product of the
Cortese grape. Gavi dei Gavi has a nip of the noted Cortese bite, but its
rich, almost Burgundian texture, depth of aroma and length of flavors
have earned it a reputation as one of Italy's most distinguished whites.
La Scolca

**Ghemme** DOC r. dr.  ★★→★★★  74 78 79 80 82 83
Among Nebbiolo-based wines of the Novara-Vercelli hills, Ghemme
ranks second to Gattinara in status but can surpass it in class. From
Nebbiolo at 60–85% with Vespolina and Bonarda, its sturdy, robust
qualities smoothen with age as it develops an elegant bouquet. Made in
limited quantity around the town of Ghemme.
Ag. 4 yrs (3 in barrel).
Antichi Vigneti di Cantalupo                Le Colline (Ravizza)
Lorenzo Bertolo                             Guido Ponti
Agostino Brugo                              G. Sebastiani & Figlio
C.S. di Sizzano e Ghemme

**Greco** w. dr.  ★  DYA
Apparently a strain of Erbaluce, Greco makes pleasant, light, rather tart
white wines in the Novara-Vercelli hills.
C.S. di Sizzano e Ghemme                    Antonio Vallana & Figlio

**Grignolino** r. dr.  ★★  DYA
Once widely planted, Grignolino has been reduced to secondary status in
Piedmont, a victim of phylloxera and shy yields. Its pale, delicate wines
seem strangely out of step in a region of bold reds, but local admirers of
"Grigno" find its almost rosy color and dry, vaguely bitter, gritty flavor
unmatchable at table. Some unclassified Grignolino, from Portacomaro
N of Asti in particular, show lovely freshness when young.
Bronda                                      Aldo Conterno
Castel di Camino                            La Spinona
Cascina Biggio                              Aldo Margarino
Cavallotto                                  Eugenio Margarino

**Grignolino d'Asti** DOC r. dr.  ★→★★★  82 83
The largest DOC zone permits 10% of Freisa in light Grignolino to drink
young and fairly cool.

| | |
|---|---|
| Balestrino & Vivalda | Contratto |
| Bersano | R. Cortese |
| Bosca | Bruno Giacosa |
| Braida (Bologna) | Moncucchetto (Biletta) |
| Carlo Brema & Figlio | Pinbologna |
| C.S. Casorzo | Renato Rabezzana |
| Cantine Bava | A.B. Ravetto |
| Giorgio Carnevale | Fratelli Rovero |
| Cascina La Spinetta (Rivetti) | Scarpa |
| Casaletto (Ronco) | Tenuta dei Re |
| Aldo Cassina | G.L. Viarengo & Figlio |
| Conte di Cavour | |

**Grignolino del Monferrato Casalese** DOC r. dr.  ★→★★★  82 83
Grown in the hills around Casale Monferrato, Grignolino (with 10% of
Freisa) is light ruby orange, refreshingly acidic, and sometimes quite
stylish. This is the classic Grignolino zone.

| | |
|---|---|
| Renzo Campagnola | Ermenegildo Leporati |
| Fratelli Cantamessa | Nuova Cappelletta |
| C.S. del Monferrato | Livio Pavese |
| C.S. di Vignale | Pio Cesare |
| C.S. Stazione Calamandrana | Poderi Bricco Mondalino |
| Cascina Belvedere | (Gaudio) |
| Castello di Gabiano | Giuseppe Ravizza |
| Castello di Lignano | Tenuta Tenaglia (Quattrocolo) |
| Giorgio Cosseta | Tenute Riccardi Candiani |
| Duca d'Asti | Valmosè |
| Franco-Fiorina | Vietti |
| Bruno Giacosa | |

**Lessona** DOC r. dr.  ★★★  70 71 74 78 79 80 82
Minuscule zone in the Vercelli hills with excellent red wine from
Nebbiolo with up to 25% Vespolina and Bonarda. Rich in bouquet and
flavor, robust, and lightly tannic, Lessona improves with 6–8 years,
sometimes more.
Ag. 2 yrs.

| | |
|---|---|
| Ormezzano | Sella Lessona |

**Malvasia di Casorzo d'Asti** DOC r. (dr.) s/sw. sw. sp.  ★→★★
DYA
Usually sweet and *spumante*, this cherry-hued wine comes from the
Malvasia Rossa vine grown around Casorzo NE of Asti. Appreciated
locally for its fragrant, grapy fruitiness.

| | |
|---|---|
| Fratelli Biletta | Livio Pavese |
| C.S. Casorzo | |

**Malvasia di Castelnuovo Don Bosco** DOC r. sw. sp.  ★  DYA
This wine from the town of Castelnuovo Don Bosco near Turin is similar
to Malvasia di Casorzo but even harder to find.

| | |
|---|---|
| Melchiorre Balbiano | Giovanni Savio |
| Cantine Bava | |

**Mesolone** r. dr.  ★★  78 79 80 82
Distinguished red from Nebbiolo and Bonarda made at Brusnengo in the
Vercelli hills. It improves with 5–8 years or more.
Armando Beccaro & Figlio

**Monfortino**
Special name for a Barolo made by Giacomo Conterno and noted for
longevity.

**Monsecco** r. dr.  ★★→★★★★  70 74 78 79 80 82
Though not enrolled as DOC, this is virtually a superior Gattinara with
an unusually long life span.
Le Colline (Ravizza)

**Moscato d'Asti–Moscato d'Asti Spumante** DOC
The DOC category for Moscato qualified as Asti Spumante is Moscato
d'Asti. Produced in quantity (45 million liters a year) in the Monferrato
hills S of Asti between Alba and Acqui Terme from Moscato Bianco or
Moscato di Canelli grapes. DOC prescribes two types of wine.

– **Asti Spumante** or **Asti** w. s/sw. sw. sp. ★★→★★★ NV
Italy's most famous sparkling wine, noted for its seductive Muscat
aroma, refreshing sweetness, and moderate alcohol. The base wine is
usually processed by *charmat*, only rarely by *méthode champenoise*. Recent
improvement in quality and consistency is due to stricter self-control
through their *consorzio* by large firms, mainly at Canelli, with the
resources to put Asti through its complex production procedures.

| | |
|---|---|
| Anforio (Premiovini) | Contratto |
| Antica Contea di Castelvero | Cora |
| Bera (Cascina Palazzo) | Duchessa Beatrice |
| Bersano | Fontanafredda |
| Lorenzo Bertolo | Fratelli Gancia |
| Felice Bonardi | Gaudenzio |
| Bosca | Graziola |
| Calissano | Clemente Guasti & Figli |
| C.S. Alice Bel Colle | Kiola |
| C.S. Canelli | Martini & Rossi |
| C.S. di Cassine | Morando |
| C.S. Dolcetto & Moscato | Ottavio Riccadonna |
| Giorgio Carnevale | Tenuta Bertulot |
| Cascina Canova (Barbero) | Valfieri |
| Cinzano | Vignaioli Piemontesi |
| Cocchi | |

– **Moscato d'Asti** or **Moscato d'Asti Naturale** w. s/sw. sw. fz.
★★→★★★ DYA
This is the base wine. After filtration, the musts are fermented into a wine
with a high degree of residual sugar. Some of this is kept aside to be
marketed as Moscato d'Asti or Moscato Naturale d'Asti, which are
usually *frizzante* through refermentation in bottle. The best have
exquisite Muscat fragrance, as little as 5% alcohol (the rest is in residual
sugar) and flavor so fresh it's like biting into a ripe grape. (Not all wine
from listed producers is DOC.)

| | |
|---|---|
| Antica Contea di Castelvero | Fontanafredda |
| Angelo Arione | Clemente Guasti & Figli |
| Balestrino | I Vignaioli di Santo Stefano |
| Bastian (Soria) | Il Cascinone di Castel Rocchero |
| Bel Colle | La Gosa |
| Bera (Cascina Palazzo) | Marenco |
| Braida (Bologna) | Vittorio & Giuseppe Mo |
| Carlo Brema & Figlio | Podere Rocche dei Manzoni- |
| C.S. Canelli | Valentino |
| C.S. di Cassine | Ronco |
| C.S. Dolcetto & Moscato | Giovanni Saracco |
| Giorgio Carnevale | Tenuta Bertulot |
| Cascina Canova (Barbero) | Traversa |
| Cascina La Spinetta (Rivetti) | Valmosè |
| Coluè | Vietti |
| De Forville | Vignaioli Piemontesi |
| Redento Dogliotti & Figli | Voerzio |

**Moscato di Strevi** w. s/sw. sw. fz. sp. ★★→★★★ NV
Strevi, a town near Acqui, is renowned for its Moscato, which is made
into wines, usually *spumante* or *frizzante*, of notable class.

| | |
|---|---|
| F. Bruni | Domenico Mangiarotti |
| Conti Valperga | Villa Banfi |
| Domenico Ivaldi | |

**Möt Ziflon** r. dr. ★★ 78 79 82
Dry red from Nebbiolo, Bonarda, and Freisa made at Suno in the
Novara hills. Medium in structure, it develops bouquet after 3–4 years.
Luciano Brigatti

**Nebbiolo d'Alba** DOC r. dr. (sw.) (sp.) ★★→★★★ 78 79 82 83
Certain Nebbiolo vineyards in the Roeri hills N of Alba and an area
between Barolo and Barbaresco produce this DOC, which applies to a
still, dry wine of good-to-excellent quality as well as *dolce* and *spumante*
versions of each. The sweet and bubbly are largely of local interest. The
dry can show the nobility of more vaunted Nebbiolo wines with the
advantage of being softer, easier to drink and less expensive. It may reach
a prime at 3–6 years, but from some vintages can last a decade. The name
should be officially changed to Roero beginning with the 1984 vintage.▶

Ag. 1 yr (*secco*).

Baracco de Baracho
Fratelli Barale
Bersano
C.S. del Nebbiolo
Ceretto
Coluè
Drago (De Giacomi)
Franco-Fiorina
Gaja (Vignaveja)
Bruno Giacosa
Malvirà (Damonte)
Marchesi di Barolo
Giuseppe Mascarello & Figlio
Pio Cesare
Produttori Montaldesi Associati
Alfredo Prunotto
Renato Ratti
Mario Savigliano & Figlio
Scarpa
Tenuta Carretta
Terre del Barolo
Sergio Vezza & Figlio
Vietti

**Nebbiolo del Piemonte** r. dr. (fz.)   ★→ ★★★   78 79 80 82 83
Name sometimes used for wine from Nebbiolo grapes not employed for
DOC. These table wines, sometimes followed by a more specific place
name, can be good to excellent.

Bersano
C.S. Tortona
Giorgio Carnevale
Cavallotto
Aldo Conterno
Fontanafredda
Gaja
Grasso
La Contea
Marchesi di Gresy
Fratelli Oddero
Renato Ratti
Francesco Rinaldi & Figli
Voerzio

**Nebbiolo delle Langhe**
Name nearing approval as a second-tier DOC for wines from Barolo and
Barbaresco vineyards from grapes not up to top standard due to a weak
harvest or left over after careful selection. Such wines would need to be of
DOC quality, though sold sooner and at a lower price.

**Orbello** r. dr.   ★★   82 83
Soft, fruity wine of good body from Nebbiolo with Bonarda, Vespolina
and Croatina grown at Bramaterra in the Vercelli hills. Drink in 2–4
years.
Sella Bramaterra.

**Pelaverga** p. dr.   ★★   DYA
Prickly pale ruby wine with a scent of currants and spices made from the
few surviving vines of the Pelaverga variety, near Saluzzo and Verduno.
Bel Colle                          Castello di Verduno

**Piccone** r. dr.   ★★   78 79 80 82 83
Sturdy red, similar to Lessona but less imposing, from Nebbiolo,
Vespolina, and Bonarda grown at Lessona in the Vercelli hills.
Sella Lessona

**Pinot** r. w. dr.   ★★   81 82 83
Both dark and light Pinot were once well known in Piedmont, but now
only a few vines can be found, mostly around Alba. New plantings
should soon result in interesting wines – red, rosé, white, still, and
sparkling. Cascina del Drago's Pinot Nero is smooth, fruity, something
like a Rully in style, to drink in 2–4 years. Fontanafredda's Pinot Bianco
is made from Pinot Nero primarily with some Pinot Bianco and Grigio
grown at Serralunga d'Alba. Pale straw green, flowery with good fruit-
acid balance, it is best in a year or two.
Drago (De Giacomi)                 Fontanafredda

**Riesling** w. dr.   ★★   DYA
Traces of Riesling Renano and Italico, along with some Müller
Thurgau, can be found in S Piedmont. More is being planted. Evidently,
the only Piedmontese Riesling on the market now is made at Gavi.
La Giustiniana

**Roero**
Designated as new name for Nebbiolo d'Alba DOC.

**Rouchet** r. dr.   ★★★   78 79 82
Rare and extraordinary red from a vine of mysterious origin known as
Rouchet or Roché grown in the highest vineyards above Castagnole
Monferrato. Scarpa's Rouchet is a strong, ruby-violet wine with bold
structure, flowery bouquet and peculiar elegance after 4–5 years.
Scarpa

**Rubino di Cantavenna** DOC r. dr.  ★★  DYA
Little-known DOC of Barbera with Grignolino and Freisa grown in the
Monferrato Casalese at Cantavenna. The wine is noted for its youthful
vigor and fresh flavor.
C. S. di Cantavenna

**Sizzano** DOC r. dr.  ★★  74 78 79 80 82 83
Limited production red from Nebbiolo at 40–60% with Vespolina and
Bonarda grown around Sizzano in the Novara hills. Robust, with fine
Nebbiolo bouquet, it lasts a decade from top vintages.
Ag. 3 yrs (2 in barrel).
Giuseppe Bianchi                     Guido Ponti
C.S. di Sizzano e Ghemme

**Spanna** r. dr.  ★→★★★  70 71 74 76 78 79 80 82 83
The name for Nebbiolo in the Novara-Vercelli hills is applied to many
unclassified wines, some mediocre, some superb, with life spans that may
range beyond 10 years to 30 or 40. Though they could be made of
Spanna alone, they most probably contain other wine from southern
regions that give body, strength, color, and longevity even to wines from
medium vintages. Indeed, the best Spanna can rival the best Gattinara
in almost every way – except authenticity. The exotically labeled
Spanna bottlings of Antonio Vallana & Figlio have provided
unsurpassed bargains in aged wines, occasionally of  ★★★★  quality.

Antonioli (Santachiara)          Luigi & Italo Nervi
Antonio Brugo                    Ermanno Rivetti
Ermanno Conti                    Travaglini
Luigi Dessilani & Figli          Antonio Vallana & Figlio
Luigi Ferrando                   Villa Era
Francoli

**Spumante**
Piedmont produces a dazzling array of bubbly wines, ranging from
lightly *frizzante* to explosively sparkling, bone dry to cloyingly sweet, and
covering all colors. Those which derive from locally grown grapes are
listed separately under Piedmont. Some of the best, the *brut spumanti*, are
from Pinot (or Chardonnay or Riesling) grapes from other regions,
chiefly Lombardy's Oltrepò Pavese, and are listed in the region of origin.

**Verbesco** w. dr.  ★★  DYA
Recently conceived light white (10% alcohol) produced by five
prominent firms in a new consortium. Made from about two-thirds dark
grapes (mainly Barbera) and processed using modern low temperature
techniques, the result is a facile, fizzy wine for carefree sipping.
Bersano                          Marchesi di Barolo
Contratto                        Volpi
Duca d'Asti

**Vermouth**
Piedmont is the world capital of vermouth, which by law must contain at
least 70% wine in intricate and often secret blends with herbs, spices and
other natural flavorings. The industry, based in Turin, Asti, and Canelli,
now usually employs wines from other regions.

**Vinòt** r. dr.  ★★★  DYA
The first *vino novello* of Italy to be vinified using carbonic maceration –
and arguably still the best in a growing field. Made from Nebbiolo, it has
fruity freshness with exceptional balance. Drink cool within 3 months.
Gaja

*Wine & Food*

Piedmontese cooking, like robust red wine, comes into its own in
the autumn. Hearty, almost chauvinistically traditional, it is
refined country cooking that follows the seasons, and fall
provides the bounty. There is game from the mountainsides;
hams, cheeses and salame matured to perfection; and a bright
array of garden vegetables augmented by what is found in woods
and fields. The multitude of antipasto, the ample pastas and
risottos, thick soups and stews, roast and boiled meats, is the kind

of fare which requires generous red wines. But the heartiness can be deceptive, for Piedmontese cooking has touches of grace distinct from, but equal to, the artistry of the provincial cooking of Burgundy and Lyonnais. The ultimate luxury is the white truffle, sniffed out by mongrels in the Langhe and shaved raw over pastas, risottos, meats, and fondues. Some of the best Piedmontese restaurants are found where the best wines are, and the time to visit is when the grapes and truffles are coming in.

**Bagna caôda** "Hot bath" of oil, garlic, and anchovies bubbling over a burner into which raw vegetables – peppers, cardoons, fennel, celery, etc. – are dipped.
    ** Freisa *secco* or ** Barbera, young and sharp.
**Brasato al Barolo** Beef marinated and stewed slowly in Barolo.
    ***→**** Barolo, well aged.
**Bollito misto alla piemontese** Boiled veal and beef, including brains and tongue, with *bagnet piemontese*, a garlicky green sauce.
    ** Boca or ** Fara.
**Camoscio alla piemontese** Chamois in a savory stew.
    *** Carema or *** Lessona.
**Capretto arrosto** Richly seasoned roast kid.
    ***→**** Barbaresco.
**Finanziera** Leftover meat and poultry together in a type of stew.
    ** Nebbiolo or ** Dolcetto.
**Fonduta** Cheese fondue based on *fontina*, often used as a sauce for pasta or risotto, and sometimes topped with shaved truffles.
    *** Dolcetto d'Alba or *** Bricco del Drago.
**Fritto misto** or **fricia** Elaborate delicacies – brains, sweetbreads, lamb cutlets, chicken breasts, eggplant, zucchini, mushrooms,

frogs' legs, sweet pastes, etc. – dipped in batter and fried.
    ** Barbera or ** Freisa *secco*.
**Insalata di carne cruda** Minced filet of beef marinated briefly with oil, lemon, and pepper, sometimes served with fine sliced mushrooms, Parmesan or truffles.
    *** Dolcetto or *** Nebbiolo.
**Lepre al sivè** "Jugged hare," marinated in wine and flavorings and stewed to rich tenderness.
    *** Gattinara or *** Carema.
**Panna cotta** Fresh cream molded with burned sugar like a crème caramel but more luxurious.
    *** Asti or *** Moscato d'Asti.
**Tajarin al tartufo** Hand-cut egg noodles with butter, Parmesan, and shaved truffles.
    **** Gavi dei Gavi.
**Tapulon** Ground donkey meat cooked with red wine, cabbage, and seasonings.
    *** Spanna or *** Ghemme.
**Tome** or **tume** Small, round sheep's milk cheeses from the Langhe, mild when young, sharp when aged.
    **→*** Dolcetto (young cheese), *** Nebbiolo (aged).
**Zabaglione** Egg yolks whipped with Marsala, other sweet wine or Barolo.
    *** Caluso Passito or *** Asti.

## Restaurants

Recommended in or near wine zones: **Alba-Langhe** *Cesare* at Alberetto Torre; *Dell'Arcangelo* at Bra; *Enoteca del Castello* at Grinzane Cavour; *Bel Sit* and *Belvedere* at La Morra; *Il Giardino di Felicin* at Monforte; *La Contea* at Neive; *Al Castello* at Santa Vittoria d'Alba. **Asti-Monferrato** *Parisio* at Acqui Terme; *Gener Neuv* and *Il Vicoletto* at Asti; *La Fioraia* at Castello di Annone; *Da Beppe* at Cioccaro di Penango; *Da Guido* at Costigliole d'Asti. **Gavi-Ovada** *Cantine del Gavi* at Gavi; *Da Pietro* at Ovada. **Novara-Vercelli hills** *Pinocchio* at Borgomanero; *La Taverna del Ricetto* at Candelo.

# Sardinia

## Sardegna

Off by itself in mid-Mediterranean, Sardinia has every reason to remain the most idiosyncratic of Italian regions. Its wines express the island's character to the letter. Several varieties are unique in Italy, brought by Phoenicians, Carthaginians, Romans, and Spaniards in particular. But over the centuries the climate (which is temperate rather than hot) and soil of the Mediterranean's second-largest island changed their nature while Sardinian concepts of taste gave them styles entirely their own.

Sardinian tastes have been changing, along with the methods which quickly revolutionized winemaking here. Though still a source of blending wines, Sardinia has become an increasingly noticed supplier of light, fresh, balanced vintages that appeal to contemporary palates. Fortunately, change hasn't swept away all the old-style character. The most typical Sardinian wines, whether sweet, semisweet, or dry, are still strong in constitution: the Sherry-like Vernaccia di Oristano, Malvasia di Bosa, and Nasco di Cagliari; the Port-like Cannonau, Monica di Cagliari and Girò di Cagliari; and the aromatic Moscatos of Cagliari and Sorso-Sennori.

But the trend is irreversibly toward dry wines of moderate strength. Nuragus, introduced by the Phoenicians and named after the *nuraghe*, the island's prehistoric conical stone towers, is the most popular of DOC wines, though the modern neutrality of this white from Cagliari's fertile Campidano plains doesn't make

**Wine Zones**

1 Campidano di Terralba
2 Carignano di Sulcis
3 Girò di Cagliari
4 Malvasia di Bosa
5 Malvasia di Cagliari
6 Mandrolisai
7 Monica di Cagliari
8 Moscato di Cagliari
9 Moscato di Sorso-Sennori
10 Nasco di Cagliari
11 Nuragus di Cagliari
12 Vermentino di Gallura
13 Vernaccia di Oristano

it the most impressive. Vermentino, from northern Sardinia (from where most of Italy's corks come), has winning character, as does the non-DOC Torbato di Alghero. Among reds, the dry versions of Cannonau, Monica, and Carignano del Sulcis combine power with finesse.

As elsewhere in the Mezzogiorno, wine production is centered in cooperatives, though here at least they seem to function. Indeed, a majority of the island's fine wines are cooperative products. But the pacesetter remains Sella & Mosca, a privately owned firm at Alghero, one of Europe's largest wine estates and producer of several outstanding wines.

Sardinia's chief tourist attraction is its clear blue sea. The Costa Smeralda is the chic place to bask in the sun, but there are many quieter and less expensive spots. The interior is noted for its sweeping views, particularly in the wild uplands around Nuoro, where stolid mountain people are the custodians of the island's traditions, including its hearty wine and food. Car ferries link Sardinia's capital, Cagliari, and the Costa Smeralda with major Mediterranean ports. There is a regular air service from the mainland to Cagliari, Alghero, Olbia, and other cities.

## Recent vintages

Few Sardinian wines require long aging, though Vernaccia di Oristano and other strong dessert or aperitif wines can last for years. Recommended vintages appear with each entry.

**Abbaia** r. dr.  **★★**  83
Vivid ruby table wine from Pascale di Cagliari and other grapes grown around Monti in NE Sardinia. Very dry, warm, and amply scented, it has attractive *gout de terroir* when young.
C.S. del Vermentino

**Aghiloia**
See Vermentino di Gallura.

**Anghelu Ruju** r. sw.  **★★★**  NV
From semidried Cannonau grapes grown near Alghero, this rich, authoritative dessert wine is named after a nearby *nuraghe*. Bright ruby-violet when young, it develops a garnet-brick color after 2–3 years in barrel and another 5 or more in bottle. It has a heady bouquet of berries and spices, and warm, lingering elegance with 18% alcohol.
Sella & Mosca

**Aragosta**
See Vermentino.

**Campidano di Terralba** DOC r. dr.  **★**  83
Ruby-crimson wine based on Bovale grapes grown in the Campidano plain S of Oristano around Terralba. Dry and soft, becoming round and tasty within 2 years.
C.S. del Campidano                    C.S. di Arborea

**Cannonau** r. (p.) (w.) dr. s/sw. sw.  **★→★★★**  79 81 83
Non-DOC wines from Cannonau abound in Sardinia under various names, dry or sweet, usually red, but also rosé and even white. Some dry reds don't qualify as DOC because they have been kept less than the required year in wood or are held under 13.5%. Some of Sardinia's best Cannonau are not DOC: Anghelu Ruju (see above), Cannonau del Goceano, Cannonau del Parteolla, Cannonau di Alghero, Cannonau Marmilla, Le Bombarde, Perda Rubia, and Rosso di Dorgali.
C.S. di Dorgali                    Consorzio per la Frutticoltura di
C.S. Dolianova                       Cagliari
C.S. Marmilla                     Mario Mereu
C.S. Riforma Agraria di Alghero    Sella & Mosca

**Cannonau di Sardegna** DOC r. p. dr. s/sw.  **★→★★★**  79 81 83
Many-faceted DOC from Cannonau grown throughout the region. The basic red *secco* must have 13.5%; it can be drunk after the required year

in barrel when it is richly robust, warm, and complete. With 3–6 years of age, the red (whether *riserva* or not) can show considerable grace as a classic *vino da arrosto*. Despite its strength, Cannonau is not generally aged very long. The *superiore* must have 15% and can be either *secco*, *amabile* or *dolce*, depending on residual sugars. *Liquoroso*, fortified with wine alcohol, must have 18% whether *secco* or *dolce naturale*. Sweet versions can show notable, Port-like class. Cannonau from Oliena (near Nuoro) and Capo Ferrato (in SE Sardinia) may carry those subdenominations.

Ag. 1 yr in barrel; *superiore* 2 yrs; *riserva* 3 yrs.

| | |
|---|---|
| C.S. di Dorgali | C.S. Sorso-Sennori |
| C.S. Dolianova | Cossu (Casa della Vernaccia) |
| C.S. di Jerzu | Fratelli Deiana |
| C.S. di Oliena | |

**Capo Ferrato**
See Cannonau di Sardegna.

**Carignano del Sulcis** DOC r. (p.) dr.  ★→★★   77 78 79 80 83
Red and rosé from Carignano grown on the isles of Sant'Antioco and San Pietro and the SW corner of the main island called Sulcis by the Carthaginians. The *rosso* is good young or, if *invecchiato*, aged 3–6 years. Both are fairly robust, garnet-hued wines, amply scented, dry, warm, generous, and spicy. Sardus Pater of C.S. di Sant'Antioco is a superior *rosso*. The *rosato* is smooth and balanced when young.
Ag. *invecchiato* 1 yr.

| | |
|---|---|
| C.S. di Calasetta | C.S. di Sant'Antioco |

**Girò di Cagliari** DOC r. dr. sw.  ★★   81 83
Rare, usually sweet red from Girò grown in the Campidano N of Cagliari. The four versions – *secco* and *dolce* of 14–14.5%, and *liquoroso secco* and *liquoroso dolce* of 17.5% – are used much as Port is. Bright ruby, warm, and smooth, it is best in 2–3 years.
Ag. *riserva* 2 yrs (1 in barrel).

| | |
|---|---|
| Vini Classici di Sardegna | Zedda Piras |

**I Piani** r. dr.  ★★   81 83
From Carignano grown near Alghero, this dry, robust table wine is warm and inviting in 2–4 years.
Sella & Mosca

**Malvasia di Bosa** DOC am. dr. s/sw. sw.  ★★→★★★   77 78 79 81 83
Prized dessert wine from Malvasia di Sardegna grown in coastal hills near Bosa in W Sardinia. The best – Salvatore Deriu Mocci's *secco* – is golden amber, suave in bouquet, with a flavor which is dry but rich and has a toasted-almond finish. *Secco* and *dolce* must have 15%, *liquoroso secco* and *dolce* 17.5%. Dry versions make fine aperitifs; the sweet are for sipping after dinner. Good in 3–5 years, sometimes much more, this expensive wine is rarely found outside the zone.

| | |
|---|---|
| Mercedes Cau Secchi | Salvatore Deriu Mocci |
| Donchessa | Fratelli Porcu |

**Malvasia di Cagliari** DOC am. dr. s/sw. sw.  ★★   77 78 79 81
From Malvasia di Sardegna grown in the Campidano, this is a good aperitif and dessert wine. There are *secco* and *dolce* of 14% and *liquoroso secco* and *dolce* of 17.5%. The *secco* is best young; the *dolce* and *liquoroso* may be kept a few years.

| | |
|---|---|
| C.S. di Serramanna | Vini Classici di Sardegna |
| C.S. Dolianova | Zedda Piras |
| C.S. Marmilla | |

**Malvasia di Planargia** am. dr.  ★★★   81 83
Virtually identical to Malvasia di Bosa *secco* and grown in the same zone of the Planargia hills, this aperitif wine shows persuasive elegance in 2–4 years.
Emilio & Gilberto Arru

**Mamuntanas Monte Oro** r. dr.  ★★   79 81 83
Cherry-crimson table wine from Carignano and Cannonau grown near Alghero. Dry, warm, of medium body but rather strong, it becomes convincing in 3–5 years, sometimes more.
Tenuta Mamuntanas

**Mandrolisai** DOC r. p. dr.  ★   81 83
Recent DOC from Bovale Sardo, Cannonau, and Monica grown around Sorgono in central Sardinia. The *rosso*, ruby, dry, and well scented with a

light bitter finish, is good in 2–3 years; the *rosato*, cherry red and grapy, is best young.
Ag. *superiore* 2 yrs. (1 in barrel.)

C.S. di Samughero                          C.S. di Sorgono Atzara

**Monica di Cagliari** DOC r. dr. s/sw. sw.  ★→★★  81 83
From Monica grown in the Campidano, the wines are more often sweet
than dry. Light ruby, soft, and delicate in scent, the *secco* and *dolce* must
have 14% and 14.5%. The *liquoroso secco* and *dolce*, of pronounced aroma
and flavor, have 17.5%.

C.S. del Campidano                         Zedda Piras
C.S. di Villacidro

**Monica di Sardegna** DOC r. dr.  ★★  81 83
Always dry, this wine is made in quantity from Monica grown
throughout Sardinia. Bright ruby, supple, medium in body, its bouquet
develops in 3–4 years.
Ag. *superiore* 1 yr in barrel.

C.S. del Campidano                         C.S. Dolianova
C.S. di Marrubiu                           C.S. Marmilla
C.S. di Sant'Antioco                       Cossu (Casa della Vernaccia)
C.S. di Serramanna                         Vini Classici di Sardegna
C.S. di Villacidro                         Zedda Piras

**Moscato di Cagliari** DOC w. sw.  ★→★★  81 83
Dessert wines from Moscato grown in the Campidano. The *dolce* has
15%, the *liquoroso dolce* 17.5%. The latter has deeper golden color, more
pronounced Muscat aroma, and smoother, richer texture.

C.S. Dolianova                             Vini Classici di Sardegna
C.S. Marmilla

**Moscato di Sardegna** DOC w. s/sw. sp.  ★→ ★★  DYA
Recent DOC for *spumante* from Moscato grown in designated vineyards
throughout Sardinia. Aromatic, fairly sweet, fruity, and bright straw
yellow, it bears a family resemblance to Asti. Moscato from Tempio
Pausania (or Tempio) and Gallura can use these subdenominations.

C.S. Gallura

**Moscato di Sorso-Sennori** DOC w. sw.  ★★  DYA
Limited production Moscato grown around Sorso and Sennori N of
Sassari. Of golden hue, it is rich (15%) and luscious with full aroma,
especially pronounced in the fortified *liquoroso dolce*.

C.S. Sorso-Sennori

**Nasco di Cagliari** DOC w. dr. s/sw. sw.  ★★  81 83
From the ancient Nasco grown in the Campidano, this may be dry,
semisweet or sweet in both the normal (14–14.5%) and *liquoroso* (16.5–
17.5%) categories. It can resemble Sherry after wood-aging, but it is
most distinctive as a lighter, drier wine with some youthful fruitiness and
subtle nutty aroma. (Sella & Mosca makes a fine non-DOC Nasco at
Alghero.)
Ag. *riserva* 2 yrs in barrel.

C.S. di Quartu Sant'Elena                  C.S. Dolianova
C.S. di Villacidro

**Nièddera** r. dr.  ★★  81 83
From Nièddera grapes of the Tirso valley near Oristano, this rare red is
very dry, strong but smooth, and fruity, best in 3–4 years.

Contini                                    Cossu (Casa della Vernaccia)

**Nuraghe Majore** w. dr.  ★★  DYA
From Clairette grapes grown near Alghero, this pale white is subtly
scented and crisply balanced, good with fish when very young.

Sella & Mosca

**Nuragus di Cagliari** DOC w. dr.  ★→ ★★  DYA
Sardinia's dominant DOC (more than 10 million liters a year), Nuragus
prevails in the Campidano. Pale straw green, dry, and neutral in scent
and flavor, it is appreciated with fish. The Consorzio per la Frutticoltura
di Cagliari makes a good non-DOC Nuragus di Sorres.

C.S. del Montiferru                        C.S. Dolianova
C.S. di Marrubiu                           C.S. Il Nuraghe
C.S. di Santadi                            C.S. Marmilla
C.S. di Serramanna                         Vini Classici di Sardegna
C.S. di Villacidro

**Oliena**
See Cannonau di Sardegna.

**Rosé di Alghero** p. dr. ★★ DYA
Consistently good pink from Cannonau and Sangiovese grown near
Alghero. Light, flowery, fresh and graceful, it is best inside a year.
Sella & Mosca

**Rosso di Berchidda** r. dr. ☐★★☐ 79 81 83
From Pascale, Cannonau, and others grown around Berchidda in N
Sardinia. Bright ruby, with well-rounded fruitiness and flowery bouquet,
it is good in 3–5 years. A *rosato* is made as well.
C.S. Cooperativa Giogantinu

**Sardus Pater**
See Carignano del Sulcis.

**S'Éleme**
See Vermentino di Gallura.

**Thaòra** p. dr. ★ DYA
Refreshing pink from Pascale grapes in NE Sardinia. Pale cherry,
fragrant, dry, and lively, it is good young.
C.S. del Vermentino

**Torbato di Alghero** w. dr. (sp.) ★★★ DYA
This table wine from Torbato grapes grown near Alghero is Sardinia's
finest white, notably in the Vigna Terre Bianche special vineyard
bottling by Sella & Mosca. Pale straw green, fragrant, it has exceptional
balance of fruit, acid and alcohol and crisp, clean finish. A recently issued
*spumante* is also convincing.
Sella & Mosca

**Vermentino** w. dr. ★→☐★★★☐ DYA
Several of Sardinia's better whites are table wines from Vermentino.
Basically dry, styles vary from rather rich, golden-yellow wines aged to
full flavor and bouquet to pale, sprightly, youthful whites. The most
impressive are Vermentino di Alghero of Sella & Mosca and the C.S.
Riforma Agraria di Alghero, which calls its wine Aragosta.
C.S. Bonnanaro                          Sella & Mosca
C.S. Dolianova                          Vini Classici di Sardegna
C.S. Riforma Agraria di Alghero

**Vermentino di Gallura** DOC w. dr. ★→☐★★☐ DYA
From Vermentino grown on the Gallura peninsula and nearby areas.
Traditionally strong, rich in flavor and low in acid, as exemplified by the
*superiore* of 7%, the old style can be tasted in the Aghiloia of the C.S. del
Vermentino and the *superiore* of the C.S. Cooperativa Giogantinu. The
trend is toward lighter, fruitier, more acidic wines to go with fish, as
noted in the S'Éleme of the C.S. del Vermentino.
C.S. Cooperativa Giogantinu          C.S. Gallura
C.S. del Vermentino

**Vernaccia di Oristano** DOC am. dr. (sw.) ★★→★★★ 71 74 75 77 79
81 83
The glory of Sardinia, this Sherry-like wine is made from overripe
Vernaccia grapes grown in the Tirso River basin near Oristano.
Vinification resembles the *solera* of Sherry, but Vernaccia's processing
involves distinct steps that need at least 2 years to complete. The best
Vernaccias are the *superiore* and *riserva*, which require long wood-aging.
Unfortified but strong (15% or more), this natural Vernaccia is bone dry
with hints of almond blossom on the nose and a lightly bitter, acidic,
woody flavor with a long finish. It needs 5 years, or considerably more, of
age. The fortified *liquoroso dolce* and *liquoroso secco* are richer and stronger
(16.5–18%) but not as refined as the others.
Ag. 2 yrs in barrel; *superiore* 3 yrs in barrel; *riserva* 4 yrs in barrel.
C.S. della Vernaccia                    Josto Puddu
Silvio Carta                            Sella & Mosca
Contini                                 Fratelli Serra
Cossu (Casa della Vernaccia)            Fratelli Zoncu
Pietro Madau

Though the island's population has shifted from the hills to the coast in recent times, the "real" Sardinian cooking is that of the back country and the open hearth: sucking pig, lamb, kid, soups of fava beans and barley, the ravioli-like *culingiones*, the piquant *pecorino sardo* and, most of all, the breads. It has been said that every Sardinian village has a bread of its own. The most sung about is *pane carasau*, also known as "music paper," because, unleavened, it is that thin. But there are hundreds, perhaps thousands, of other breads of every size and shape. Fish on the menu is a relatively recent exploitation of a source that was always there in the deep waters off the island's rocky coasts. Almost every Mediterranean species can be savored, sometimes together in the fish soup known as *cassòla*. The most prized bounty of the sea are *aragosta*, small, tasty lobsters, and the exotic *bottarga originaria*, dried slabs of mullet eggs from the fishing grounds off Oristano.

**Agnello con finocchietti** Lamb stewed with onion, tomato, and fennel.
  ★★★ Cannonau di Sardegna *secco*.
**Aragosta arrosta** Rock lobster grilled.
  ★★★ Aragosta or ★★★ Torbato di Alghero.
**Bottarga** Dried mullet eggs sliced thin on toast or in salad.
  ★★★ Vernaccia di Oristano *superiore* or *riserva*.
**Cassòla** One of the most lavish Mediterranean fish soups.
  ★★→★★★ Vermentino or ★★ Nuragus.
**Culingiones** Ravioli filled with *ricotta* and greens, and served with tomato sauce and grated *pecorino*.
  ★★ Rosé di Alghero.
**Favata** Rich stew of fava beans and pork.
  ★★ Monica di Sardegna.
**Malloreddus** Tiny gnocchi of semolina, dressed with meat or tomato sauce and grated *pecorino*.
  ★ Cannonau *rosato*.
**Pilau** Kid or lamb with pilaf rice.
  ★★★ Carignano del Sulcis.
**Porceddu** Sucking pig spit roasted slowly on an open fire.
  ★★★ Cannonau di Oliena.
**Sebadas** or **seadas** Pastry with cheese and bitter honey.
  ★★ Moscato di Sorso-Sennori.
**Su farru** Mint and barley soup.
  ★★ Vermentino di Gallura *superiore*.
**Zuppa cuata** Thick soup of meat, cheese, and bread.
  ★★ Rosso di Berchidda.

### Restaurants

Recommended: **North** *Ai Tuguri* at Alghero; *Da Franco* at Palau; *Da Petronilla* at Porto Cervo; *Sa Posada* near Sassari; *Canne al Vento-Da Brancaccio* at Santa Teresa Gallura. **Center** *Sa Funtà* at Cabras; *Su Gologone* near Oliena; *Da Giovanni* and *Il Faro* at Oristano. **South** *Dal Corsaro* and *Sa Cardiga e Su Schironi* at Cagliari; *Su Meriagu* at Quartu Sant'Elena; *Palmas* at Sorrich.

# Sicily

Sicilia

The revolution in Italian wine has unfolded most dramatically in Sicily, where in 20 years, from a step beyond medieval, enology has leapt headlong into the future. But the regional program which has transformed vineyards and cooperative wineries beyond recognition could hardly be labeled a resounding success. Nowhere are surpluses more voluminous than in Sicily, where production nearly doubled from the 642 million liters of 1964 to the 1.26 billion liters of 1979, the most of any region that year.

Still, wine drinkers have much to savor in Sicily's conversion. A decade ago, light, dry, fruity wines were the exception; now they're the rule. Even those potent dessert and aperitif wines, such as Marsala and Moscato, which have long been the island's forte, have improved remarkably. The most qualified products are awarded the region's *Q* for quality.

Production is concentrated in Sicily's westernmost province of Trapani, which turns out more wine than do most Italian regions. Besides three DOCs – Marsala, Alcamo, and Moscato di Pantelleria – Trapani generates awesome amounts of blending and table wines, which often end up in storage in the province's

**Wine Zones**
**1** Faro
**2** Regaleali

50 cooperatives. One problem is that Sicilians drink less wine per capita (about 50 liters a year) than do other Italians, so markets are by definition distant.

Sicily, Italy's largest region and the Mediterranean's largest island, still bears the stamps of Greeks, Arabs, Normans, Spaniards, and all manner of other peoples who imposed their wills and ways here. The major Greek ruins are at Siracusa

(Syracuse), Agrigento, Segesta, and Erice – all conveniently
near wine zones. Palermo, the capital and busiest port, and
nearby Monreale with its cathedral, are on the edge of the
Marsala and Alcamo zones. The active volcano of Mt Etna has a
DOC zone on its lower slopes. The Lipari Islands are also noted
for wine.

Sicily is served by regular air services between major Italian
cities and Palermo, Catania, and Trapani. Ships arrive daily
from Naples, Genoa, Cagliari and other ports. The chief link to
the mainland is the car ferry, which shuttles between Messina
and Calabria's Villa San Giovanni.

## Recent vintages

Data applies chiefly to red wines for aging, such as Etna, Corvo,
and Regaleali.

1983   Drought was less severe than in '82, favoring a larger harvest and
often very good wines.
1982   Sharply reduced by drought and heat, but irrigated and high
altitude vineyards made good wines.
1981   Substandard, though wines from select grapes were satisfactory.
1980   Late, reduced harvest with fair-to-good results.
1979   Bumper crop; very good quality throughout the island.
1978   Generally good, normal vintage.
1977   Small crop of excellent wines.
1976   Below average.
1975   Fine, bountiful harvest.

**Ala** r.–am. sw.  ★★  NV
From semidried grapes of Nero d'Avola, Perricone, and Frappato
vinified in an old way and fortified, it has intense aroma from barrels of
bitter cherry wood. Warm, rich, with unique bittersweet flavor and
amber-red color, its strength (19%) permits it to last for decades.
Duca di Salaparuta

**Alcamo** or **Bianco Alcamo** DOC w. dr.  ★→★★  DYA
Dry white based on Catarratto Bianco from a large zone of W Sicily with
axis in the town of Alcamo. Pale straw green, neutral in odor and flavor,
bone dry, yet rather soft. Better examples have a hint of fruit and
crispness. See also Rapitalà and Rincione.

C.S. Paladino                        Duca di Castelmonte (Pellegrino)
C.S. Sant'Antonio (Virzi)            Martinico & Figli
Conte de la Gatinais                 Fratelli Montalto
Cooperative Agricola Aurora          Tenuta Rincione (Papè)
D'Angelo Vini (Gebbia)

**Ambrato di Comiso** am. s/sw. sw.
Curious amber wine from Frappato di Vittoria and other grapes,
strengthened by cooked musts that gave a caramel-like flavor and light
sweetness. Once a DOC candidate it now seems headed for extinction.

**Carboj** r. p. w.  ★→★★  79 81 83
Brand name for table wines from Sciacca in SW Sicily. Rosso di Sciacca
is most impressive. From Barbera with Nero d'Avola and Nerello
Mascalese, it is bright garnet, generous in scent and body with rustic
goodness that improves with 2–5 years. Rosato di Sciacca, from the same
grapes and the white Trebbiano di Sicilia are table wines to drink young.
C.S. Enocarboj

**Cerasuolo di Vittoria** DOC r. dr.  ★★  81 83
Cherry-red wine from Calabrese and Frappato grown around Vittoria in
SE Sicily. Light red, almost rosé, it can take a few years of aging, though
when drunk young and on the cool side it is fragrant with good
body and balance despite strength (13% or more). Production is still
very limited. See also Stravecchio Siciliano.
Giuseppe Coria                       Nino Rallo
Biagio Giudice

**Cerdèse** r. p. w. dr.  ★→★★  79 81
Table wines made at Cerda near Palermo. The rosso, from Nerello

Mascalese and Perricone, is the best of the trio, structured, rounded and refined in 3–4 years. The *rosato* and *bianco* are refreshing young.
Fontanarossa

**Corvo**
Brand name applied to several wines made by Duca di Salaparuta at Casteldaccia from grapes gathered in various parts of the island.
– **Corvo Bianco** w. dr.  ★★→★★★  DYA
Made from the free-run musts of Inzolia, Trebbiano, and Catarratto, there are two versions. Marca Verde Prima Goccia has a light straw-gold color with medium body and refined, balanced flavor. Colomba Platino is more delicate in color, odor, and flavor – to drink very young. Though the grapes may not be the noblest, for consistency of results in Sicily's hot climate, Corvo whites are admirable.
– **Corvo Rosso** r. dr.  ★★★  78 79 80 81 83
From Nerello Mascalese, Perricone, and Nero d'Avola, this red is remarkably consistent. Dark ruby with orange highlights, generous and smooth, with bouquet developing after barrel and bottle age.
– **Corvo Spumante** w. dr. s/sw. sp.  ★★  DYA
Good *charmat* sparklers from the same grapes as Corvo *bianco*. The Brut, dry and refreshing, makes a good aperitif. The Demi-sec, soft and lightly sweet, goes well with fruit.
– **Corvo Stravecchio di Sicilia** am. dr.  ★★★  NV
Fortified wine from Inzolia, Catarratto, and Grillo aged for years in barrels to refined, dry, amber-gold richness with exquisite bouquet.
Duca di Salaparuta

**Donzelle** r. w. dr.  ★→★★  81 83
Table wines from Partana in W Sicily. The *rosso* is bright cherry red, tautly satisfying in 2–3 years. The *bianco* is light, brisk, rather neutral,
C.S. La Vite

**Draceno** r. p. w.  ★→★★  81 83
Table wines from the Belice valley near Partanna in W Sicily. The *rosso*, based on Perricone, is deep garnet, strong, amply scented, robustly dry with a bitter background, to drink in 3–5 years. The *rosato*, also from Perricone, is refreshing young. The *bianco*, from Catarratto, is delicately fruity yet vivacious, the most attractive of the trio.
C.S. Saturnia

**Eloro di Casale** r. dr.  ★★  79 81 83
Good red from Nero d'Avola grown at Noto in SE Sicily. Ample in body, fine in bouquet, its ruby-violet color turns garnet with age.
A. Modica di San Giovanni

**Etna** DOC r. p. w. dr.  ★→★★★  78 79 80 81 83
The three types of wine made in this zone on the E slopes of Mt Etna benefit from cool climate with plenty of sunshine. The *rosso*, from Nerello Mascalese, dominates production. Deep ruby tending to garnet, with 3–4 years or more it develops deep bouquet and warm, full-bodied flavor with sound equilibrium. The *rosato*, also from Nerello Mascalese, is a versatile meal wine. The *bianco*, from Carricante and Catarratto, is straw gold, fresh in scent, dry, and delicate. The *bianco superiore*, grown in the community of Milo and containing at least 80% Carricante, is fruitier, somewhat stronger, and more elegant. Only Villagrande makes *superiore*.
Berbero (Vignaioli Etnei)  Solicchiata (C.S. di Torrepalino)
Linguaglossa (Le Vigne dell'Etna)  Villagrande (Nicolosi Asmundo)
Diego Rallo & Figli  Villa Iolanda

**Faro** DOC r. dr.  ★★  79 81 83
Red based on Nerello grown at the island's NE tip around Messina. Ruby taking on brick tones with 3–5 years, it develops lovely bouquet and finesse. Unfortunately, very little is made.
Spinasanta

**Faustus** r. p. w.  ★★→★★★  79 81 83
Brand name for three wines made at Casteldaccia, E of Palermo, by Giuseppe Mazzetti. The *rosso*, from Nero d'Avola, Nerello Mascalese, and Perricone, is garnet, elegant, and full, with attractive herb-like bouquet after 3–5 years. The *rosato*, from the same dark grapes with a little light Inzolia, is lively and fragrant, one of S Italy's better rosés when young. The *bianco*, from Inzolia, is pale greenish and dry.
Azienda Vinicola Grotta

**Frappato di Vittoria** r. dr.  ★★  79 81 83
Rich amber-red wine from Frappato grapes grown at Vittoria in SE
Sicily. Grapy and lively young, it transforms to a slightly maderized
aperitif wine with age.
Giordano

**Gemme** w. dr.  ★★  DYA
Lively white from several grapes from high vineyards of the Alto Belice in
central Sicily. Light, clean but unusually perfumed and acidic, it has a
refreshing spritz. An alternate trademark is Baronessa Ancá.
Donnafugata

**Grecanico di Sicilia** w. dr.  ★★  DYA
From Grecanico grapes grown in the Marsala zone, this bright, straw-
yellow table wine is faintly scented, clean, and dry, good young.
Fratelli Montalto                    Carlo Pellegrino

**Grottarossa** r. p. w. dr.  ★★  DYA
Table wines from the Colli Nesseni near Caltanissetta designed to drink
within a year or two. The red is sturdy and smooth, the white and rosé
fruity, zesty, refreshing.
C.S. Enopolio di Caltanissetta

**Libecchio** w. dr.  ★★  DYA
Recently conceived and highly publicized white from Trebbiano and
Inzolia made at Menfi. The truly distinguishing feature of this light,
crisp, blossomy wine is the label by Renato Guttuso.
Barone di Turolifi

**Luparello** p. dr.  ★★  81 83
Dark pink table wine from Calabrese grown near Pachino in SE Sicily.
Aged 2 years in oak, it is rich in nuance with hints of bitter and sweet.
Azienda Vitivinicola Luparello

**Malvasia delle Lipari** DOC am. s/sw. sw.  ★★→★★★★  80 81 83
Two versions of this exquisite wine are made from Malvasia di Lipari
grapes grown on the Lipari or Aeolian isles N of Messina. The basic type
of 11.5% is moderately sweet and aromatic, epitomized by the Capo
Salina of Carlo Hauner with its seductive scents of apricots and citrus.
The *passito* (18%) and *liquoroso* (20%) are richer, sweeter, longer lived.
Capo Salina (Hauner)                 F. Moccotta
Nino Lo Schiavo

**Mamertino** am. s/sw.  ★  NV
Antique wine of Messina, now made from semidried Catarratto, Inzolia,
and Grillo. Lightly sweet with a raisiny aroma and old-gold color.
Spinasanta

**Marsala** DOC
Created for the English market in 1773 by John Woodhouse, Marsala
has since had its ups and downs. Recently, its fortunes have revived. The
*vergine* and *superiore* of certain houses are prized for their burnished-
amber color, rich wood-and-caramel aroma and luxuriantly smooth
flavor, whether naturally dry or fortified and sweet. Marsala is made
from Catarratto and/or Grillo and Inzolia grown in a vast zone of W
Sicily in the provinces of Trapani, Palermo, and Agrigento. The industry
is based in the port of Marsala. Processes vary from firm to firm, but often
the natural wine is blended with what are known as *sifone* (sweet wine
and wine alcohol) and *cotto* (cooked down musts). Production of some 35
million liters annually is not all sold as DOC. The four basic categories
take in some of the old commercial names and initials. The terms *vecchio*,
*riserva*, and *stravecchio* which may be used on labels have no significance.
– **Marsala Fine** am. dr. s/sw. sw.  ★  NV
The common grade of 17% is made by blending base wine with more
*cotto* than *sifone*. Old names include Italy Particular (IP) and Italia.
Ag. 4 months in barrel.
– **Marsala Speciale**  ★  NV
Marsala of 18% alcohol flavored with egg, cream, coffee, etc., which so
alters color, texture, and taste that it hardly qualifies as wine. Such
concoctions may state that they are prepared with Marsala DOC.
Ag. 6 months in barrel.
– **Marsala Superiore** am. dr. sw.  ★★→★★★★  NV
Regaining its lofty past reputation, this takes in the traditional Superior

Old Marsala (SOM), London Particular (LP) and Garibaldi Dolce (GD). With 18% alcohol (some left in residual sugars in sweet versions), it is blended according to house formulas and can last for decades. The dry is very dry with aromas of wood, nuts, citrus and spices and a velvety yet austere flavor.

**– Marsala Vergine** am. dr. **★★→★★★★** NV
The lightly fortified, "virgin" product is now the most prestigious. Dry to bone dry, it contains neither *sifone* nor *cotto* but is made by blending wines aged in barrels for different lengths of time, sometimes by *solera*, though not necessarily. Light amber gold, exquisitely scented, it has the breed, tone, and complexity of aromas and flavors to stand with the world's great aperitif wines. Some like it with sharp or strong cheeses.
Ag. 5 yrs in barrel.

| | |
|---|---|
| V. Giacalone Alloro & C. | Fratelli Mineo |
| Vito Curatolo Arini | Mirabella |
| De Vita | Fratelli Montalto |
| Fratelli Fici | Fratelli Oliva |
| Florio & C | Carlo Pellegrino & C. |
| Ingham Whitaker & C. | Diego Rallo & Figli |
| Francesco Intorcia & Figli | Sala Spanò |
| Lilibeo | Solero & Gill |
| Fratelli Martinez | Woodhouse |

**Moscato di Noto** DOC w. am. s/sw. sw. (sp.) **★★** NV
From Moscato Bianco grown around Noto in SE Sicily, this dessert wine comes in three versions rarely seen in commerce. The basic Moscato is semisweet, fragrant, and golden, to drink young. The *spumante* is pale yellow, delicately sweet, and aromatic. The *liquoroso* of 22% is mellifluous and warm, with plush Muscat aroma.
Cantina Sperimentale di Noto

**Moscato di Pantelleria** DOC w. am. s/sw. sw. sp. **★★→★★★** NV
From Zibibbo (large Moscato) grapes grown on gnarled vines trained low in the volcanic soil of this island off the coast of Tunisia, Italy's most remote DOC zone. This most vaunted of Sicilian Moscatos has several styles. The basic Moscato di Pantelleria from normally ripe grapes has four types: *naturale* (softly sweet, fragrant, 12.5%), *naturalmente dolce* (richer, sweeter, 17.5%), *spumante naturale* (sparkling versions of the previous), and *liquoroso* (fortified with wine alcohol). Passito di Pantelleria from semidried grapes has three types: *naturalmente dolce* (14%), *liquoroso* (fortified to at least 21.5%), and *extra* (23.5%). All *passito* types are very sweet and rich. Much of the one million liter annual production is sold by the Agricoltori Associati cooperative whose *passito extra* is called Tanit and *spumante naturale* Solimano.
Ag. *passito extra* 1 yr.
Agricoltori Associati di Pantelleria     Diego Rallo & Figli
F. Maccotta

**Moscato di Siracusa** DOC am. sw.
Why a DOC was granted to a wine that no longer exists is puzzling. The zone comprises the community of Siracusa in SE Sicily where Moscato Bianco is prescribed for golden-yellow to amber, sweet wine of 16.5%.

**Moscato di Villa Fontane** w. sw. **★★** 75 77 78 79 81
Dessert wine from Moscatello grown near Vittoria in SE Sicily. Golden, luscious, and richly aromatic, it can age a decade or more.
Giuseppe Coria

**Nérello Siciliano** r. dr. ★★ 80 81 83
Generous, warm table wines from Nerello Mascalese grapes made in W Sicily become fairly smooth and elegant with 3–5 years of age.
Marino                            Fratelli Montalto

**Normanno** r. w. dr. ★★ 80 81 83
Popular table wines of consistent quality. The *rosso*, of Nerello and Frappato from the Agrigento area, is dark ruby, robust, smooth, and well scented in 3–5 years. The *bianco*, from Catarratto grown near Marsala, is pale straw green, finely scented, crisp, and poised.
Diego Rallo & Figli

**Pignatello** r. (p.) dr. ★→★★ 81 83
Table wines from the Pignatello (or Perricone) grape grown in W Sicily

are usually red but sometimes rosé. The red can acquire an attractive
bitter cherry aspect with 3–4 years of age.
Martinico & Figli                    Carlo Pellegrino & C.

**Rapitalà** w. dr.  ★★★  DYA
Though it qualifies as Bianco Alcamo, this white from Camporeale SW
of Palermo has character all its own: bright golden color, fine balance
between youthful buoyancy and nutty, lightly bitter maturity.
Conte de la Gatinais

**Regaleali** r. p. w. dr.  ★★→★★★  78 79 80 81 82 83
Table wines firmly established among Sicily's elite originate in high
vineyards at Sclafani Bagni, SE of Palermo. The *rosso*, from Nerello
Mascalese and Perricone, is bright ruby, robust, soft, and scented after
3–4 years. The Rosso del Conte, a special reserve of the same grapes, is
more elegant and longer lived (a decade or more from some vintages),
perhaps Sicily's grandest red. The *rosato*, from the dark grapes, is
fragrant and classy when young. The *bianco*, from Catarratto, Inzolia,
and Sauvignon, is pale, clean, and as brisk and fruity as alpine whites.
Conte Tasca d'Almerita

**Rincione** r. p. w. dr.  ★★  81 83
Table wines from Calatafimi in W Sicily. The *rosso* and *rosato*, from Nero
d'Avola and Nerello Mascalese, are fine examples of their types. The
*bianco* is similar to Alcamo, but Trebbiano gives it more fruit and finesse.
Tenuta Rincione (Papè)

**Rosso di Menfi** r. dr.  ★★  81 83
Good red from Nerello Mascalese, Nero d'Avola and Sangiovese grown
near Menfi in S Sicily. Bright ruby, lightly scented, full and warm; best
in 2–5 years. The Settesoli cooperative also makes a Bianco di Menfi and
Feudo dei Fiori white of more than routine interest.
Bonera (C.S. Settesoli)

**Solicchiato Bianco di Villa Fontane** am. s/sw.  ★★★  75 77 78 79 81
Unique dessert wine made near Vittoria in SE Sicily from light grapes
dried in the sun. After a year in barrel, it is golden, fruity, and
moderately sweet; after a decade it becomes amber and luxuriant.
Giuseppe Coria

**Solimano**
See Moscato di Pantelleria.

**Steri** r. w. dr.  ★★  81 83
Table wines from the Comarca di Naro E of Agrigento. The *bianco*, from
Trebbiano, Inzolia, and Vernaccia di San Gimignano, is light straw
yellow, mild in scent, and clean and fresh in flavor. The *rosso*, from Nero
d'Avola, Barbera, and Lambrusco, is bright ruby vermillion, soft, warm
and ample. Steri *riserva speciale*, from Lambrusco Salamino and Barbera,
is dense, rich in extract, and generous, singular among the island's reds.
Giuseppe Camilleri

**Stravecchio Siciliano di Villa Fontane** am. dr.  ★★★  NV
Reserve wine from Cerasuolo grapes grown near Vittoria in SE Sicily is
aged 20, 30 years or more in casks, which makes it similar to very old dry
Sherry. A small quantity of wine from one barrel of this Stravecchio is
drawn off each year and replaced with new wine. This endless supply is
known as Perpetuo.
Giuseppe Coria

**Tanit**
See Moscato di Pantelleria.

**Torre Marina** r. w. dr.  ★★  82 83
Table wines from W Sicily. The *bianco*, from grapes grown around
Marsala, is light and zesty. The *rosso*, from dark grapes in neighboring
zones, is smooth and sturdy enough for some aging.
Vito Curatolo Arini

**Vecchio Samperi** am. dr.  ★★★★  NV
Practically a Marsala, made from the preferred Grillo grapes in the
DOC zone, but put through a personalized *solera* process that doesn't
conform to the norms (i.e., it is not fortified with alcohol). This is a
superb aperitif wine.
De Bartoli

**Verdello Siciliano** w. dr. ⬛**★★**⬛ DYA
Crisp white from Verdello grapes grown in W Sicily. Light and finely
balanced, they are noted for a hint of salt on the tongue.
Marino

**Zibibbo**
This strain of large Moscato makes golden to amber dessert wines in
several parts of Sicily, notably Pantelleria.

Sicily is the alleged cradle of all sorts of good things to eat, among
them pasta (unlikely, even if Italy's first such paste may have
been rolled here), innumerable sweets (including sherbet, thanks
to Etna's year-round snow), and various fish and vegetable
dishes. Fairly recent times have also witnessed the rise of the
pizza (though Naples usually gets credit for that) and that other
symbol of Italo-American culinary artistry, the meatball. The
island's natural endowments of sunshine on fertile volcanic soil
combined with the multitude of ethnic influences have left Sicily
with an unrivalled heritage of foods. Sadly, many dishes are now
neglected. But the basics are as flavorsome as ever: citrus fruit,
olives, brilliant vegetables, herbs, spices, lamb, sheep's cheeses,
grain for pasta, and a multitude of breads and pastries. Then
there is the sea brimming full of fish, offering tuna, swordfish, and
sardines, to name but a few. Sicily reigns as capital of Italian
sweets, the encyclopedic array of which culminates in *cassata*.

**Beccaficu** Sardines either stuffed
and baked or breaded and fried.
   **★★** Normanno *bianco*.
**Braccioli di pesce spada**
Swordfish filets wrapped around a
cheese-bread-vegetable stuffing
and grilled.
   **★★★** Regaleali *bianco*.
**Caponata** Eggplant and other
ripe vegetables in a rich stew.
   **★★** Cerasuolo di Vittoria.
**Cassata** The island's pride:
opulent array of candied fruit and
chocolate on a sponge-cake.
   **★★★** Moscato *dolce*.
**Cùscusu** Of Arab origin,
couscous-style fish stew with
semolina.
   **★★★** Rapitalà.
**Farsumagru** Braised veal roll
stuffed with meat, cheese, and
vegetables.
   **★★★** Regaleali *rosso*.

**Pasta con la Norma** Spaghetti
with eggplant, basil, tomato,
garlic, and cheese: a homage to
Catania's Vincenzo Bellini and his
opera *La Norma*.
   **★★** Etna *rosato*.
**Pasta con le sarde** Palermo's
classic pasta flavored with sardines
and wild fennel has become an
island-wide speciality.
   **★★★** Corvo *bianco*.
**Peperonata** Peppers stewed with
tomato, onion, and green olives.
   **★** Alcamo.
**Polpettone** The fabled meatballs,
possibly even with tomato sauce on
pasta.
   **★★★** Corvo *rosso*.
**Tonno alla siciliana** Fresh tuna
cooked with white wine, fried
anchovies, herbs, and spices.
   **★★★** Faustus *bianco*.

### Restaurants

Recommended in or near wine zones: **Etna** *Timeo* at Taormina. **Faro** *Da
Alberto* and *Pippo Nunnari* at Messina. **Lipari** *Filippino* at Lipari.
**Marsala** *Zio Ciccio* at Marsala. **Noto-Vittoria** *Alberto il Mago del Pesce* at
Marina di Ragusa: *Al Sorcio* at Donnalucata; *Trattoria dei Due Mari* at
Porto Palo. **Pantelleria** *Hotel Cossyra* at Pantelleria; *Le Lampare del
Mursia* at Mursia. **Siracusa** *Jonico 'a Rutta e Ciali* at Siracusa.

# *Trentino-Alto Adige*

Trentino-Alto Adige

This northernmost point of Italy, with its perfumed white wines and German as a second language, can't avoid being compared with Alsace. They have numerous vines in common – Riesling, Sylvaner, Pinot Blanc, Pinot Noir, Pinot Grigio (Tokay d'Alsace), and Muscat – and it is said that Traminer, a clone of which became Gewürztraminer in Alsace, originated in the South Tyrolean village of Tramin. But the analogy should not be overdrawn, for Trentino-Alto Adige has distinctive styles in wines that carry over to a notable production of reds and rosés..

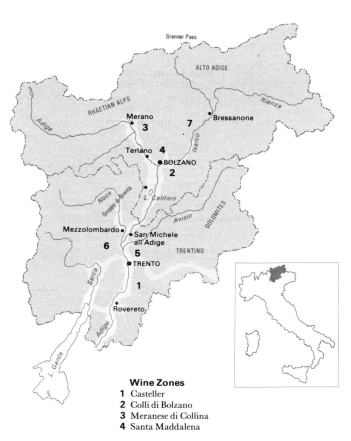

**Wine Zones**
1 Casteller
2 Colli di Bolzano
3 Meranese di Collina
4 Santa Maddalena

Trentino (the southern province of Trento or Trent) and Alto Adige (the province of Bolzano or Bozen, also known as the South Tyrol) share a gorgeous region of Alps drained by the Adige River. Despite ethnic contrasts between the Italians and the German-speaking minority (the latter clings tenaciously to proud traditions), the region is a model of enological efficiency. Two records are unsurpassed: some 55% of wine is DOC and more than 35% of production is exported. Most exports depart from Alto Adige to Germany, Switzerland, and Austria – often labeled in German and even carrying the QbA (*Qualitätswein bestimmter Anbaugebiete*) in place of DOC. In the past, very little found its way to other parts of Italy, though the demand, especially for white wines, has begun to reverse that pattern.

Vineyard space is confined (only 15% of the land can be cultivated). The cool climate is conducive to fruity, acidic whites and fragrant reds marked by an attractively bitter undertone. The region is northern Italy's leading source of rosé.

Most white varieties were imported long ago from France or Germany. The Pinots, with the increasingly noticeable Chardonnay, go into some of Italy's best sparkling wines. Outstanding Riesling, Müller Thurgau, Sylvaner and Sauvignon are also produced, notable for their fragrance and uncanny capacity to retain freshness with age. Among reds, Schiava dominates in the popular Caldaro or Kalterersee and the renowned Santa Maddalena. Cabernet, Merlot, Pinot Nero, and the indigenous Teroldego, Lagrein and Marzemino further enhance the region's reputation for reds.

Trentino-Alto Adige with its towering Dolomites, glacier lakes and deep forests is one of central Europe's favorite vacation spots. Millions of tourists a year cross the Brenner Pass from Austria or venture up from Milan, Venice, Verona, and Lake Garda to ski, climb, and relax amidst the beauty of Gothic and Romanesque villages nestled into green mountainsides. Wine is a major attraction. The Adige valley is traversed by wine roads in both provinces, leading to an imposing array of wines, some of which are never better than here at home. Alto Adige's wines are displayed at the *enoteca* in the Castel Mareccio.

### Recent vintages

1983  Memorable for reds and whites from high altitude vines, though heat caused problems with ripening and fermentation.

1982  What at first seemed an excellent year was often disappointing; whites, though fragrant, may be short-lived due to low acidity.

1981  Frost, then drought, then rot before the harvest cut the crop by nearly half, but some of what remained was satisfactory or better.

1980  Average year of fair-to-good wines with some notably perfumed whites.

1979  Large harvest of generally high quality.

1978  Small crop with mixed results; some Trentino reds, particularly Teroldego, were memorable.

1977  Uneven; the few good wines made are not for long aging.

1976  Generally good year for reds; memorable for Alto Adige whites.

1975  Good-to-excellent results in all zones.

1974  Fine harvest with some memorable reds.

Earlier fine vintages: '71, '70, '69, '64.

*Note: Kellereigenossenschaft, German for cooperative winery, is abbreviated as K. in this chapter*

**Alto Adige (Südtiroler) DOC**
This zone, which covers much of the vine land of Alto Adige through the Adige and Isarco valleys, boasts 17 types of wine, more than any other DOC zone. They include reds, rosés, and whites, mostly dry but also sweet – all varietals which must contain at least 95% of the grape. Total production is about 13 million liters a year. Because the zone overlaps six others and part of a seventh, it is sometimes thought of as a catch-all, though it shouldn't be; some of Italy's best wines carry the appellation.

– **Cabernet** r. dr.  $\boxed{\text{**}\rightarrow\text{****}}$  74 75 76 78 79 80 82 83
Cabernet Sauvignon and/or Cabernet Franc make appealing deep ruby wines with herby bouquet, whether light and fruity or ample, elegant, and complex. The bigger wines can take from 4 to 10 years to mature into some of Italy's finest Cabernet.
Ag. *riserva* 2 yrs.

– **Chardonnay** w. dr.
Expected to join the list in 1984, this may be the nation's most promising Chardonnay source.

– **Lagrein Dunkel (Scuro)** r. dr.  ★★→★★★★  79 80 82 8?
Deep ruby wine of fine bouquet and soft, smooth, generous style which can attain remarkable class with 4–5 years of aging, as shown by Klosterkellerei Muri-Gries, Schloss Schwanburg and Josef Niedermayr. Ag. *riserva* 1 yr.

– **Lagrein Kretzer (Rosato)** p. dr.  ★★→★★★  DYA
Delightful rosé from Lagrein: cherry pink, fragrant, and fruity, with balanced acidity.

– **Malvasia (Malvasier)** r. dr.  ★  DYA
Malvasia Nera makes a ruby-garnet wine, well scented and generously mellow in its youth.

– **Merlot** r. dr.  ★→ ★★  80 81 82 83
Bright ruby, usually grapy with scent and flavor of herbs whether drunk young or aged for 3–5 years. Ag. *riserva* 1 yr.

– **Moscato Giallo (Goldenmuskateller)** w. sw.  ★★  DYA
Locally prized dessert wine from Moscato Giallo. Golden yellow, aromatic, sweet but not cloying, it is best very young.

– **Moscato Rosa (Rosenmuskateller)** r. p. s/sw. ★★→★★★★ 8? ?3
This rare *amabile* is as flowery and graceful as its pretty ruby-rose color indicates. Young, it makes a charming sipping wine; with some age it gets smoother and more elegant but loses some of its exceptional fruity fragrance. Graf Eberhard Kuenburg's Schloss Sallegg stands out.

– **Müller Thurgau** w. dr.  ★★→★★★  80 81 83
Though the popular style is for attractively tart whites to drink young, this Riesling-Sylvaner cross develops depth, fragrance and tone with age.

– **Pinot Bianco (Weissburgunder)** w. dr.  ★★→★★★★  79 80 81 83
Pinot Grigio and Chardonnay win the popularity contests, but there is more good, often excellent, Pinot Bianco here than any other variety. If convincing in *spumante* and young still wines, it gets more impressive with age, retaining qualities of youth for a decade or longer.

– **Pinot Grigio (Ruländer)** w. dr.  ★→ ★★★  8?
Though overtaxed due to public demand, the variety can produce admirable wines here, with more backbone and lasting power than the flowery but often fragile Pinot Grigio of Friuli. Usually vinified light, it has a pale bronze color, delicate fragrance and smooth texture.

– **Pinot Nero (Blauburgunder)** r. dr.  ★→ ★★★  79 80 ?1 82 83
Though this rarely lives up to expectations, some producers manage soft, fruity wines of medium ruby color and a hint of mint in the bouquet after 2–3 years in bottle. A rare few achieve grander things, such as Hofstätter's '74 and '69, which compare with good Burgundy.

– **Riesling Italico (Welschriesling)** w. dr.  ★  DYA
Little of this wine is made, and probably just as well, for Riesling Renano is clearly superior here. Still, when young, it has a zestful, fruity charm.

– **Riesling Renano (Rheinriesling)** w. dr.  ★★→★★★★  DYA
The true Riesling thrives here as nowhere else in Italy. The normal style is very dry in straw-green wines, fresh, fruity, and finely scented. Some producers (Hofstätter, Bellendorf, Lageder, Tiefenbrunner) reach more impressive levels in wines that hold well with age.

– **Sauvignon** w. dr.  ★★→★★★  82 83
New interest in this variety may lead to noble results. The small amount made is usually light and dry, with delicate gunflint scent.

– **Schiava (Vernatsch)** r. dr.  ★→★★  DYA
The popular family of vines makes light, almondy, garnet-cherry hued wines to drink young and cool. The best-known subvariety is Schiava Grigia or Grauvernatsch.

– **Sylvaner** w. dr.  ★→ ★★★  81 82 83
Though often made as a light, simplistic white, this can show unexpected style from high altitude vineyards in wines that need 2–3 years or more to express the aromatic, fruity qualities. Tiefenbrunner's '81 stands out.

– **Traminer Aromatico (Gewürztraminer)** w. dr.  ★→ ★★★ 81 82 83
Though it often lacks the weight of Alsatian Gewürz, the variety can do enviably well around its home town of Tramin, where Anton Dissertori and Tiefenbrunner excel. When young, it is straw-green and fruity. Aged

for 2 years, it tends toward gold as the aroma becomes opulently spicy
and the silky flavor gains length. Often confused with the commoner
Traminer, which makes mediocre wines.

Bellendorf
Josef Brigl
Castel (Schloss) Rametz
Della Staffa (Premiovini)
Anton Dissertori
Karl Franceschini
Alfons Giovanett
Herrnhofer
Hirschprunn
Kehlburg
K. Baron Di Pauli
K. Girlan (C.S. Cornaiano)
K. Kaltern (C.S. Caldaro)
K. Margreid-Entiklar
  (C.S. Magré-Niclara)
K. Marling (C.S. Marlengo)
K. Nals (C.S. Nalles)
K. St. Michael-Eppan (C.S.
  San Michele-Appiano)
K. St. Pauls (C.S. San Paolo)
K. Schreckbichl (C.S. Colterenzio)

K. Tramin (C.S. Termeno)
Kettmeir
Klosterkellerei Muri-Gries
Alois Lageder
Laimburg
Anton Lindner
H. Lun (Sandbichler)
Karl Martini & Sohn
Josef Niedermayr
Hans Rottensteiner
Heinrich Rottensteiner
Santa Margherita
Schloss Sallegg (Kuenburg)
Schloss Schwanburg
Quinto Soini & Figli
J. Tiefenbrunner (Schloss
  Turmhof)
Trattmannhof
Von Elzenbaum
W. Walch

*( Note: More than half the wines of Alto Adige are produced
by cooperatives and marketed by the Verband der Kellereigenossenschaften
Südtirols or Consorzio Viticoltori Alto Adige.)*

## Cabernet
Both Cabernets Sauvignon and Franc are widely grown, as DOC Alto
Adige and Trentino, also in table wines with Merlot and others.

**Caldaro** or **Lago di Caldaro (Kalterersee)** DOC r. dr. ★→ ★★ DYA
Alto Adige's *gemütlich* quaffing wine is better known in German-speaking
lands as Kalterersee than it is elsewhere in Italy. Made in quantity (25
million liters a year) from Schiava Grossa, Gentile and Grigia grown
along the Adige valley, its name comes from the pretty lake SW of
Bolzano. Light garnet to almost pink, it has the noted Schiava grapy
fragrance and unusually refreshing verve and fluidity with an almondy
finish. It is best young – inside 2–3 years – and cool. Wine from the
original zone around the lake may be called *classico* or, with 10.5%
alcohol and some refinement, *classico superiore*. With 11% alcohol, it may
be called *scelto* or *Auslese*, suggesting it comes from late harvested grapes.

Ambach
Bellendorf
Càvit
Cantina Produttori Mezzocorona
Castel (Schloss) Rametz
Gaierhof
Hirschprunn
J. Hofstätter
K. Baron di Pauli
K. Girlan (C.S. Cornaiano)
K. Gries (C.S. Gries)
K. Kattern (C.S. Caldaro)
K. Margreid-Entiklar
  (C.S. Magré-Niclara)
K. St. Michael-Eppan
  (C.S. San Michele-Appiano)

K. St. Pauls (C.S. San Paolo)
K. Schreckbichl (C.S. Colterenzio)
K. Tramin (C.S. Termeno)
Klosterkellerei Muri-Gries
Alois Lageder (Römigberg)
Laimburg
Anton Lindner
Karl Martini & Sohn
Josef Niedermayr
Hans Rottensteiner
Schloss Kaltenburg (Brigl)
Schloss Sallegg (Kuenburg)
Schloss Schwanburg
W. Walch

**Castel San Michele** r. dr. ★★★ 79 80 81 82 83
Fine Cabernet-Merlot from San Michele all'Adige N of Trento,
produced at the noted agricultural school. Deep ruby to garnet,
generous, and herby, its tannic harshness mellows in 5–6 years or more.
Istituto Agrario Provinciale (San Michele all'Adige)

**Casteller** DOC r. p. dr. ★ DYA
Trentino's everyday wine from Schiava, Merlot, and Lambrusco grown
in hills along the Adige from N of Trento S to the Veneto. Light ruby to
bright pink, vinous, dry, and light – drink inside 2 years.

Càvit
Lagariavini

La Vinicola Sociale Aldeno
Fratelli Pedrotti

**Chardonnay** w. dr.  ★→ ★★★  81 82 83
Though headed for DOC in Alto Adige and Trentino, Chardonnay has
been issued as a growingly fashionable table wine in Italy and abroad.
Some superior wines have emerged, usually from high altitude vineyards
in both provinces – Pojer & Sandri and Zeni in Trentino; Tiefenbrunner
and Lageder in Alto Adige. But much of the wine is aimed at the popular
markets – Santa Margherita, Càvit and Bollini, which sell well in the
U.S.A., offer a light, fruity alternative to the weightier, woodier
California style. There are also questionable products capitalizing on the
name. (See also Spumante.)

| | |
|---|---|
| Bollini | K. Schreckbichl (C.S. Colterenzio) |
| Cantina Produttori Mezzocorona | Kettmeir |
| C.S. Cooperativa Mezzocorona | Lagariavini |
| C.S. Lavis-Sorni-Salorno | La Vinicola Sociale Aldeno |
| Castel (Schloss) Rametz | Alois Lageder |
| Càvit | Lechthaler (Sonnenkuss) |
| Barone De Cles | Novaline |
| Della Staffa (Premiovini) | Fratelli Pedrotti |
| Fratelli Dorigati | Pojer & Sandri |
| Alfons Giovanett | Santa Margherita |
| Istituto Agrario Provinciale | J. Tiefenbrunner (Schloss Turmhof) |
| (San Michele all'Adige) | Zeni |
| K. St. Michael-Eppan | |
| (C.S. San Michele-Appiano) | |

**Colli di Bolzano (Bozner Leiten)** DOC r. dr.  ★→★★  DYA
All-purpose Schiava from hills surrounding Bolzano. Light ruby-garnet,
soft and easy, it can be delightful young.

| | |
|---|---|
| K. Gries (C.S. Gries) | Alois Lageder |
| K. Terlan (C.S. Terlano) | Karl Martini & Sohn |

**de Vite** w. dr.  ★★★  82 83
Exquisite white from Kerner, a cross between Riesling Renano and
Schiava (or Trollinger). Pale straw green and perfumed, it has
precocious charm which can extend a few years.
J. Hofstätter

**Edelweisser** w. dr.  ★★  DYA
Also from Kerner, though designed to drink in its zesty youth.
Von Elzenbaum

**Foianeghe** r. w. dr.  ★★→★★★  76 77 78 79 80 82 83
Special table wines from Isera near Rovereto. Foianeghe Rosso, in which
Merlot dominates Cabernet, is a deep ruby-garnet color, generous,
complex and poised, it develops bouquet over 4–5 years. Foianeghe
Bianco from Chardonnay and Traminer is full and fruity to drink within
2 years.
Conti Bossi Fretriotti

**Fontane d'Oro** w. dr.  ★★★  82 83
Fine white from Pinot Bianco with some Müller Thurgau and Nosiola to
distinguish it. Its flowery scent and smooth fruitiness, good young, can be
enhanced with age.
Istituto Agrario Provinciale (San Michele all'Adige)

**Goldmuskateller** w. dr.  ★★★  81 82 83
This exceptional table wine from Moscato Giallo grapes grown near
Entiklar in Alto Adige is full of Muscat aroma but unexpectedly dry in
flavor. Its rich and complex bouquet improves with 3–4 years of age.
J. Tiefenbrunner (Schloss Turmhof)

**Grauvernatsch**
German for Schiava Grigia. DOC wines can carry the name under Alto
Adige Schiava.

**Kolbenhofer** r. dr.  ★★★  82 83
From Schiava grown at the Kolbenhof vineyard above Tramin, this is
similar to Caldaro but more elegant. Garnet red and fragrantly fruity, it
is graceful and smooth inside 3 years.
J. Hofstätter

**Lagrein**
Popular variety of Bolzano now used for red and rosé throughout the
region. DOC under Alto Adige, Trentino, and Valdadige.

**Malvasia (Malvasier)**
Red wine from Malvasia Nera is DOC under Alto Adige.

**Maso Lodron** r. dr.   ★★★   78 79 81 83
Cabernet-Merlot from Nogaredo S of Trento. Deep ruby, herby in its full
aroma and flavor, it becomes smooth and deep with 4–6 years, or more.
Letrari

**Meranese di Collina (Meraner Hügel)** DOC r. dr.   ★   DYA
Merano's local red from Schiava grown in the hills around the city. Light
ruby, lightly scented, easy, and tasty, it is best on the cool side in a year or
two. Wine from a small territory known as the Contea di Tirol may
qualify as Burgravio or Burggräfler.

Castel (Schloss) Rametz          K. Meran (C.S. Merano)
K. Algund (C.S. Lagundo)         Torggler
K. Marling (C.S. Marlengo) ·

**Merlot**
DOC as a varietal under Alto Adige, Trentino, and Valdadige, Merlot is
often blended with Cabernet in table wines.

**Mori Vecio** r. dr.   ★★→★★★   78 79 81 83
Cabernet-Merlot from Mori S of Trento. Ruby tending to garnet, with
5–6 years or more of age it is elegant in structure and bouquet.
Lagariavini

**Morlacco** r. dr.   ★★→★★★   78 81 82 83
Interesting combination of Pinot Nero, Marzemino, and Cabernet from
the Vallagarina S of Trento. Ruby to garnet, soft, and full-bodied, its
prime is reached in 4–6 years, sometimes more.
Fratelli Pedrotti

**Moscato (Muskateller)**
Both Moscato Giallo (Goldenmuskateller) and Moscato Rosa
(Rosenmuskateller) are DOC under Alto Adige; only the white Moscato
is DOC under Trentino.

**Müller Thurgau** w. dr.   ★★→★★★★   80 81 82 83
Though DOC under Alto Adige, Terlano, Trentino Riesling, Valle
Isarco and Valdadige, Müller Thurgau has reached its grandest heights
as a table wine. In Trentino, Pojer & Sandri make a remarkably fragrant
and fruity version at Faedo. But the foremost Müller is Tiefenbrunner's
Feldmarschall, grown at 1,000 meters above Entiklar in Alto Adige.

C.S. Mori                          Carlo Rossi
K. Cembra (C.S. Val di Cembra)     J. Tiefenbrunner (Feldmarschall)
Pojer & Sandri

**Nosiola** w. dr.   ★★→★★★   DYA
Table wine of unique personality from Nosiola grown in Trentino. Light
straw-green with a special fruity aroma which carries over into its dry,
smooth flavor with bitter background, it is exhilarating in its youth.

Cantina di Toblino                 Giovanni Poli
Giuseppe Fanti                     Zeni
Pojer & Sandri

**Novaline Rubino** r. dr.   ★★→★★★   81 82 83
Cabernet-Merlot grown at Mattarello in Trentino vinified in a light style
that shows elegance in bouquet with 3–4 years.
Novaline

**Pinot Bianco (Weissburgunder)**
DOC in Alto Adige, Terlano, Trentino, and Valdadige. Much of what
was formerly believed to be Pinot Bianco has lately been revealed as
Chardonnay, most notably in Trentino.

**Pinot Grigio**
DOC in Alto Adige, Valle Isarco, and Valdadige, Pinot Grigio may be
used at 50% in Trentino Pinot Bianco. But much of it is table wine, which
may be called Pinot Grigio delle Venezie or with some other vague
geographical reference that doesn't guarantee authenticity. Still, along
with the mediocre products designed to meet excessive demand, some
good table wine is produced, though it is usually wiser to select DOC.

**Pinot Nero (Blauburgunder)**
DOC under Alto Adige, Trentino, and Valdadige, Pinot Nero is also
mixed with other varieties, sometimes in white, sparkling wines.

**Pragiara** r. dr.  ★★★  79 82 83
Minute production of Cabernet-Merlot aged in casks at Isera in
Trentino to a robust, deep ruby-garnet wine that needs at least 5 years to
attain elegance.
De Tarczal

**Riesling**
Both Riesling Renano (Rheinriesling) and Riesling Italico
(Welschriesling) are recognized as DOC under Alto Adige, Terlano,
Trentino (which permits Müller Thurgau as a Riesling), and Valdadige.
The Rieslings are also used for table wines.

**San Leonardo** r. dr.  ★★★  78 79 80 81 82 83
Fine Cabernet-Merlot from San Leonardo vineyards in the Vallagarina,
S of Trento. Rich in color and body, balanced, it needs 4–5 years for its
noble tannin to mellow and bouquet of herbs and berries to develop.
Tenuta San Leonardo (Guerrieri Gonzaga)

**San Zeno** r. dr.  ★★  79 80 82 83
Merlot dominates Cabernet in this table wine from Aldeno S of Trento.
The result is a softer, lighter, somewhat earlier-maturing wine than most
other Bordeaux-style blends.
La Vinicola Sociale Aldeno

**Sandbichler**
Brand name of H. Lun's Alto Adige DOC Pinot Nero and Riesling
Renano.

**Santa Maddalena (St Magdalener)** DOC r. dr.  ★★→★★★  82 83
Once the region's premier wine, Santa Maddalena is still adored in
Bolzano and neighboring German-speaking nations, though it hardly
rates as one of Italy's three great wines (along with Barolo and
Barbaresco) as determined under Mussolini in 1941. Made in quantity
(4 million liters a year) from various Schiava grapes in a hilly zone above
Bolzano, it ranges from dark ruby to garnet with pronounced almond
and violet bouquet typical of Schiava. Dry, round, at best velvety with
an enticing bitter background, it reaches peaks in a year or two, though
it can last longer. *Classico* (or *Klassisches Ursprungsgebiet*) applies to a
restricted area around the village of Santa Maddalena.

| | |
|---|---|
| Bellendorf | Kettmeir |
| Josef Brigl | Klosterkellerei Muri-Gries |
| Castel (Schloss) Rametz | Alois Lageder |
| J. Hofstätter | H. Lun |
| K. Gries (C.S. Gries) | Karl Martini & Sohn |
| K. St. Magdalena (C.S. | Henrich Plattner |
| Santa Maddalena) | Hans Rottensteiner |
| K. St. Michael-Eppan | Heinrich Rottensteiner |
| (C.S. San Michele-Appiano) | Schloss Schwanburg |
| K. Terlan (C.S. Terlano) | W. Walch |

**Sauvignon**
DOC under Alto Adige and Terlano. This noble vine is gaining favor.

**Schiava (Vernatsch)**
By far the most heavily planted vine here in Schiava Gentile, Grigia,
Grossa, Media, Piccola, and Tschaggeler. DOC under Alto Adige and
Valdadige, it is the base of DOC Caldaro, Casteller, Colli di Bolzano,
Meranese di Collina, Santa Maddalena, and Sorni *rosso*.

**Schiava di Faedo** p. dr.  ★★★  DYA
Schiava rosé from Faedo N of Trento. Of light cherry hue and blossomy
scent, it is crisply acidic with that supple but vital tone of good Schiava –
when young and fresh.
Pojer & Sandri

**Sorni** DOC r. w.  ★→★★  DYA
Recent DOC from around village of Sorni N of Trento. The *rosso*, from
Schiava, Teroldego, and Lagrein, is light ruby, subtly perfumed, soft,
and eminently quaffable when young. The *bianco*, based on Nosiola, is
pale straw and subtly scented with fresh, soft flavor when very young.
White of 11% may be called *scelto*.
C.S. Lavis-Sorni-Salorno                Moser
Maso Poli (Gaierhof)

**Spumante** w. (p.) dr. (s/sw.) sp. ★★→★★★★
Grapes – prevalently Chardonnay, Pinot Bianco, and Pinot Nero – for some of Italy's finest sparkling wines made by both *méthode champenoise* and *charmat* are grown in the region. Several producers, including Ferrari of Trento, long a leader in the nation's Champagne field, have headquarters here. Others buy grapes or wine and process them elsewhere. Those not marked *m.c.* for *méthode champenoise* are presumably made by *charmat*.
– **Arunda Brut (m.c.), Arunda Extra Brut (m.c.)**
Arunda
– **Bisol Brut (m.c.), Bisol Brut Nature (m.c.)**
Desiderio Bisol & Figli (Veneto)
– **Brut del Concilio (m.c.), Brut Rosé del Concilio (m.c.)**
Lagariavini
– **Carlozadra Brut (m.c.)**
Perlage (Lombardy)
– **Carpenè Malvolti Brut (m.c.)**
Carpenè Malvolti (Veneto)
– **Castel Monreale (m.c.), Schloss Konigsberg Brut (m.c.)**
Castello (Schloss) Rametz
– **Cesarini Sforza Brut Riserva (m.c.), Cesarini Sforza Brut Riserva dei Conti (m.c.)**
Cesarini Sforza
– **Della Staffa Brut**
Premiovini (Lombardy)
– **Dolzan Brut (m.c.)**
Dolzan
– **Équipe 5 Brut Riserva (m.c.), Équipe 5 Brut Rosé (m.c.)**
Équipe Trentina Spumante
– **Ferrari Brut (m.c.), Ferrari Brut de Brut (m.c.), Ferrari Brut Rosé (m.c.), Ferrari Nature (m.c.), Riserva Giulio Ferrari (m.c.)**
Spumante Ferrari
– **Frescobaldi Brut (m.c.)**
Marchesi de' Frescobaldi (Tuscany)
– **Gran Le Brul (m.c.)**
Le Brul
– **Gran Càvit Brut, Gran Cavit Brut Brut, Novella Fronda Chardonnay Brut**
Càvit
– **Haderburg Brut (m.c.), Haderburg Nature (m.c.)**
Haderburg (Ochsenreiter)
– **Kettmeir Brut Grande Cuvée**
Kettmeir
– **Lageder Brut**
Alois Lageder
– **Marchese Antinori Nature (m.c.)**
Marchesi Antinori (Tuscany)
– **Maria Theresia (m.c.)**
Masetto
– **Marone Cinzano Pas Dosé (m.c.), Pinot Chardonnay Atesino**
Cinzano (Piedmont)
– **Maschio Metodo Classico (m.c.)**
Maschio (Veneto)
– **Novaline Brut (m.c.)**
Novaline
– **Pisoni Brut Gran Spumante (m.c.)**
Fratelli Pisoni
– **Praeclarus Brut (m.c.)**
Kledona
– **Rotari Brut (m.c.)**
C.S. Cooperativa Mezzocorona
– **Spagnolli Brut (m.c.)**
Cantine Spagnolli
– **Vivaldi Brut (m.c.)**
Vivaldi

**Sylvaner**
The chief varietal of Valle Isarco (Eisacktaler) DOC, it is also classified under Alto Adige, Terlano, and Valdadige.

**Terlano (Terlaner)** DOC
The zone in hills along the Adige NW and SW of Bolzano comprises
seven white wines. Limited production is centered in the towns of
Terlano and Nalles, where wines may be called *classico*.
– **Müller Thurgau** w. dr. ★★ DYA
The small amount made is crisp, light, and refreshing when young.
– **Pinot Bianco (Weissburgunder)** w. dr. ★★→★★★★ 81 82 83
The prevalent variety, Pinot Bianco (with some Chardonnay) can rival
all the finest of Alto Adige.
– **Riesling Italico (Welschriesling)** w. dr. ★→★★ DYA
Good workaday white which occasionally rises above the ordinary.
– **Riesling Renano (Rheinriesling)** w. dr. ★★→★★★ 82 83
Fruity, finely scented wine of straw-green color; though light it shows
distinctive varietal character.
– **Sauvignon** w. dr. ★★→★★★ 82 83
Though limited in quantity, this shows outstanding promise. Better
examples have the greenish highlights, gunflint bite, and elegant
fruitiness typical of the grape.
– **Sylvaner** w. dr. ★→★★ DYA
Though it doesn't reach heights here, it can be an amply scented wine of
more than everyday appeal.
– **Terlano (Terlaner)** w. dr. ★→★★ 82 83
Light sipping wine from at least half Pinot Bianco with any or all other
varieties. Pale straw, fruity, refreshingly acidic.

| | |
|---|---|
| Josef Brigl | K. Terlan (C.S. Terlan) |
| K. Andrian (C.S. Andriano) | Klosterkellerei Muri-Gries |
| K. Gries (C.S. Gries) | Alois Lageder |
| K. Nals (C.S. Nalles) | Anton Lindner |
| K. St. Michael-Eppan | Hans Rottensteiner |
| (C.S. San Michele-Appiano) | Schloss Schwanburg |

**Teroldego Rotaliano** DOC r. p. dr. ★★→★★★★ 79 80 82 83
Wine from this vine, found only in the gravelly plain known as the
Campo Rotaliano where the Noce River joins the Adige between
Mezzolombardo and San Michele all'Adige, can stand with the grandest
reds of NE Italy. Dark ruby violet to garnet, depending on vintage, it is
generous, robust, and slightly tannic, with a bitter undertone and
splendid bouquet of flowers and berries after 2–3 years or, from
outstanding vintages, up to a decade of age. A vivacious *rosato* is included
in production of some 2 million bottles a year.
Ag. *superiore* (12%) 2 yrs.

| | |
|---|---|
| Barone De Cles | V. Foradori & Figli |
| Cantina Cooperative Rotaliano | Gaierhof |
| Cantina Produttori Mezzocorona | Istituto Agrario Provinciale (San |
| C.S. Cooperativa Mezzocorona | Michele) |
| Càvit | Lechthaler |
| Conti Martini | Maso Donati |
| Fratelli Delana | Moser |
| Dolzan | Alfonso Rossi |
| Fratelli Dorigati | Zeni |
| Fratelli Endrizzi | |

**Traminer Aromatico (Gewürztraminer)**
DOC under Alto Adige, Trentino, and Valle Isarco, this native of Alto
Adige is growing in popularity elsewhere, though the noble
Gewürztraminer is too often confused with the common Traminer.

**Trentino** DOC
The zone covers much of the grape-growing territory of Trentino,
through the Adige, Sarca, and Avisio valleys, where some 5.5 million
liters a year are now produced. Currently there are 10 types of wine,
chiefly varietals, though proposed modifications could expand the
number to 19. The listing includes the proposed types without star
ratings or vintages.
– **Bianco** w. dr. (sp.)
Proposed white would be at least half Chardonnay with Pinot Bianco.
– **Cabernet** r. dr. ★★→★★★ 78 79 81 82 83
Now usually a blend of Cabernet Franc with Cabernet Sauvignon, this is
among the most consistent Italian Cabernets. Rich in color and bouquet,

its marked herb and pepper qualities mellow after 3–4 years and peak at 10. Classics are Conti Bossi Fedrigotti and Tenuta San Leonardo.
Ag. *riserva* 2 yrs.
– **Cabernet Franc** r. dr.
This already dominant clone may be labeled separately.
– **Cabernet Sauvignon** r. dr.
When vinified separately, this might prove to be more elegant than the Franc alone.
– **Chardonnay** w. dr. (sp.)
Already prominent, when classified this might become the dominant white variety of Trentino.
– **Lagrein** r. p. dr.  ★→ ★★★   79 80 82 83
Both the persuasive *rosso* and the fragrant *rosato* can rival all but the finest Lagrein of Bolzano. Barone De Cles and Conti Martini stand out.

– **Marzemino** r. dr.  ★→ ★★★   79 81 82 83
This native can show Beaujolais-like charm when young, though its full-bodied, grapy softness evolves toward a deeper, richer, almost aristocratic tone accented by a bitter finish. The best comes from Isera where De Tarczal and Simoncelli excel.
Ag. *riserva* 2 yrs.
– **Merlot** r. dr.  ★→ ★★   80 81 82 83
The most popular Trentino varietal, Merlot makes ruby-garnet wines – scented and soft, with the typical herby flavor – usually best expressed in 2–4 years, though *riserva* can be kept longer.
Ag. *riserva* 2 yrs.
– **Moscato** w. am. s/sw. sw.  ★★
Dessert wines made mainly from Moscato Giallo grapes grown in limited quantities in S Trentino. Though often drunk young, the richer, sweeter *liquoroso* and *riserva* versions take some age. (Under proposed changes this will become Moscato Giallo.)
– **Moscato Rosa** p. s/sw. sw.
Proposed as a separate entity here, Moscato Rosa is a proven dessert wine in Alto Adige.
– **Müller Thurgau** w. dr.
Now permitted under Riesling Trentino, this promising cross should blossom on its own.
– **Nosiola** w. dr.
The revival of this native white deserves confirmation in DOC.
– **Pinot Bianco** w. dr. (sp.)  ★→ ★★★   81 82 83
The appellation now permits the inclusion of Pinot Grigio, as well as Chardonnay. But the modified rules would separate the three and let Pinot Bianco express its eminent potential.
– **Pinot Grigio** w. dr. (sp.)
Gaining as a varietal, the proposed discipline of DOC should help keep the records straight.
– **Pinot Nero** r. p. dr.  ★→ ★★   79 80 82 83
Though some producers achieve soft, plush, fragrant wines good for 3–6 years, most Pinot Nero is inconsequential, though it makes good rosé.
Ag. *riserva* 2 yrs.
– **Riesling** w. dr.  ★→ ★★   DYA
The name now applies to Riesling Renano and Italico plus Müller Thurgau, too many options to determine personality. But proposed modifications will separate the three.
– **Rosso** r. dr.
This propitious proposal would consummate the marriage of Cabernet (at 50–85%) and Merlot in what will make many of the province's better red wines DOC.
– **Traminer Aromatico** w. dr.  ★→ ★★   82 83
If they rarely approach the class of Alto Adige Gewürztraminer, some Traminers here can hold their distinct virtues for 3–4 years.
– **Vino Santo** am. sw.  ★★   74 78 79 82 83
The limited production of this prized sweet wine is concentrated in the Lake Toblino area. After aging in small barrels, it turns golden amber and aromatic, developing a velvety texture with many years in bottle. New proposals would confine the grape source to Nosiola and exclude Pinot Bianco.
Ag. 3 yrs.

Barone De Cles                          Riccardo Battistotti
Baroni a Prato (Castel Segonzano)   Conti Bossi Fedrigotti            ▶

Conti Martini
Cantina di Toblino
Cantina Produttori Mezzocorona
C.S. Colli Zugna
C.S. Cooperativa Mezzocorona
C.S. di Isera
C.S. di Mori
C.S. Lavis-Sorni-Salorno
C.S. Riva del Garda
Càvit
Del Poggio
De Tarczal
Dolzan
Fratelli Endrizzi
V. Foradori & Figli
Gaierhof
Istituto Agrario Provinciale
   (San Michele all'Adige)
Lagariavini

La Vinicola Sociale Aldeno
Letrari
Longariva
Maso Cantghl
Maso Donati
Novaline
Fratelli Pedrotti
Gino Pedrotti
Fratelli Pisoni
Giovanni Poli
Fratelli Rigotti
Alfonso Rossi
Carlo Rossi
Armando Simoncelli
Società Agricoltori Vallagarina
E. Spagnolli
Tenuta San Leonardo
   (Guerrieri-Gonzaga)
Villa Borino

**Valdadige (Etschtaler)** DOC
Though only *rosso* and *bianco* are specified under the terms of this zone, which follows the Adige from Merano S almost to Verona in the Veneto, varietals may also be mentioned on labels. Some 10 million liters of DOC wine flow annually from high-yield vineyards here, much of it to neighboring countries.
– **Bianco** w. dr.  ★→★★  DYA
Wine can derive from Pinot Bianco or Grigio, Riesling Italico, Müller Thurgau, Bianchetta Trevigiana, Trebbiano Toscano, Nosiola, Vernaccia, Sylvaner, and Veltliner alone, or in combinations. When varietal names appear separately, this indicates some personality. Valdadige is the source of growing amounts of Pinot Grigio.
– **Rosso** r. p. dr.  ★  DYA
Nondescript red or rosé from various combinations of Lambrusco, Schiava, Merlot, Pinot Nero, Lagrein, Teroldego, and Negrara.

Bollini
Cantina Produttori Mezzocorona
C.S. Cooperativa Mezzocorona
Càvit
Fratelli Delana

Fratelli Endrizzi
Gaierhof
Fratelli Pasqua
Santa Margherita
Scamperle

**Valle Isarco (Eisacktaler)** DOC
Small production of five white varietals grown at high altitude along the Isarco (Eisack) River NE of Bolzano past Bressanone (Brixen) in Italy's northernmost DOC zone.
– **Müller Thurgau** w. dr.  ★★→★★★  82 83
Delicate and flowery, it is good young, but from some vintages develops grace over 2–4 years.
– **Pinot Grigio (Ruländer)** w. dr.  ★→★★  DYA
Well-rounded wine of pale roseate yellow color, fine scent, and fresh flavor.
– **Sylvaner** or **Silvaner** w. dr.  ★★→★★★  81 82 83
The local favorite, Sylvaner thrives here as nowhere else in Italy, achieving style similar to German Franken wines. Though some prefer it young when it is pale and snappy, with age it acquires elegant aromas and flavors.
– **Traminer Aromatico (Gewürztraminer)** w. dr.  ★★  82 83
Though similar in style to that of Tramin, here the wine develops ethereal aroma and a supple fragility when young.
– **Veltliner** w. dr.  ★  DYA
The small volume produced of this green-tinted wine – which is DOC only here – is light and appealingly fruity in scent and flavor.

K. Eisacktaler (C.S. della Valle
   d'Isarco)
Alois Lageder
Pacherhof (Huber)

Stiftskellerei Neustift (Abbazia di
   Novacella)
Karl Vonklausner

**4 Vicariati** r. dr.  ★★★  78 79 81 82 83
From Cabernet and Merlot, this premium red of the region's largest cooperative is selected vineyard by vincyard, then reselected before being aged 2 ycars in *barriques*. Deep ruby, robust, and somewhat tannic

but smooth, it needs 4–5 years to reach its best.
Càvit

**Vin dei Molini** p. dr. *** DYA
Singular rosé from Schiava crossed with Riesling in vineyards 720 meters
high at Faedo, N of Trento. Light coral garnet and subtly flowery, its
piquant dryness is enhanced by high acidity and charming freshness with
a vaguely bitter finish. Best inside a year.
Pojer & Sandri

## Wine & Food

The cooking of Trentino and Alto Adige derives from distinct
heritages, one Italo-Venetian, the other Germanic-Tyrolean.
But the intermingling of peoples drawing on shared resources
along the Adige valley has taken the sharp edges off the contrasts.
Something akin to a regional style of cooking has emerged. True,
the Italian-speaking population still relies more heavily on
polenta, gnocchi, and pasta, the German-speaking on wursts,
black bread, and soups. But the fare found in *ristoranti* and
*Gasthäusen* here has been enriched by the points in common. The
*Knödel*, for example, has become *canederli* in Italian and savored
just as avidly. The same can be said for *sauerkraut* or *crauti*. Game,
trout, *speck* (smoked bacon), and Viennese-style pastries are
further evidence of a unity of taste that makes the long hours
spent at table in the warm, wood-paneled *Stübe* so enjoyable.

**Biroldi con crauti** Blood sausages
with chestnuts, nutmeg, and
cinnamon, served with *sauerkraut*.
  * Casteller.
**Canederli/Knödel** Among many
dumplings, perhaps the tastiest are
with calf's liver served in broth.
  ** Lagrein Kretzer.
**Gemsenfleisch** Chamois cooked
Tyrolean style with red wine
vinegar and served with polenta.
  *** Lagrein Dunkel
or *** Cabernet.
**Gerstensuppe** Barley soup with
bacon, onions, and celery.
  * Meranese di Collina (Meraner
Hügel)
**Gröstl** Beef, potatoes, and onions,
cooked together in a cake-like
mold.
  ** Merlot or ** Pinot Nero.

**Blau Forelle** Alpine trout boiled
with white wine and flavorings.
  **→*** Müller Thurgau.
**Krapfen Tirolese** Fried paste
with marmalade and powdered
sugar.
  **→*** Moscato Rosa
or ** Moscato Giallo.
**Sauresuppe** Flavorsome tripe
soup traditionally eaten at mid-
morning on market days and
holidays.
  * Colli di Bolzano (Bozner
Leiten).
**Smacafam** Buckwheat cake with
sausages, onion, lard, and cheese.
  ** Marzemino.
**Speck** Smoked bacon sliced onto
black bread.
  ** Caldaro (Kalterersee).

### Restaurants

Recommended in or near wine zones: **Alto Adige** *Greif* at Bolzano;
*Elefante* and *Fink* at Bressanone (Brixen); *Forstlerhof* at Burgstall (Postal);
*Völserhof* at Fiè allo Sciliar (Völs am Schlern); *Andrea* and *Hotel Villa
Mozart* at Merano. **Trentino** *Concorde* at Calceranica al Lago; *Maso
Cantanghel* near Civezzano; *All'Olivo* at Faver; *Al Paròl* at Mesiano di
Povo; *Da Valentino* at Padergnone; *Albergo Ristorante al Ponte* at Pergine;
*Hotel Rovereto* and *Sisler* at Rovereto; *Da Silvio* at San Michele
all'Adige; *Castel Toblino* at Sarche; *Chiesa* and *Vecchia Trento* at Trento;
*Doss Pules* at Verla di Giovo.

# _Tuscany_

## Toscana

Tuscany is identified as intimately with wine as it is with art, language, crafts, and ideas, all of which over the centuries it has exported prodigiously. This is the domain of Sangiovese, the hearty, sometimes noble mainstay of every Tuscan DOC red wine from Chianti to Brunello di Montalcino, Vino Nobile di Montepulciano, Carmignano, and less lofty appellations. Chianti might still be the world's most widely known name in wine, even if, after some six centuries of fluctuating fame and fortune, its popularity has declined of late. While Chianti's cheerful flask has been gradually replaced by the standard bottle, surpluses have been mounting in the cellars of central Tuscany. This malaise has been felt throughout the industry.

Chianti's problems are due in part to modern preference for white, light, fresh, bubbly wines over more imposing reds. But there is also a crisis of identity. Producers themselves seem undecided about Chianti's personality and their differences in concepts, techniques and, most conspicuously, skills in winemaking are reflected in the variable quality. Some Chianti, with its unmistakable Bordeaux-like structure, ranks with Italy's greatest reds; other wine of the name is barely tolerable plonk.

Some other Tuscan wines have troubles, too, though on a much smaller scale, for Chianti in its seven geographical units accounts for some 90% of the wine produced among the region's 24 DOCs and, indeed, for about one-sixth of the national DOC total. Though Tuscany ranks only seventh among the regions in total production, it contends with the Veneto as top producer of DOC with some 170 million liters a year. Brunello and Vino Nobile, among Italy's first four DOCGs, enjoy reasonably sound markets, as does the elite DOC Carmignano. But it is the unclassified wines such as Sassicaia, Tignanello and a galaxy of other new stars that are showing how brilliant Tuscan red wines can be.

Tuscan whites are also resurging, thanks to increasing consumer demand and a handy surplus of white grapes no longer used in Chianti. Most noticeable is Galestro, produced by a consortium of large firms. But there are so many innovations or revised whites that only a choice few have been cited this time.

Tuscan wine flows from vineyards that cover hillsides from the Tyrrhenian to the Apennines – a rural civilization shaped over centuries into a landscape of extraordinary harmony. Visitors come to see the Florence of the Medici, the Palio of Siena, and the towers of Pisa and San Gimignano. But Tuscan wine, despite its exciting possibilities, has scarcely been tapped as a tourist attraction. Still, there is plenty to see and taste by the wine lover with time to explore. The prime wine road is the Chiantigiana, which cuts through the enchanting heart of Chianti to link Florence with Siena (home of the _Enoteca Italica Permanente_ – the national wine library – in the Medici fortress). Also worth visiting are the _enoteche_ at Montalcino, Carmignano, and Terricciola in the Colline Pisane. Among shops recommended are _Enoteca Nebraska_ at Camaiore, _Bottega del Vino-Casanova_ at Chianciano Terme, _Enoteca Mora_ at Ponte a Moriano and _Punto di Vino_ at Viareggio. _Enoteca Gallo Nero_ at Greve sells nearly all Chianti Classico. In Florence, good collections can be found at _Enoteca Nazionale Pinchiorri_ and _Enoteca Murgia_.

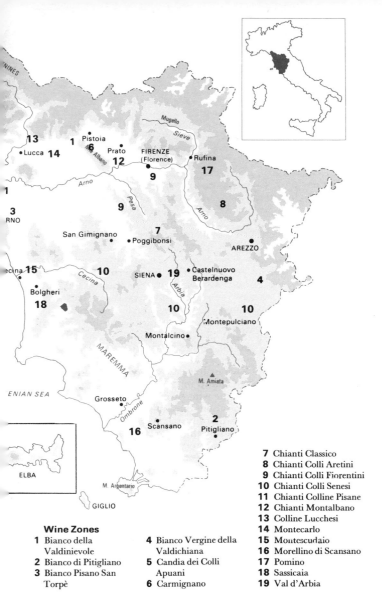

**Wine Zones**

1 Bianco della Valdinievole
2 Bianco di Pitigliano
3 Bianco Pisano San Torpè
4 Bianco Vergine della Valdichiana
5 Candia dei Colli Apuani
6 Carmignano
7 Chianti Classico
8 Chianti Colli Aretini
9 Chianti Colli Fiorentini
10 Chianti Colli Senesi
11 Chianti Colline Pisane
12 Chianti Montalbano
13 Colline Lucchesi
14 Montecarlo
15 Montescudaio
16 Morellino di Scansano
17 Pomino
18 Sassicaia
19 Val d'Arbia

### Recent vintages

Chianti *riserva*, Vino Nobile, and Carmignano approach primes around 4–7 years, though some vintages favor aging of a decade or more. Brunello needs 6–10 years to begin opening up, and great vintages can last for decades.

1983 Extreme heat caused uneven ripening, but top producers made good to very good wines with select grapes.
1982 Large, first-rate vintage of big, balanced red wines, the best in a string of good harvests.
1981 Reduced but in some cases very good; Brunello, Vino Nobile and Chianti from Siena province fared well.
1980 Large, uneven crop, average quality with a few towering exceptions in Chianti and Carmignano.
1979 Record harvest of good to very good wines; early charm points to rather short life spans.

1978    Reduced, but some outstanding, long-lived wines were made,
        notably Brunello, Carmignano, and Chianti Classico.
1977    Below normal in size but memorable for Brunello, Vino Nobile,
        and certain Chiantis.
1976    A write-off – except for Sassicaia and some Brunello.
1975    Fine vintage; exceptionally good for Brunello, Vino Nobile, and
        Chianti from Siena province.
1974    Spotty; unremarkable, except for some superb Chianti Rufina.
1973    Below average, though excellent for Carmignano.
1972    Generally poor, but a grand year for Sassicaia.
1971    Good to excellent but uneven; some great Chianti, but there were
        disappointments in Montalcino and Montepulciano.
1970    Fine harvest; outstanding Brunello and Vino Nobile.
Earlier fine vintages: (Brunello) '64, '61, '55, '45; (Chianti) '64, '62;
(Vino Nobile) '67, '58.

**Aleatico** r. sw.
From the ancient Aleatico vine grown on Elba and in the Maremma, this
rich red dessert wine is becoming a rarity.

**Ansonica del Giglio** am. dr.  ★ DYA
Curiosity from Ansonica grown on the isle of Giglio off the Argentario
promontory. Amber, ample in scent, its rustically suave dryness makes it
good with fish soup.
Le Cannelle

**Barco Reale** r. dr.  ★★  83
This new red wine named for the Medici park that covered the zone has
become a lighter, fresher version of Carmignano, probably to serve as a
second-tier DOC if Carmignano becomes DOCG. Producers are the
same as for Carmignano.

**Bianco del Chianti** w. dr. (fz.)  ★★→★★★  DYA
The name Chianti applies by law only to reds, though whites are made
throughout the seven zones. Some are covered by separate DOCs –
Bianco Pisano San Torpè, Bianco Vergine della Valdichiana, Val
d'Arbia, Vernaccia di San Gimignano – but many more are table wines.
They are usually made from Trebbiano and Malvasia, grapes used
decreasingly in Chianti, sometimes with other varieties added. Though
customarily rather light, neutral and fragile (if not sour), new cellar
techniques have brought out more fruit and aromas than previously in
whites of surprisingly appealing tone, with good balance and sometimes
a hint of *pétillance*. A few of the better examples tasted recently are listed.
(See also Bianco della Lega and Galestro.)

| | |
|---|---|
| – **Bianco del Beato** | – **Capezzana Bianco** |
| Fattoria dei Barbi (Colombini) | Tenuta Capezzana |
| – **Bianco dell'Amorosa** | – **Colline di Ama** |
| Fattoria L'Amorosa | Castello di Ama |
| – **Bianco di Castellare** | – **Eburneo** |
| Castellare di Castellina | Podere di Cignano |
| – **Bianco di Coltibuono** | – **Ginestra** |
| Badia a Coltibuono | Patriarca (Lucherini) |
| – **Bianco di Montosoli** | – **Riecine Bianco** |
| Altesino | Riecine |
| – **Bianco di Volpaia** | – **Trebianco** |
| Castello di Volpaia | Castello dei Rampolla |
| – **Bianco Le Torri** | – **Vigna Nuova** |
| Le Torri (Campigliano) | Vignavecchia |
| – **Brolio Bianco** | – **Vigneto della Rosa Bianca** |
| Barone Ricasoli | Podere Il Palazzino |
| – **Capannelle Bianco** | – **Vin Brusco** |
| Capannelle | Montenidoli (Fagiuoli) |

**Bianco della Lega** w. dr.  ★→★★  DYA
Recent unofficial appellation for white table wine based on Trebbiano
and Malvasia grown in Chianti Classico and supervised by the *consorzio*.
Usually light in color, scent, and flavor, it is rather neutral but, when
well made, fruity and balanced.

| | |
|---|---|
| Castello di Querceto | Fattoria La Ripa |
| Fattoria di Ama | Fontodi |
| Fattoria di Montagliari | Melini |
| Fattoria di Selvole | Pagliarese |

▶

| Palazzo al Bosco (Olivieri) | Conti Serristori |
| Savignola Paolina | Villa Cerna |

**Bianco della Val d'Arbia**
See Val d'Arbia.

**Bianco della Valdinievole (and Vin Santo)** w. dr. (am.)
(sw.) ★ DYA
Simple white from Trebbiano grown around Montecatini Terme and
Pescia where most is consumed. Pale straw yellow, it is light with a hint of
prickle. Vin Santo della Valdinievole is DOC but rarely seen.
Adolfo Giannini

**Bianco di Pitigliano** DOC w. dr. ★→★★ DYA
Trebbiano, Grechetto, and others combine in a neutral, clean,
sometimes fruity white from Pitigliano in S Tuscany.
C.S. Cooperativa di Pitigliano      Podere Scansanaccio

**Bianco Pisano San Torpè** DOC w. dr. ★→★★ DYA
Recent DOC of Trebbiano, Canaiolo Bianco, and Malvasia grown SE of
Pisa in a zone overlapping Chianti Colline Pisane. Straw green, lightly
fragrant, dry, round, and slightly bitter at the finish.

| Badia di Morrona (Gaslini) | Fattoria di Piedivilla |
| Barone Hostini di Sant'Ermo | Fattoria Usigliano del Vescovo |
| Cantina delle Colline Pisane | Fratelli Salvadori |
| Fattoria di Gello | San Giacomo |

**Bianco Vergine della Valdichiana** DOC w. dr. ★→★★★ DYA
From Trebbiano chiefly with Malvasia and Grechetto grown in the
Chiana valley between Arezzo and Chiusi. Straw yellow, it is usually soft
and dry with hints of both sweet and bitter. Avignonesi's fragrant, fruity
version, with its hints of almonds and honey, stands above the crowd.

| Avignonesi | Fattoria Santa Vittoria |
| Baldetti | Luca della Robbia |
| C.S. Colli Aretini | Molino della Vecchia |
| C.S. di Cortona | Spalletti |
| Aldo Casagni | Tenuta di Vitereta |
| Fattoria delle Maestrelle | Vecchia Cantina di |
| Fattoria di Manzano | Montepulciano |

**Bolgheri** DOC p. w. dr. ★ →★★ DYA
New DOC for rosé and white wines from Bolgheri SE of Livorno. The
*rosato*, from Sangiovese and Canaiolo, is exemplified by Marchesi
Antinori's well-known Rosé di Bolgheri. The *bianco*, from Trebbiano and
Vermentino, is not yet clearly identifiable. Sassicaia (not DOC) is grown
nearby.
Marchesi Antinori

**Brunello di Montalcino** DOC–DOCG r. dr. ★★→★★★★ 70 71 75 77
78 79 80 81 82 83
This long-lived red from Brunello (a strain of Sangiovese Grosso) grown
in the community of Montalcino S of Siena has emerged only in recent
times as one of Italy's most prized and, from some producers, among the
world's most expensive wines. Powerfully structured, tannic and deep
ruby, after 5–6 years it matures towards an austere, warm, ample flavor,
brick-red color and rich bouquet (known to last for 50 years or more).
Though Brunello is capable of grandeur with great age (notably from
Biondi-Santi, which originated the wine late last century), rapid
expansion has confused production. DOCG may help align general
quality with great expectations, though not everyone agrees that the
established methods of Biondi-Santi, Fattoria dei Barbi and the late
Emilio Costanti should prevail. Tastings of relatively recent Brunello from
Altesino, Argiano, Caprili, Case Basse, Mastrojanni, Tenuta Caparzo
and Il Poggione indicate that superb Brunello can be achieved by
traditional methods. But the new wave, led by Villa Banfi, Castelgiocondo
and Col d'Orcia might influence others toward a more approachable
contemporary style. Production is increasing beyond 2 million liters a
year. DOCG takes effect with the '80 vintage issued in 1985 and could be
applied retroactively to '79 and '78. (See also Rosso di Montalcino.)
Ag. 4 yrs. ($3\frac{1}{2}$ in barrel); *riserva* 5 yrs.

Altesino                              Argiano                              ▶

Biondi-Santi (Il Greppo)
Camigliano
Campogiovanni
Canalicchio (Lambardi)
Canalicchio di Sopra (Pacenti)
Capanna
Caprili
Casale del Bosco (Nardi)
Casanova (Neri)
Case Basse
Castelgiocondo
Castiglion del Bosco
Colombaio di Montosoli
Fattoria dei Barbi
Fattoria Poggio Antico

Fattoria Val di Suga
San Filippo dei Comunali
Il Greppone Mazzi
La Chiesa di Santa Restituta
Lisini
Mastrojanni (Loreto)
Pertimali
Poderi Emilio Costanti
Poggio alle Mura
Tenuta Caparzo
Tenuta Col d'Orcia
Tenuta Il Poggione
Tenuta di Sesta
Tenuta Valdicava
Villa Banfi

**Brusco dei Barbi** r. dr.  ★★★  79 81 82 83
Special wine from Brunello grapes of Montalcino processed by *governo*
(refermentation induced by semidried grapes) to be ready sooner than
Brunello, though it has similar size and livelier character. Usually to
drink inside 4–5 years, but it can age.
Fattoria dei Barbi

**Ca' del Pazzo** r. dr. 82 83
An innovation of winemaker Vittorio Fiore, blending declassified
Brunello with Cabernet Sauvignon aged 6–7 months in small, new oak
barrels. Early tastings of the '82 indicated excellent potential.
Tenuta Caparzo

**Cabernet**
Cabernet Sauvignon (and some Franc) seems to have a bright future in
Tuscany as a varietal and in blends. After the pioneering of Sassicaia,
others have followed suit: Antinori with Solaia, Castello dei Rampolla
with Sammarco, Fonterutoli with Concerto, Capezzana with Ghiaie
della Furba (Cabernet-Merlot), Villa Banfi with Tavarnelle. Antinori's
Tignanello started another trend of Sangiovese with Cabernet, now
found in Avignonesi's Grifi, Tenuta Caparzo's Ca' del Pazzo,
Lungarotti's San Giorgio (in Umbria) and more than a few Chiantis.

**Candia dei Colli Apuani** DOC w. dr.  ★  DYA
From Vermentino and Albarola grown above Massa and Carrara in
NW Tuscany, this still-obscure DOC is straw colored, lightly aromatic,
and dry but soft with a hint of bitterness.

**Carmignano** DOC r. dr.  ★★★→★★★★   73 75 77 78 79 80 81 82 83
Recognized as one of the world's first wine zones of controlled name and
origin by the Grand Duchy of Tuscany in 1716, Carmignano is noted
chiefly for its aristocratic red. Recently the tiny zone W of Florence was
expanded to take in *rosato* and Vin Santo. The red is similar to Chianti,
but with Cabernet at 6–10% for a touch of elegance, Carmignano is
bright ruby tending to garnet and orange with age. Its smooth, dry,
complex flavor and flowery bouquet show finesse similar to wines of the
Haut Médoc. Though well expressed after 4–10 years, certain vintages
(Villa di Capezzana 1931, for example) hold admirably for 50 years. The
130,000 liters a year of Carmignano red show the most consistency of any
Tuscan DOC, because only wines approved by experts at an annual
tasting can carry the name. (See also Barco Reale.)
Ag. 18 months (1 yr in barrel); *riserva* 3 yrs (2 in barrel).
– **Rosato** p. dr. (fz.) (sp.)  ★★  DYA
Lovely rosé often called Vin Ruspo from Carmignano grapes processed
in a special way to attain youthful freshness. Flowery and fruity, it can be
*frizzante* or even *spumante*.
– **Vin Santo** am. dr. s/sw.  ★★→★★★
Some of the best Tuscan Vin Santo originates in this zone, where it is
now confirmed as DOC. Aged several years in small barrels, it can age
5–10 years in bottle.

Fattoria Ambra
Fattoria di Artimino
Fattoria di Bacchereto
Fattoria di Calavria
Fattoria Il Poggiolo
Fattoria Le Farnete

Podere Le Poggiarelle
Villa di Capezzana (Contini
  Bonacossi)
Villa di Trefiano (Contini
  Bonacossi)

**Cepparello** r. dr.  ★★★  80 82
Pure Sangiovese selected in the Isole e Olena vineyards in Chianti
Classico and aged 10–11 months in *barriques* by winemaker Paolo De
Marchi. Early tastings of the amply structured '82 pointed to a well-
rounded ★★★★ after 3–4 years.
Isole e Olena

**Chardonnay**
This seems to be preferred among noble vines for white wines being
planted or grafted in Tuscany. Villa Banfi was among the first out with a
varietal Chardonnay called Fontanelle, though others were on the way.
Chardonnay is also being used in blends.

**Chianti** DOC
The renowned red comes from the dark Sangiovese grape with Canaiolo
and (required but not always included) some light Trebbiano and
Malvasia. Partitioned into seven zones which cover much of central
Tuscany, Chianti is the largest DOC in size and volume with an average
of 130 million liters a year from nearly 7,000 registered vineyards. Each
zone has distinct terrains and microclimates, and since well over 1,000
producers tend to express individual attitudes and styles, Chianti is not
one wine but many. It may be a light wine freshened by *governo* (a
refermentation induced by adding semidried grapes to the new wine) to
drink from the flask, or a medium-bodied, flexible red to drink in 2–5
years, or a complex, austere, barrel-aged reserve wine in the claret mold.
As with Bordeaux, though, it would take a lifetime to get to know all the
names, places, and tastes. Despite remarkable expansion through the
1970s, culminating in a record crop of 180 million liters in 1979, Chianti
has slumped, forcing some estates out of business and others to reassess
aims. The trends to eliminate white grapes and to modernize wineries
have improved general quality, making Chianti one of the best values in
premium wine anywhere. DOCG is slated to take effect soon, though
serious doubts have arisen about the prospects of guaranteeing the wine
of such a vast and varied territory. Among other questionable norms, the
use of up to 17% of wines or must from outside the zones is permitted.
DOCG would reduce this allowance, while limiting maximum grape
yields and cutting use of white grapes. At present, much production is
supervised by the consortiums of Chianti Classico (symbolized by a black
rooster) and, in the other six zones, Chianti Putto (symbolized by a
cherub). Though Chianti Classico and Rufina are generally cited on
labels, producers in other districts often opt to call their wine simply
Chianti without naming the zone.

– **Chianti Classico** r. dr.  ★★→★★★★  71 75 77 78 79 80 81 82 83
The heart of Chianti between Florence and Siena, this picturesque zone
includes Castellina, Radda, and Gaiole, where the original Chianti
League was formed in the 13th century. Though character varies from
sector to sector, quality is more consistent here than in other zones. Much
of the best, longest-lived *riserva* originates here. Most Chianti Classico is
good in 2–5 years, *vecchio* in 3–7, and *riserva* in 4–8, though some estates'
wines can age well beyond a decade from good vintages. (Producers
listed in the seven zones do not include all bottler and shipper brands,
which could also be dependable.)

| | |
|---|---|
| Aziano (Ruffino) | Il Guerrino |
| Baccio da Gaiuole (Gittori) | Isole e Olena |
| Badia a Coltibuono | La Bricola |
| Berardenga | La Loggia |
| Bertolli | La Massa |
| Bibbiani | Lamole |
| Borgianni | La Pagliaia |
| Brolio (Ricasoli) | La Quercia |
| Caggiolo | La Selvanella (Melini) |
| Campomaggio | Le Masse di San Leolino |
| Capannelle | Le Piazze |
| Carobbio | Lilliano |
| Casalgallo | Lo Spugnaccio |
| Casalino | Lornano |
| Casa Sola | Luiano |
| Casavecchia di Nittardi | Machiavelli (Serristori) |
| Casa Volterrani | Melini |

▶

Castagnoli
Castelgreve
Castellare di Castellina
Castell'in Villa
Castello dei Rampolla
Castello di Ama
Castello di Bossi
Castello di Cacchiano
Castello di Cerreto
Castello di Fagnano
Castello di Fonterutoli
Castello di Gabbiano
Castello di Meleto
Castello di Monterinaldi
Castello di Mugnana
Castello di Querceto
Castello di Rencine
Castello di San Donato in
   Perano
Castello di San Polo in Rosso
Castello di Uzzano
Castello di Verrazzano
Castello di Volpaia
Castello Vicchiomaggio
Castel Ruggero
Castelvecchi
Catignano
Cellole
Cennatoio
Cerbaiola
Chianti Geografico
Fattoria Casenuove
Fattoria della Aiola
Fattoria delle Corti
Fattoria delle Lodoline
Fattoria di Rosennano
Fattoria di Petroio
Fattoria di Selvole
Fattoria di Tizzano
Fattoria di Vistarenni
Fattoria Granaio (Melini)
Fattoria La Pesanella
Fattoria Le Pici
Fattoria Montecchio
Fattoria Poggiarello
Filetta
Fontodi
Fortilizio il Colombaio
Fossi
Gaiello dell Filigare
Grignanello
I Sodi
Il Campino di Mondiglia

Mocenni
Monsanto
Montagliari
Montemaggio
Montepaldi
Montesassi
Monte Vertine
Montoro
Montoro e Selvole
Nozzole
Ormanni
Pagliarese
Palazzo al Bosco
Petroio alla Via della Malpensata
Pian d'Albola
Podere Il Palazzino
Poggio alla Croce
Poggio al Sole
Poggiolino
Poggio Rosso
Quercesola
Quornia
Giorgio Regni (Valtellina)
Riecine
Riseccoli
Rocca delle Macie
Ruffino Riserva Ducale
San Cosma
San Felice (Il Grigio)
Santa Cristina (Antinori)
Santa Lucia
Santo Stefano
San Vito in Berardenga
Savignola Paolina
Straccali
Tenuta di Vignole
Terrarossa (Melini)
Terre di Melazzano
Tiorcia
Tomarecchio & Miscianello
Valiano
Vecchie Terre di Montefili
Vignamaggio
Vignavecchia
Villa Antinori
Villa a Sesta
Villa Banfi
Villa Cafaggio
Villa Calcinaia
Villa Cerna
Villa Montepaldi
Villa Rosa
Villa Terciona

– **Chianti Colli Aretini** r. dr.  ★→ ★★★  81 82 83
Soft, well-scented Chianti from hills overlooking the Arno E of Chianti
Classico. Most is of medium body to drink in 1–4 years, but some ages.

C.S. Colli Aretini
Castello di Montegonzi
Fattoria dell'Albereto
Fattoria di Chiaravalle
Fattoria di Marcena
Fattoria di Santa Vittoria
Fattoria La Trove
I Selvatici

Monte Petrognano
Podere di Cignano
San Fabiano
Sant'Elena
Savoia Aosta
Villa Cilnia
Villa Fabbriche
Villa La Selva

– **Chianti Colli Fiorentini** r. dr.  ★→★★★★  75 77 78 79 81 82
Source of much of the flask Chianti consumed in Florence, this zone in
hills S and E of the city and down along the Arno and Pesa valleys, also
makes some of the finest estate-bottled *riserva*. The flask wine, still
sometimes made by *governo*, is light, soft, and round when young. The
aging wine, of ruby-garnet color, later takes on amber-orange highlights;

it can be robust, austere, aristocratic, and complete in bouquet and
flavor, to drink in 5–10 years. Producers include several from the fringes
of the zone with the right to call their wine Chianti.

| | |
|---|---|
| Bracciolino | Granaiolo & Coiano |
| Ottorino Buti | I Golli |
| Casalbosco | La Marta |
| Castello di Poppiano | La Querce |
| Chianti Pillo | La Tassinara |
| Collazzi | Le Chiantigiane |
| Conti Lucchesi Palli | Le Torri (Campiglioni) |
| Dianella Fucini | Le Torri a Mosciano |
| Fattoria Cabbiavoli | Montegufoni (Posarelli) |
| Fattoria dell'Ugo | Nardi-Dei |
| Fattoria di Loro | Pasolini Dall'Onda Borghese |
| Fattoria di Mandri | Passaponti |
| Fattoria di Poggio Capponi | Poggio Romita |
| Fattoria di Sammontana | San Vito in Fior di Selva |
| Fattoria Gigliola | Tenuta Corfecciano |
| Fattoria Il Corno | Tenuta Il Monte |
| Fattoria Il Palagio | Tenuta Ribaldaccio |
| Fattoria La Tancia | Torgaio di San Salvatore (Ruffino) |
| Fattoria Montellori | Torre a Decima |
| Fattoria Pagnana | Uggiano |
| Fattoria Terranova | Ugolino |
| Fattorie Giannozzi | Villa dell'Olmo |

– **Chianti Colli Senesi** r. dr.   ★→ ★★★★   75 77 78 79 81 82

This zone, the largest, is split into three sectors: one around Montalcino,
one around Montepulciano, and the rest in an arc S of the Classico zone
from San Gimignano eastwards past Siena and Castelnuovo Berardenga.
Chianti here ranges from some of the most elegant and long-lived down
to the wine factory variety with price to match quality (that industry is
centered in Poggibonsi and Castellina Scalo). Variations in conditions
and techniques result in a wide range of styles.

| | |
|---|---|
| Avignonesi | Il Poggiolo (Bonfio) |
| Casale del Bosco | La Foce Castelluccio |
| Castello di Montauto | La Muraglia |
| Castelpugna | La Suvera |
| Cecchi | Le Portine (Bonfio) |
| Cercignano | Majnoni Guicciardini |
| Chigi Saracini | Montenidoli |
| Riccardo Falchini | Patriarca (Lucherini) |
| Fanetti | Podere Santa Croce |
| Farneta | Poderi Boscarelli |
| Fassati | Poderi Emilio Costanti |
| Fattoria Casabianca | Poliziano |
| Fattoria di Monte Oliveto | Rosso di Casavecchia |
| Fattoria di Pancole | Tenuta di Gracciano (Della Seta) |
| Fattoria di Pietrafitta | Tenuta La Lellera |
| Fattoria di Santo Pietro | Fratelli Vagnoni |
| Fattoria L'Amorosa | Vecchia Cantina di |
| Fattoria La Torre | Montepulciano |
| Il Macchione | Villa Cusona (Guicciardini Strozzi) |
| Il Palagetto | Villa Montemorli |

– **Chianti Colline Pisane** r. dr.   ★→★★   82 83

From hills around Casciana Terme SE of Pisa, this zone has a mild
maritime climate and its Chianti is the lightest, softest and, as a rule, the
shortest-lived, though its round fruitiness makes it a versatile meal wine.

| | |
|---|---|
| Badia di Morrona (Gaslini) | Fattoria di Piedivilla |
| Barone Hostini di Sant'Ermo | La Suvera |
| Benagotti | Tenuta di Ghizzano |
| Cantina delle Colline Pisane | Usigliano del Vescovo |
| Cittadella | Vino del Caratello (Salvadori) |
| Fattoria Cempini Meazzuoli | |

– **Chianti Montalbano** r. dr.   ★→★★★   80 82 83

The Montalbano balcony of hills W of Florence and S of Pistoia is more
noted for Carmignano, but Chianti can also reach admirable levels here,
usually in soft, fruity wines to drink in 1–5 years.

| | |
|---|---|
| Bibbiani | Fattoria di Montorio |
| Fattoria Belvedere | Fattoria Il Poggiolo |
| Fattoria di Artimino | Tenuta di Capezzana |
| Fattoria di Bacchereto | Tenuta di Lucciano (Spalletti) |

**– Chianti Rufina** r. dr. ★★→★★★★
The smallest zone, in hills above the Sieve River E of Florence, produces some of the most grandiose Chianti. Rufina's vineyards lie at a relatively high altitude, which can be sensed in the rarefied bouquet and lingering elegance of well-aged wines, notably Selvapiana, Fattoria di Vetrice, Castello di Nipozzano and the special vineyard Montesodi.

Antiche Fattorie
Busini
Camperiti
Castello di Nipozzano (Frescobaldi)
Fattoria Altomena
Fattoria di Bossi
Fattoria di Vetrice
Fattoria Parga

Grignano
Montesodi (Frescobaldi)
Petrogano
Poggio a Remole (Frescobaldi)
Poggio Reale (Spalletti)
Pomino (Frescobaldi)
Selvapiana
Tenuta di Poggio
Vitirufina

**Colline Lucchesi** DOC r. w. dr. ★→★★★ 81 82 83
Rosso delle Colline Lucchesi, a good Chianti-style red grown in the hills around Lucca now shares its zone with a white based on Trebbiano. The red can be soft and lively to drink in a year or two or, in some cases, as durable and elegant as a fine Chianti. The white is an unknown entity.

Alberto Bertolli
Fattoria Bruguier
Fattoria di Forci
Fattoria di Fubbiano

Fattoria I Tre Cancelli
Maionchi
Tenuta Maria Teresa

**Coltassala** r. dr. ★★★→★★★★ 80 81 82 83
A special vineyard red from Sangiovese and Mammolo grown at Volpaia in Chianti Classico and seasoned in small, new oak barrels. Rich and refined, it has the complexity of bouquet and flavors to add a new dimension to Tuscan red wines.
Castello di Volpaia

**Concerto** r. dr.
A newly conceived Cabernet from near Castellina in Chianti. Tasters of the wine in *barrique* indicate it has remarkable potential.
Castello di Fonterutoli.

**Elba** DOC r. w. dr. (sp.) ★→★★★ 79 81 82 83
The island where Napoleon encouraged viticulture during his brief exile is noted for iron-rich soil which lends vigor to wines. The *rosso*, from nearly the same grapes as Chianti, is usually bright ruby and grapy, an all-purpose wine to drink young, though the red of Tenuta La Chiusa stands out for its full body, depth, and bouquet, reaching peaks of elegance in 4–8 years. The *bianco*, from Procanico (Trebbiano) chiefly, is light straw gold, delicately scented, dry but rather full-bodied, and soft, though the best have a crisp finish. A *spumante* is also permitted.

Azienda Agricola di Mola
M. Gasparri & C.
Podere La Pianella

Tenuta Acquabona
Tenuta La Chiusa
Vinicola Elbana

**Flaccianello della Pieve** r. dr. 81 82 83
One of a growing number of new-style red wines about to debut in Chianti. This is a pure Sangiovese aged in new oak.
Fontodi

**Fontanelle Chardonnay** w. dr. 82 83
Banfi's Ezio Rivella pioneered this California-style, wood-aged Chardonnay from new vineyards at Montalcino. Too novel to rate definitively, its oaky character impressed some experts as showing the style that will make it a sure winner on the international market.
Villa Banfi

**Galestro** w. dr. ★★ DYA
New-style white backed by a consortium of producers equipped to vinify this basically simple but technologically advanced product. Based on Trebbiano with other light grapes grown in central Tuscany, it puts to profitable use the excess of light grapes in Chianti. Uniquely among Italian wines it has a maximum alcohol grade of 10.5% and must be processed and bottled entirely at low temperature. The result is a light, dry, pale, modern wine, attractively fresh and fruity and made in growing volume with exemplary consistency.

Agricoltori di Chianti Geografico
Barone Ricasoli

C.S. Colli Aretini
Cecchi

Fattoria Fonti
Fattorie Giannozzi
Il Raccianello
Le Chiantigiane
Marchesi Antinori

Marchesi de' Frescobaldi
Rocca del Macie
Ruffino
Teruzzi-Puthod (Ponte a Rondelino)

**Ghiaie della Furba** r. dr. ★★★→★★★★ 78 79 81 82 83
Newly conceived red of Cabernet Sauvignon and Cabernet Franc with
Merlot grown in low-lying, gravelly vineyards near Carmignano. Early
vintages of this racy, Bordeaux-style wine are still immature, but with
time they promise to reinforce the estate's already lofty status.
Tenuta di Capezzana

**Granato di Scarlino** r. dr. ★★ 81 82 83
Tasty red in the Chianti mold made at Scarlino near Grosseto. Of
bright ruby-garnet color, it has full bouquet and lively warm flavor after
3–4 years, sometimes more.
Righetti-Lancione

**Grattamacco** r. w. dr. ★★→★★★ 81 82 83
Inspired wines made by Piermario Meletti Cavallari near Castagneto
Carducci in coastal hills SE of Livorno. The *rosso*, from Colorino,
Sangiovese, and light varieties, has irresistible berry-like goodness in its
youth. The *bianco*, of Trebbiano, Malvasia and others, is fruity, zestful, as
poised as whites of supposedly nobler breed. The estate is also preparing
a red based on Cabernet and aged in new oak.
Podere di Grattamacco

**Grifi** r. dr. ★★★★ 81 82 83
Recently conceived red of Sangiovese and a localized clone of Cabernet
grown near Montepulciano and aged in new *barriques*. The limited
bottling of '81 showed race and splendor which should reach prime in
5–8 years.
Avignonesi

**I Sodi di San Niccolò** r. dr. ★★★→★★★★ 79 80 81 82 83
In the new wave of single-vineyard Tuscan reds aged in new French oak,
this has moved quickly to the forefront. From Sangiovese, Canaiolo and
Malvasia Nera grown near Castellina in Chianti, it has the depth and
complexity to improve for 6–8 years or more.
Castellare di Castellina

**La Corte** r. dr. ★★★ 78 79 81 82 83
A special vineyard Sangiovese grown in Chianti Classico, aged in *barrique*
and fined in bottle. The '78 from this progressive estate was delicate and
finely tuned like a Pauillac.
Castello di Querceto

**Le Crete** w. dr. ★★★ DYA
Brisk and flowery with well-balanced fruit and green apple aspect make
it very nice young.
Tenuta Caparzo

**Le Pergole Torte** r. dr. ★★★→★★★★ 77 78 79 81 82 83
This might have been Chianti Classico if winemaker Sergio Manetti had
not preferred to use Sangiovese alone in this prototype single-vineyard
bottling. Aged in small, new oak barrels, it has the breed and
equilibrium to expect a long and splendid life.
Monte Vertine

**Malvasia** w. dr. (r.) (sw.)
The ancient vine has many clones grown in Tuscany, used in Chianti
(alas) but more suitably in white wines both dry and sweet (Vin Santo).
Though rarely noteworthy on its own, Avignonesi's '83 Malvasia (★★★) –
dry, smooth, silky, even elegant – hints that better things might be
coming.
Avignonesi

**Maremma** r. p. w. dr. ★→★★ 81 82 83
Wines from the coastal Maremma hills of Grosseto province have
attracted notice for their sound virtues. The *rosso*, from Sangiovese and
others, is bright ruby, fragrant, and round, good in 1–4 years. The *rosato*,
from dark grapes, is lively when young. The *bianco*, from Procanico
(Trebbiano), Ansonica, and Vermentino, is light and fruity, ideal with
fish inside a year. Of note are the wines of Capalbio, Montepescali and

the Val di Cornia

| | |
|---|---|
| Alberese | Montepescali Cantina |
| Jacopo Banti | Cooperativa |
| C.S. Capalbio | Monte Santo (Cordella) |
| Fattoria Poggeti | Podere San Luigi |
| A. Lippi | Tenuta di Montecucco |
| Marruchetone | |

**Monte Antico** r. w. dr.  ★→★★★   75 77 78 79 81 82 83
DOC has been requested for wines from Monte Antico in hills between
Siena and Grosseto, adjacent to Montalcino. The *rosso*, from Sangiovese,
Canaiolo, and light varieties, is deep ruby tending to garnet-orange with
5–6 years, dry, elegant, with deep bouquet and long finish. The *bianco*,
from Trebbiano and Malvasia, is pale gold, soft, and scented when
young. Castello di Monte Antico red stands out.

| | |
|---|---|
| Ardenghesca | Fattoria La Pievanella |
| Castello di Monte Antico | |

**Montecarlo** DOC r. w. dr.  ★★→★★★  82 83
The zone E of Lucca is known for its white. Though based on Trebbiano,
the supplementary varieties – Sémillon, the Pinots, Vermentino,
Sauvignon, Roussanne – distinguish it and give producers a chance to
create styles. Bright straw, delicate and flowery, it is suavely fruity and
sumptuous with a crisp finish. Some vintages improve beyond a year or
two. DOC has expanded to include a red based on Sangiovese, which
shows promise (see Rosso di Cercatoia) even if it isn't established yet.

| | |
|---|---|
| Buonasola | Fattoria La Torre |
| Cerruglio (Tori) | Fattoria Manzini |
| Eredi di Carmignani | Fattoria Michi |
| Fattoria del Buonamico | Romano Franceschini |
| Fattoria del Teso | Poderi San Luigi |
| Fattoria di Montecarlo | |

**Montescudaio** DOC r. w. dr. (am.) (sw.)  ★→ ★★   79 81 82 83
This hilly zone inland from Cecina in Pisa province has three types of
wine. The *rosso*, from Sangiovese and light grapes, is bright ruby,
scented, and soft, good in 2–5 years. The *bianco*, based on Trebbiano, if
rarely inspiring can be tasty young. The rare Vin Santo, from semidried
light grapes, must be aged in small barrels in the traditional way and
have 17% alcohol, whether sweet or dry.

| | |
|---|---|
| Fattoria San Giovanni | La Rinserrata |
| Fattoria Santa Maria | Podere Morazzano |

**Morellino di Scansano** DOC r. dr.  ★★→★★★   77 78 79 81 82 83
Recent DOC from hills SE of Grosseto around Scansano, this is the only
classified Tuscan red besides Brunello that may be made entirely from
Sangiovese. Deep ruby tending to garnet, it develops big bouquet and
dry, warm, austere, fairly robust balance with long finish in 4–5 years,
sometimes more. An appellation to watch.
Ag. *riserva* 2 yrs.

| | |
|---|---|
| Banditaccia | C.S. del Morellino di Scansano |
| Erik Banti | Sellari Franceschini |
| Fattoria Palazzaccio | |

**Morillone** r. dr.  ★★  83
From Sangiovese, Cabernet, Montepulciano and more grown at San
Giamignano, this is a supple, mouth-filling red of youthful appeal.
Terruzzi & Puthod (Ponte a Rondolino)

**Moscadello di Montalcino** DOC w. s/sw. sw. fz.  ★★  DYA
Of ancient renown, this sweet Moscato from Montalcino has been
revived as a DOC, thanks largely to the American giant Villa Banfi and
its heavy investment in a futuristic winery and vast vineyards. Though
aimed at the U.S. market, Moscadello should find admirers elsewhere,
for its Muscat fragrance, clean sweetness and bubbles seem to be in
vogue. There is also a still and sweeter version, though rarely seen.

| | |
|---|---|
| Tenuta Il Poggione | Villa Banfi |

**Palazzo Altesi** r. dr.  ★★★→★★★★  80 81 82 83
Another in the new breed of Tuscan reds, this comes from Brunello
grapes grown at Montalcino but vinified in a Burgundy style and aged in
small barrels of Limousin oak. Soft and smooth, precociously elegant, it
should hold its charm for up to a decade.
Altesino

**Parrina** DOC r. w. dr.  ★★  81 82 83
Tiny zone in hills E of the Argentario promontory in S Tuscany. The
*rosso*, based on Sangiovese, is bright ruby, fruity, neatly dry, balanced,
and tasty in 2–4 years. The *bianco*, from Procanico (Trebbiano), is light
golden and grapy with a bitter undertone, good young.
Fattoria del Chiusone          Fattoria La Parrina

**Pomino** DOC r. w. dr. (s/sw.)  ★★→★★★  82 83
New DOC for red, white and Vin Santo made in one of the oldest
recognized wine areas of Tuscany in the Chianti Rufina area. The *rosso*,
from Sangiovese with Canaiolo, Cabernet and Merlot, is enticingly
smooth and round, to enjoy in 2–6 years, sometimes considerably more.
The *bianco*, already renowned from Frescobaldi, is based on Pinot Bianco
and Chardonnay with Trebbiano. Pale golden, flowery, smoothly dry
with polish, it has the stuff to last several years. A special reserve bottling
known as Il Benefizio was barrel fermented from '73 and '78 and
rounded out in *barriques* to give an oaky, richly scented wine that
promises ★★★★ when it mellows into form. The Vin Santo from raisined
grapes follows traditional standards.
Ag. 1 yr; *riserva* 3 yrs; Vin Santo 4 yrs in barrels.
Marchesi de'Frescobaldi

**Rosato** or **Rosé**
Many rosés are made in Tuscany, usually from Sangiovese blended with
other varieties. Most popular is Ruffino's simplistic Rosatello. Antinori's
Rosé di Bolgheri (now DOC) and Frescobaldi's Villa di Corte show
blossomy class. Impressive rosés have been issued in Chianti Classico by
Badia a Coltibuono and Castello di San Polo in Rosso. Among the
artisanal-style rosés, two from the Montescudaio zone stand out: Rosato
da Morazzano and Rosato La Rinserrata. Vin Ruspo, now Carmignano
DOC as Rosato, is also noteworthy.

**Rosso dei Vigneti di Brunello**
Forbidden name for young red wine from Brunello grapes grown in
Montalcino. The new DOC Rosso di Montalcino replaces the name,
though bottles from vintages previous to 1983 may still be seen.

**Rosso della Lega** r. dr.
Proposed appellation to be used by members of the Chianti Classico
*consorzio* for red wine not classified as Chianti.

**Rosso delle Colline Lucchesi**
This long-standing DOC now comes under Colline Lucchesi.

**Rosso di Cercatoia** r. dr.  ★★→★★★★  75 77 78 79 81 82 83
Fine red made at Montecarlo near Lucca from Sangiovese and other
varieties selected in top vintages and aged in oak casks. Deep ruby-
garnet, over 3–6 years it develops rich bouquet and, from Fattoria del
Buonamico, the velvety texture of good red Burgundy. This may now
qualify as Montecarlo Rosso DOC.
Eredi di Carmignani          Fattoria del Buonamico

**Rosso di Montalcino** DOC r. dr.  ★★→★★★★  83
New appellation for red wine from Brunello grapes of Montalcino not
aged long enough to qualify as Brunello di Montalcino. This serves as a
second-tier DOC. Though lacking the austere, tannic complexity of aged
Brunello, this Rosso can make eminently delightful drinking at much
lower cost. Generous in color, bouquet and body, round, complete, even
noble – some prefer this style to Brunello, which has been criticized for
having too much cask age. Good young, some versions could age.

| | |
|---|---|
| Altesino | Fattoria Val di Suga |
| Argiano | La Chiesa di Santa Restituta |
| Camigliano | La Magia |
| Campogiovanni | Lisini |
| Capanna | Mastrojanni |
| Casanova | Poggio alle Mura |
| Case Basse | San Filippo dei Comunali |
| Col d'Orcia | Tenuta Caparzo |
| Colombaio di Montosoli | Tenuta Il Poggione |
| Fattoria Poggio Antico | Villa Banfi |

**Rubizzo** r. dr.  ★★  DYA
Youthful, light ruby wine from red grapes for Chianti vinified under a
modern *governo* method that leaves it soft, fruity, full of brio – "the perfect

wine for spicy food", as estate owner Italo Zingarelli puts it.
Rocca delle Macìe

**Sammarco** r. dr. ★★★→★★★★  80 81 82 83
This fine Cabernet Sauvignon-Franc aged in new oak barrels has
convinced owner Alceo Di Napoli that his future is in Cabernet and not
Chianti Classico. A big red with the pronounced grass and pepper
character of young Cabernet, its type is closer to Napa than Bordeaux,
though time should bring out its own brand of style.
Castello dei Rampolla

**San Angelo Pinot Grigio** w. dr.  ★★  DYA
From young vines planted at Montalcino, this Pinot Grigio debuted
from the '83 vintage. Already impressive – with good fruit and balance
and a pale brass color – it could rival top Pinot Grigio from the north.
Villa Banfi

**San Giocondo** r. dr.  ★★  DYA
Italy's most popular *vino novello*, like Beaujolais *nouveau* its sprightly,
grapy freshness is best within 3–4 months. (See also *Vini novelli*.)
Marchesi Antinori

**Sangiovese** or **Sangioveto della Toscana** r. dr.
The mainstay of most Tuscan DOC red wines, Sangiovese in its various
clones is also used in non-classified bottlings ranging from ordinary *vino
da tavola* to the new-style *barrique*-aged reds (sometimes blended with
Cabernet) that are revolutionizing Tuscan viniculture.

**Sangioveto delle Torri** r. dr.  ★★★  82 83
Pure Sangioveto Grosso grown in the Colli Fiorentini near Barberino
Val d'Elsa is seasoned in small, new oak barrels. Supple but well
structured with deep ruby-garnet color, it needs 2–3 years to develop
bouquet and possibly another 5 to reach perfection.
Le Torri (Campiglioni)

**Sanjoveto di Coltibuono**
Pure Sangiovese grown in Chianti Classico and aged in new oak. Badia a
Coltibuono's old vines give wine of great authority that should be among
the most durable of the new Tuscan reds. Early tastings point to ★★★★.
Badia a Coltibuono

**Sassicaia** r. dr. ★★★→★★★★  72 76 77 78 79 80 81 82 83
This Cabernet Sauvignon from the Tenuta San Guido at Bolgheri SE of
Livorno is a contemporary legend, admired in Italy and abroad
("Perhaps Italy's best red wine" – Hugh Johnson) despite limited
production of 50,000–60,000 bottles a year. A curiosity in Tuscany, it
thrives in weak vintages ('72, '76) for other reds. Aged 2 years in
*barriques*, this full ruby-garnet wine needs 5 years in bottle to bring out
deep, herby bouquet and rich, velvety, warm flavor with Bordeaux-like
breed and California-like structure. The '81 vintage was outstanding.
Marchesi Incisa della Rocchetta

**Solaia** r. dr. 79 81 82 83
Selected from the Solaia plot in Chianti Classico, this Cabernet
Sauvignon from barrels showed style, depth and power of top-notch
Napa and Sonoma bottlings – though it will need several years more to
prove its certain ★★★★ as the best evidence yet that Chianti can produce
superb Cabernet.
Marchesi Antinori

**Tavernelle Cabernet Sauvignon** r. dr. 82 83
From Cabernet Sauvignon grown at Montalcino and aged in new
French oak, barrel samples showed the youthfully awkward vigor of the
variety. Guided by Ezio Rivella's expert hands, this should emerge in
time as a noteworthy Cabernet in the California style.
Villa Banfi

**Tignanello** r. dr.  ★★★★  75 77 78 79 80 81 82 83
From Sangiovese grown in Chianti with about 10% Cabernet, this is
among the most admired and imitated reds of Italy, the brainchild of
Antinori enologist Giacomo Tachis. Despite the mixed background,
Tignanello has aristocratic breed with complexity – from aging in small
oak barrels – that should reach a peak in 7–10 years.
Marchesi Antinori

**Torricella** w. dr.   ★★★   77 81
Extraordinary white made only in years when conditions were ideal
(recently '77 and '81) from Malvasia grown at Brolio in Chianti Classico.
Left briefly in oak casks and then for a decade or more in bottle, which
heightens its bouquet and refines its smoothly dry, lingering flavor.
Barone Ricasoli

**Trebbiano** w. dr. (fz.) (sw.) DYA
The overwhelming light variety turns up in nearly every white of
Tuscany, usually in unremarkable but zesty wines to drink quickly.
Some *vino da tavola* carries the varietal name, though usually Trebbiano is
used anonymously in both DOC and table wines, and also Vin Santo.

**Val d'Arbia** DOC w. dr. (s/sw.)   ★→★★   DYA
New DOC for dry white and Vin Santo grown in the Arbia valley
between Radda in Chianti and Montalcino. Bianco della Val d'Arbia –
based on Trebbiano and Malvasia – is delicate, dry, clean and fruity
when vinified at low temperature. Vin Santo follows the usual lines.

| | |
|---|---|
| Barone Ricasoli | Pieve a Barca |
| Casale del Bosco (Nardi) | San Felice |
| Castell'in Villa | Tolomei |
| Fattoria di Vistarenni | Villa di Radi |

**Vernaccia di San Gimignano** DOC w. dr. (sw.) (fz.) (sp.)
★→★★★   81 82 83
Ancient white from Vernaccia grown around the towered hill town. For
years made by traditional methods into a golden wine of some aging
capacity, the trend is toward clean, pale, flowery wines to drink young.
Leading producers are Falchini, with a smooth-textured style, and
Teruzzi & Puthod, whose singular *riserva* from Ponte a Rondolino has
brought out Vernaccia's too often hidden charms. Bubbly versions are
increasing; the *liquoroso* seems nearly extinct.
Ag. *riserva* 1 yr.

| | |
|---|---|
| Castello di Montauto | Il Palagetto (Frigeni-Sonzogni) |
| Castello di Pescile | Guicciardini-Strozzi (Cusona) |
| Riccardo Falchini (Casale) | Il Palagio |
| Fattoria della Quercia | Il Raccianello |
| Fattoria di Fugnano | La Quercia di Racciano |
| Fattoria di Monte Oliveto | Montenidoli (Fagiuoli) |
| Fattoria di Pancole | San Quirico |
| Fattoria di Pietrafitta | Teruzzi & Puthod |
| Fattoria La Torre | (Ponte a Rondolino) |
| Fattoria Tollena | Fratelli Vagnoni |
| Giulio Frigeni | |

**Villa Antinori Bianco** w. dr.   ★★★   82 83
Impeccable white from Trebbiano and nobler varieties grown on
Antinori estates in Chianti Classico. Pale golden and delicate in scent, it
has some of the refinement of a good, dry white Graves.
Marchesi Antinori

**Vin Ruspo or Vinruspo**
See Carmignano Rosato.

**Vin Santo** am. (r.) s/sw.   ★★→★★★
This traditional sipping wine ("holy wine" probably refers to use in the
Mass) is made all over Tuscany from grapes semidried on racks or by
hanging from rafters, pressed, and sealed in *caratelli* (small barrels) in
lofts for at least 3 years. Vintages vary intricately from place to place,
though good Vin Santo can last for years. Most comes from Malvasia
and Trebbiano, but dark grapes and red wine also figure. Whether
sweet, semisweet or austerely dry, Vin Santo should be clear golden-
amber, generously aromatic, strong (14–17%), and velvety. At best (the
maximum ★★★★ is Avignonesi's luxuriant Vin Santo), it can be one of
Italy's great dessert wines. But too often it is crudely improvised,
oxidized, unpleasant. Industrial imitations (often from S Italian
Moscato) are widespread. A regionwide classification has been delayed,
but Vin Santo is DOC under Bianco di Valdinievole, Carmignano,
Montescudaio, Pomino and Val d'Arbia, so producers in those zones are
listed there. Every Tuscan farm has its own production, so only a choice
few are cited.

| | |
|---|---|
| Avignonesi | Brolio (Ricasoli) |
| Badia a Coltibuono | Giovanni Cappelli   ▶ |

Aldo Casagni
Castell'in Villa
Castellare di Castellina
Castello di Uzzano
Castello di Volpaia
Cennatoio
Riccardo Falchini (Casale)
Fattoria dei Barbi
Fattoria di Martignana
Fattoria Pagnana

Guicciardini Strozzi (Cusona)
Lisini
Marchesi Antinori
Marchesi de'Frescobaldi
Monte Vertine
Pagliarese
Poggio al Sole
San Giorgio a Lapi
Tenuta Il Poggione
Tenuta La Lellera

**Vinattieri Rosso** r. dr. 82 83
From Sangiovese Grosso selected in Montalcino and Chianti and aged in
new French oak by winemaker Maurizio Castelli. Before release, the
authoritative, richly complex '82 vintage promised a top ranking among
Tuscany's new reds.
Vinattieri

**Vino della Signora** w. dr.  ★★  82 83
From Traminer grown in Chianti Classico, this golden-green wine is
typically aromatic, smooth, and softly attractive in 1–2 years.
Poggio al Sole

**Vino Nobile di Montepulciano** DOC-DOCG r. dr.  ★→ ★★★★
70 75 77 78 79 80 81 82 83
The hill town of Montepulciano in SE Tuscany is the home of this red
with the resounding name and the honor of having been Italy's first
DOCG (in 1983). But the modern version of what the poet Redi
described in the 17th century as "king of all wines" lacks consistency.
Though it can be splendid on rare occasions, it is more often rustic,
oxidized, astringent – a direct result of faulty vinification and aging
techniques. DOCG might have helped weed out inferior products, but
instead early examples often showed traditional flaws. Vino Nobile
resembles Chianti *riserva* in grape content – a clone of Sangiovese,
Prugnolo Gentile, dominates the blend of red and white varieties – as
well as in character. Deep garnet turning to brick red with age, it is noted
for a trace of violets in bouquet and an austerely dry, somewhat tannic
flavor, which can become truly noble after 3–4 years and stay so for over
a decade. Recent tastings have shown inherent class from Avignonesi,
Poderi Boscarelli, Fassati, Fattoria di Fognano, Montenero, Casella, and
the rapidly improving Poliziano. But some of the established names seem
rather stagnant. Annual production is about 1.8 million liters.
Ag. 2 yrs; *riserva* 3 yrs; *riserva speciale* 4 yrs.

Avignonesi
Fratelli Bologna Buonsignori
Carletti della Giovanpaola
Casella (Carpini)
Fassati
Fattoria del Cerro
Fattoria di Fognano
Fattoria di Gracciano
  (Mazzucchelli)

Gattavecchi
Il Macchione
Montenero
Poderi Boscarelli
Poggio alla Sala
Poliziano
Giuseppe Raspanti & Figli
Tenuta di Gracciano (Della Seta)
Tenuta Sant'Agnese (Fanetti)

**Vini Novelli** r. dr.  ★→★★  DYA
The *nouveau* reds to drink within weeks after the harvest are burgeoning
in Tuscany, as elsewhere, though there are signs that the fad might be
fading. After Antinori's San Giocondo, there is Frescobaldi's Nuovo
Fiore, Villa Banfi's Santa Costanza, Col d'Orcia's Novembrino,
Monsanto's Primizio, Rocca delle Macie's Dicembrino, and more. Their
fragility should prevent them from being exported extensively.

## Wine & Food

Contemporary Tuscan food is a triumph of nature: simplified
country cooking, it lacks imagination, but is an accurate
expression of the almost mystical equilibrium Tuscans maintain
with their land. The elaborations exported to France by the
Medici are long gone and mostly forgotten. Also vanishing,

sadly, are the inspired dishes that used to take cheerful Tuscan mammas all morning to create. But the basics are still there: bread and the emerald-green *extra vergine* olive oil that combine so well in *bruschetta* and *panunto*; exquisite vegetables and greens that make a *minestrone* easy (Tuscans have always been more resourceful with soups than pasta); the rosemary, garlic, onion, sage, basil, bay leaves, and tarragon that heighten flavor; and, of course, the bean, so adored that when detractors couldn't think of anything worse they called the Tuscans *mangiafagioli* (bean eaters). Meat, simply grilled or roasted, is essential in the diet: chicken, pork, duck, and Florence's highly rated *bisteca alla fiorentina* (the hefty slab of beef from native Chianina steers). Boar and game birds are also prized in this most wooded Italian region. Some of Italy's tastiest *pecorino* comes from sheep grazed in the stark *crete* hills of Siena province, notably around Pienza.

**Acquacotta** "Cooked water," soup of vegetables in season and mushrooms.
 ★★ Parrina *bianco*.
**Arista** Pork loin roasted with rosemary and garlic.
 ★★★ Vino Nobile di Montepulciano.
**Bistecca alla fiorentina** Thick steak charred on the outside, pink inside, served with beans and oil.
 ★★★→★★★★ Chianti *riserva*.
**Cacciucco alla livornese** Piquant fish soup with garlic toast.
 ★★★ Grattamacco *bianco*.
**Cenci** Twists of fried dough with powdered sugar.
 ★★ Vin Santo.
**Crostini di fegato** Breadcrusts with chicken liver paté.
 ★★ Chianti young.
**Fegatelli di maiale** Pork livers spit-roasted with bay leaves.
 ★★→★★★ Morellino di Scansano.

**Gramugia** Ancient soup of Lucca with onions, artichokes, fava beans, asparagus, and bacon.
 ★★ Montecarlo *bianco*.
**Panzanella** Stale bread soaked with water and crumbled with chopped tomatoes, onions, basil, oil, and vinegar in a sort of salad.
 ★★→★★★ Vernaccia di San Gimignano.
**Pappardelle alla lepre** Wide ribbon noodles with rich hare sauce.
 ★★ Chianti Colli Aretini.
**Ribollita** Hearty *minestrone* with beans, black cabbage, and other vegetables, thickened at the end with bread.
 ★★ Chianti Colli Senesi
**Tordi allo spiedo** Spit-roasted wood thrush.
 ★★★→★★★★ Brunello di Montalcino or
 ★★★→★★★★ Carmignano.

## Restaurants

Recommended in or near wine zones: **Bolgheri** *Gambero Rosso* at San Vincenzo, *Il Biondo* at Sassetta. **Carmignano** *Da Delfina* at Artimino; *Cantina di Toia* at Bacchereto; *Erta del Moro* at Carmignano. **Chianti Classico** *La Torre* at Castellina in Chianti; *Badia a Coltibuono* and *Spaltenna* at Gaiole; *Giovanni da Verrazzano* at Greve; *La Biscondola* at Mercatale Val di Pesa; *Montagliari* and *Villa Le Barone* at Panzano; *La Baracchina* and *Tavernetta Serristori* near San Casciano Val di Pesa; *La Taverna* at Vagliagli. **Colli Aretini** *Castello di Sorci* at Anghiari; *Vicolo del Contento* at Castelfranco di Sopra. **Colli Fiorentini** *La Tavolozza* at Grassina; *Belvedere* at Impruneta. **Colli Senesi** *La Frateria di Padre Eligio* at Cetona; *La Casanova* at Chianciano Terme; *Il Patriarca* near Chiusi; *La Chiusa* at Montefollonico; *Il Pozzo* at Monteriggioni; *Antica Trattoria Bottega Nova* near Siena; *Locanda L'Amorosa* near Sinalunga. **Lucca-Montecarlo** *Forassiepi* and *La Nina* at Montecarlo; *Vipore* at Pieve Santo Stefano; *Trattoria La Mora* at Ponte a Moriano; *Solferino* at San Macario in Piano. **Montalcino** *Edgardo* and *Il Giglio* at Montalcino. **San Gimignano** *Le Terrazze* and *Ponte a Rondolino* at San Gimignano.

Umbria's special aptitude for wine is not as widely noted as it might be. The only name of enduring fame is Orvieto, from the hill town where Etruscans mastered winemaking techniques two millennia before its golden nectar inspired Renaissance artists. After a lapse, Orvieto has bounded back as one of Italy's most exported whites. But the region's grandest *crus* flourish at Torgiano, though their reputations lag behind their remarkable class. The only other name known beyond the region is Colli del Trasimeno, wines from the basin of central Italy's largest lake.

Umbria is a treasure trove of local wines. Three promising DOCs have been added recently – Colli Altotiberini, Colli Perugini and Montefalco. But the rest, including some rarities, oddities, and antiquities, comprise a jumble of names and types, ranging from inspired, sometimes superb examples of wine-making skills down to the hit-and-miss results of the undying peasant tradition.

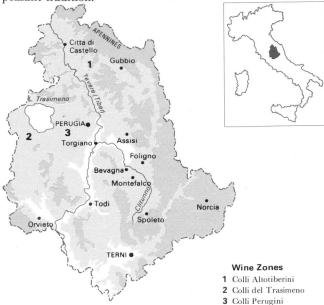

**Wine Zones**
1 Colli Altotiberini
2 Colli del Trasimeno
3 Colli Perugini

A startling variety of vines grows here. Besides the standard Sangiovese, Canaiolo, Trebbiano, and Malvasia, there are Grechetto, Montepulciano, Verdicchio, and intriguing out-siders, some of which have been here since the last century, some just introduced: Merlot, Cabernet, Barbera, Tocai, Traminer, Garganega, Gamay, Nebbiolo, Dolcetto, the Pinots, Chardon-nay, Riesling, and more. It will be fascinating to see what becomes of them as techniques improve.

Discovering Umbria's wines can be as exciting as exploring its ancient towns. Halfway between Rome and Florence, crossed by the *Autostrada del Sole* and other fast roads, the region mixes art and history with the bucolic attractions of a countryside noted as "the green heart of Italy." Perugia, the capital, has splendid museums, Orvieto its Duomo, Spoleto its "Festival of the Two Worlds," and Assisi its religious shrines. Then there are Gubbio, Spello, Todi, Narni, Città di Castello, and other places where history is not a thing of the past. Enophiles should not miss the *Museo del Vino* at Torgiano, a model of the genre, or the *Enoteca Regionale* at Perugia. Interesting *enoteche* have also opened recently at Città di Castello and Orvieto. The *Enoteca Vino Vino* at Terni provides a sage selection.

## Recent vintages

Umbria has cool, damp winters and warm, dry summers, one of Italy's most consistently favorable climates for wine. For instance, from 1970 through 1983, Orvieto reported good to excellent harvests every year except 1972 and 1976. Torgiano was also weak in 1972 and 1976, but had good to very good results in other years, exceptional in 1970, 1971, 1975, 1980 and 1982.

**Almonte** r. dr. ★→★★ 81 82 83
From Sangiovese, Barbera, and light grapes grown at Frontignano near Todi, this medium, ruby-garnet wine is nicely fragrant, though its innate goodness may be disturbed by lack of balance. Drink inside 4 years.
Vagniluca

**Assisi** r. p. w. dr. ★→★★★ 81 82 83
The hills around the famous shrine have been producing good wines for years, recently consistent enough to aspire to DOC. Rosso di Assisi (Merlot and others) is deep purple, mellow, juicy and mouth-filling, best in 2–4 years. The *rosato*, from the same dark grapes, is fresh and tasty young. Bianco di Assisi, from Grechetto Trebbiano, Malvasia and others, can be round and smooth when young.
Sasso Rosso                                     Tili

**Bianco d'Arquata** w. dr. ★→★★ 80 81 82 83
From Grechetto, Trebbiano, and others grown near Bevagna, S of Perugia. From the 1977 and 1980 vintages, this light golden-green wine had perfumed, textured suavity and range of nuances strikingly Burgundian in style.
Adanti

**Cabernet Sauvignon di Miralduolo** r. dr. ★★★ 77 78 79 80 81 82 83
This Cabernet from Torgiano is deep garnet purple, generous in herby, berry-like bouquet, dry but fat, and still a touch assertive because Cabernet vines – and wines – need time to mature. With time, this could equal the glories of Torgiano Rubesco *riserva*.
Lungarotti

**Castel Grifone** p. dr. ★★ DYA
Brilliant pink from the same grapes as Torgiano *rosso* fermented at low temperature to crisp, fruity goodness.
Lungarotti

**Castello di Montoro** r. dr. ★★→★★★ 75 77 78 79 80 81 82 83
Winning composite of Sangiovese, Merlot, Barbera, and Montepulciano grown at Montoro di Narni near Terni. Ruby red tending to garnet, with 5–8 years, its subtle bouquet and warm, lingering flavor show elegant complexity.
Marchesi Patrizi Montoro

**Chardonnay di Miralduolo** w. dr. ★★→★★★ 82 83
Impressive wood-aged Chardonnay from a special plot at Torgiano. Flowery and finely balanced, it has the structure to improve over 2–3 years. With time, this could become an exemplary Chardonnay.
Lungarotti

**Colle del Cardinale** r. dr. ★★ 79 80 81 82 83
Good red from Sangiovese, Merlot, and Barbera grown just outside Perugia. Its early robustness smoothens with 5–6 years of age.
Podere Collecorno

**Colli Altotiberini** DOC r. p. w. dr.　★→[★★★]　80 81 82 83
Recent DOC in the upper Tiber valley around Città di Castello applies
to three types, some well made, some decidedly countryish. The *rosso*,
from Sangiovese and Merlot, is ruby red, pleasantly vinous when young,
fairly robust, with enough tannin to take 3–4 years of age, sometimes
more. The *rosato*, from the same grapes, is bright roseate, clean, fragrant
and fruity within a year or two – notably from Colle del Sole and
Castello di Ascagnano. The *bianco*, based on Trebbiano, varies so much
that it is hard to define a style.

| | |
|---|---|
| Bizzi | Carlo Ferri |
| Gino Campanelli & Figli | Silvio Nardi (Montione) |
| Castello di Ascagnano | Panicale |
| Colecchio (Cristini) | Pie' di Murlo (Tondini) |
| Donini | Colle del Sole (Polidori) |
| Enoagricola-Montone | Fratelli Renzacci |
| Roscetti | Tenuta di Montecorona |
| San Rocco (Gasperini) | Antognolla |

**Colli del Trasimeno** DOC r. w.　★→[★★★]　79 81 82 83
This vast zone which surrounds Lake Trasimeno has two types of wine
and an emerging reputation. The *rosso*, from Sangiovese, Ciliegiolo, and
Gamay, is bright ruby tending to garnet with 2–6 years of age, with fine,
flowery scent and lively, fruity flavor. The *bianco*, from Trebbiano,
Malvasia, Verdicchio, and Grechetto, is light straw, subtle in scent, with
fresh, balanced crispness when young.

| | |
|---|---|
| Belvedere (Illuminati) | Lamborghini (La Fiorita) |
| C.S. del Trasimeno | Po' del Vento (Anichini) |
| Fattoria San Litardo | Sovrano Militare Ordine di Malta |
| Grifo di Boldrino (La Querciolana) | |

**Colli Perugini** DOC r. p. w. dr.　★→[★★]　82 83
Umbria's newest DOC covers *rosso*, *rosato* and bianco grown in the hills
along the Tiber between Perugia and Todi. The *rosso* and *rosato* are based
on Sangiovese, the *bianco* on Trebbiano Toscano.

**Corbara** or **Lago di Corbara** r. dr.　[★★]　81 82 83
Red wine based on Sangiovese grown near Lago di Corbara SE of
Orvieto. Ruby, smooth, and lightly bitter, it is best in 3–4 years.

| | |
|---|---|
| Barberani | Bigi |

**Decugnano dei Barbi Rosso** r. dr.　★★★　81 82 83
Stunningly fruity red from Sangiovese and Cabernet grown near Lake
Corbara. Deep ruby, fresh in bouquet and grapy in flavor, it has the
finesse of a fine Beaujolais.
Decugnano dei Barbi

**Fior di Mosto** p. dr.　★★　DYA
Pleasantly fragile rosé from dark grapes grown at Pierantonio, N of
Perugia. Bright pink, its fruity liveliness is best within months of the
harvest. Each vintage carries an original artist's label.
Castello di Ascagnano

**Grechetto** or **Greco** w. dr. (sw.)　★→[★★]　81 82 83
Grechetto grapes make dry wines in several places S of Perugia, notably
around Foligno and Todi. Light golden green, seductively perfumed,
velvety, and fruity with a hint of both sweetness and bitterness, they are
good in 1–3 years. The variety is also used for Vin Santo.

| | |
|---|---|
| C.S. Todi | Tardioli |
| Caprai | Vagniluca |
| Enopolio di Foligno | |

**Merlot** r. dr.　★→★★★　79 81 82 83
Grown in Umbria for at least a century, Merlot is used in both varietals
and blends. Ruggero Veneri's Merlot from Spello stands out. Deep ruby-
garnet with herby bouquet, its robust, soft smoothness is good for 4–5
years or more.

| | |
|---|---|
| Agraria Ponteggia | La Paciana |
| Castello di Ascagnano | Ruggero Veneri |

**Montefalco** DOC
Recent appellation comprises two distinct reds from hills around
Montefalco and Bevagna between Foligno and Todi.

– **Montefalco Rosso** r. dr.  ★→ ★★★   81 82 83
From Sangiovese with some Sagrantino for mouth-filling tone, this is a
soft, ruby violet wine, its dryness rounded out by a mellowing sweet and
bitter undertone. Adanti and Fongoli make impressive wine, usually to
drink inside 4 years.
– **Sagrantino di Montefalco** r. dr. sw.  ★★→★★★   81 82 83
From the venerable Sagrantino grape which was usually made into sweet
*passito* wines, this full-bodied red is now often dry. Both have a dark
purple-garnet color, rich, berry-like scent and warm, rich, full flavor
with a light bitter undertone. The *passito* is aromatic, strong and
exquisitely *abboccato*. Both versions are best inside 4 years. Adanti is the
outstanding producer.
Ag. *passito* 1 yr.

| | |
|---|---|
| Adanti | Angelo Fongoli |
| Domenico Benincasa | La Paciana |
| Enopolio di Foligno | Tardioli |

**Orvieto** w. dr. s/sw.  ★→ ★★★   DYA
Umbria's renowned white comes from Trebbiano, Verdello, Grechetto,
Malvasia, and others grown in a large zone around the striking hill town
of Orvieto (the *classico* area), extending N along the Paglia and S along
the Tiber into Latium. Historically *abboccato*, most Orvieto is now dry,
polished, and rather neutral in odor and flavor due to modern
processing, though the best producers of Orvieto *classico* – Antinori,
Barberani, Cotti, and Decugnano dei Barbi – give it some fruit and
personality. The *abboccato*, golden and softly textured in the past, has
come back paler and lighter in body but fruity and silky as tasted in
Antinori's Castello della Sala. Antinori also makes small quantities of a
barrel-seasoned *abboccato* and Decugnano dei Barbi does a remarkable
*pourriture noble*, both of which rate ★★★★. Of some 6 million liters a year,
much is exported by Chianti firms. (Producers do not include all bottler
and shipper brands, which could also be dependable.)

| | |
|---|---|
| Barberani | Achille Lemmi |
| Bigi | Papini |
| Castello della Sala (Antinori) | Petrurbani |
| Centrale Cantine Cooperative | Tenuta Le Velette |
| Vincenzo Cotti | Conte Vaselli |
| Decugnano dei Barbi | |

**Rosso di Assisi**
See Assisi.

**Rubesco**
See Torgiano *rosso*.

**Rubino** r. dr.  ★★★   77 79 81 82 83
Fine red from Sangiovese, Merlot, and others grown near Umbertide in
the Colli Altotiberini. With 4–7 years, more from top vintages, it
develops deep bouquet, authority, and finesse, while its rich ruby color
takes on hints of garnet.
Colle del Sole (Polidori)

**Sagrantino**
See Montefalco.

**San Giorgio** r. dr.  ★★★→★★★★   77 78 79
The latest example of Giorgio Lungarotti's innovative spirit, this
combines the basic Torgiano *rosso* varieties with 20–22% Cabernet
Sauvignon. Bold, slightly aggressive in its youth, this will need years to
mellow and perhaps a decade or more to reach its prime. Rich in
bouquet, body and flavor, it remains to be seen if this will be Lungarotti's
best.
Lungarotti

**Solleone** am. dr.  ★★★   NV
Sherry-like aperitif wine from Trebbiano and Grechetto made by a
modified *solera* method. Light amber, bone dry, and strong (18%), its
ethereal bouquet of almonds and wood can last for many years.
Lungarotti

**Torgiano** DOC r. w. dr.  ★★→★★★★   70 71 73 74 75 77 78 79 80 81 82 83
The zone SE across the Tiber from Perugia is noted for both red and
white wines, particularly the *riserva* that carries Giorgio Lungarotti's
trademark Rubesco. The *bianco* (Lungarotti's is Torre di Giano), from

Trebbiano and Grechetto, is pale, flowery, with polished fruit-acid balance – to drink young. The *riserva* Torre di Giano from the Vigna Il Pino plot is aged briefly in wood and develops uncommon finesse with 3–4 years. The *rosso*, from Sangiovese, Canaiolo, Montepulciano, and Ciliegiolo, is ruby red, round, and smoothly persuasive in 2–5 years. Rubesco *riserva*, numbered from the Monticchio vineyard, is one of Italy's most distinguished reds. It needs 6–7 years to develop opulent bouquet and the aristocratic combinations of tastes and textures rarely sensed outside the Haut Médoc. From great vintages, such as 1971 and 1975, it needs a decade or more to reach prime as its color mellows to rich garnet with a trace of *pelure d'oignon*.
Ag. *riserva* 3 yrs.
Lungarotti

**Vernaccia di Cannara** r. s/sw. sw. fz.  ★  DYA
*Simpatico* dessert wine from Cometta and Corvetta grown around Cannara and Bevagna. Inky and fragrant, with thick, grapy sweetness, usually *frizzante*, it is drunk locally, especially around Easter.

**Vin Santo** am. s/sw. sw.  ★→★★★
Made nearly everywhere from Grechetto, Malvasia, Trebbiano and other grapes semidried (preferably hanging from rafters near a fireplace to pick up a smoky flavor) and aged in small, sealed barrels. Golden to amber, aromatic, and fairly strong (14%), at best it is velvety and softly sweet, capable of aging.
Adanti                                    Lungarotti

## Wine & Food

Umbrians can relate as humbly as Franciscans how they eat only what their good earth provides. Granted, menus are spare, repetitive, and orthodox – in other words, highly selective. Here seasonal produce is prepared in streamlined ways by country people without much time to spend in the kitchen – something like *nouvelle cuisine*, except that it has scarcely changed since the Middle Ages. Oil is so good it has been called Umbria's "liquid gold," though it is never used so sparingly. There are thick soups and a limited few pastas, including the always reliable home-made *tagliatelle* strewn across oval platters and mixed with *ragù* which often contains chicken livers. Meat and game are *di rigore* in this landlocked region: prized Perugina beef, farm poultry, wood pigeons, and lamb. Pork is so artfully prepared in the town of Norcia that pork butcher shops throughout Italy are known as *norcinerie*. Among things that grow, a special place is reserved for cardoons, the artichoke-like thistles known here as *gobbi*. But the most delicious irony of this region's "modest" cuisine is the truffle – whether black or white it is so prolific that Umbria has become the nation's (if not the world's) leading supplier.

**Anguille alle brace** Grilled eels from the Tiber or Lake Trasimeno.
  ★★ Colli del Trasimeno *rosso*.
**Cicerchiata** Carnival cake with honey, almonds, and candied fruit.
  ★★★ Sagrantino di Montefalco *passito*.
**Gobbi alla perugina** Fried cardoons with meat *ragù*.
  ★★ Torgiono *rosso*.
**Mazzafegati** Piquant pork liver sausages, served around Christmas
  ★★ Colli Altotiberini *rosso*.
**Minestra di farro** Soup of semolina cooked with tomatoes, onions, etc., in broth of a *prosciutto* bone.

  ★★ Castel Grifone or  ★★ Colli Altotiberini *rosato*.
**Palomba alla ghiotta** Spit-roasted wood pigeon with *ghiotta*, an intricate sauce of wine, vinegar, ham, livers, and herbs.
  ★★★★ Rubesco *riserva* or ★★★ Castello di Montoro.
**Porchetta alla perugina** Whole young pig roast in a wood oven with wild fennel, rosemary, and garlic.
  ★★★ Rubino.
**Spaghetti alla norcina** The sauce of sausages cooked with onions in cream may be topped with grated cheese or white truffles.
  ★★★ Orvieto *classico secco*.

**Stringozzi** Short noodles dressed with garlic, oil, and sometimes tomatoes.

★★ Torgiano *bianco*.

**Torcolo** Sponge cake to be dipped in Vin Santo.

★★★ Vin Santo.

## Restaurants

Recommended in or near wine zones: **Assisi-Montefalco** *Buca di San Francesco* and *Umbra* at Assisi; *La Bastiglia* and *Il Mulino* at Spello. **Colli Altotiberini** *Castello di Ascagnano* at Ascagnano; *L'Enoteca* at Città di Castello. **Colli del Trasimeno** *Sauro* on Trasimeno's Isola Maggiore; *Cacciatoreda Luciano* at Passignano sul Trasimeno. **Colli Perugini-Torgiano** *Umbria* at Todi; *Le Tre Vaselle* at Torgiano. **Orvieto** *La Badia, Morino* and *Villa Ciconia* at Orvieto.

# Valle d'Aosta
## Vallè d'Aosta

Italy's smallest region has little space for vines amidst its massive Alps. Most vineyards grow on terraces hewn out of stone on south-facing slopes along the Dora Baltea River, which flows from Mt Blanc's glaciers past Aosta and on into Piedmont. Wine production of 3.5 million liters a year (Italy's lowest volume) isn't adequate for 110,000 people drinking 130 liters a year (Italy's highest rate).

The few wines of this French-speaking region are made by plucky and persevering *vignerons*, especially those in Europe's highest vineyards at Morgex. There are only 2 DOCs – Donnaz and Enfer d'Arvier – but a campaign is underway for a regionwide DOC to take in various appellations. Production now consists mainly of a little galaxy of *crus* drawing luster from both Italian and French varieties.

The only way to taste Aosta's products is to visit. As Italy's gateway to France (the Mt Blanc tunnel) and Switzerland (the Great St Bernard tunnel) Valle d'Aosta is host to throngs of visitors. Some hurry through, others come to ski or take in the dramatic scenery of chalets and castles among Europe's highest peaks.

### Recent vintages

Recommended years of wines for aging appear with each entry.

**Aymaville** r. dr. **→*** 75 78 79 80 82
From Petit Rouge and Fumin grown at Aymaville SW of Aosta, this bright ruby wine needs a couple years in barrel to develop fine, raspberry-like bouquet and lightly acidic but elegantly balanced flavor that can last admirably for 2–5 years, sometimes more.
La Sabla (Charrère)

**Blanc de Cossan** w. dr. ** DYA
Sprightly white from dark Grenache grown at Cossan outside Aosta. Light gold with rosy glints, its tart, fresh fruitiness is best very young. The Reserve du Prieur from the same grapes is semisweet with 15%.
Institut Agricole Régional Aoste

**Blanc de La Salle** w. dr. (sp.) ** DYA
From Blanc de Valdigne grown at 1,000 meters at La Salle SE of Mt Blanc, this pale greenish wine is delicate in scent and flavor with a clean, acidic finish. A little Champagne-method *spumante* called Blanc du Blanc de La Salle is also made.
Association des Viticulteurs          Celestino David

**Blanc de Morgex** w. dr. ** DYA
From Blanc de Valdigne above Morgex in Italy's highest vineyards, it resembles its neighbor Blanc de La Salle but can be more rarified with low alcohol (9.5–10.5%), very high acidity and a hint of bitter almond at the finish. Good young, though some vintages last well.
Association Viticulteurs Morgex      Albert Vevey
Marcello Quinson

**Chambave Rouge** r. dr. **→*** 71 74 78 79 82
From Gros Vien, Dolcetto, and Barbera grown in gravelly terrain near Chambave, this distinguished wine is ruby tending to garnet with age. Its ethereal bouquet and dry, rather acidic flavor give it personality.
Ezio Voyat

**Creme du Vien de Nus** r. dr. ** 78 79 82 83
From Vien de Nus, this dark red wine has grapy fragrance and rich flavor, good in 3–5 years. Made by the village priest at Nus, E of Aosta.
Augusto Pramotton

**Donnaz** DOC r. dr.   ** 74 78 79 82 83
The region's lone Nebbiolo, Donnaz is similar to its Piedmontese
neighbor Carema – i.e. lighter than Nebbiolo from lower altitudes but
noble all the same. Garnet with fine bouquet it needs 5–6 years to
develop. About 50,000 bottles are produced annually.
Ag. 3 yrs (2 in barrel).
Caves Cooperative de Donnaz

**Enfer d'Arvier** DOC r. dr.   *→**\*\*** 79 82 83
The zone at Arvier W of Aosta is a rocky, terraced mountainside known
to get so torrid that it's called *l'Enfer*. Nonetheless, the permitted yield of
Petit Rouge grapes is one of the lowest among DOCs; production is only
about 6,000 bottles a year. Dark red to medium garnet, its rich, berry-
like bouquet and rather sharp, grapy taste smoothens with 3–5 years.
Co-Enfer                                   Maurizio Thomain
Giuseppe Thomain

**Gamay della Valle d'Aosta** r. dr.   *→**\*\*** 82 83
Introduced recently, the Beaujolais grape has done well on its own as a
fruity, smooth red to drink in 1–4 years (see Vin des Chanoines). It also
blends well with Petit Rouge and Pinot Nero.
Clos Gerbore                               Aldo Perrier

**Gamay-Pinot Nero** r. dr.   * 82 83
This Burgundian combination renders bright garnet wines of fruity scent
and dry, light, balanced flavor, to drink in 2–4 years.
Luigi Ferrando

**La Colline de Sarre et Chesallet** r. dr.   **\*\*** 82 83
Gamay and Petit Rouge combine W of Aosta in this bright garnet wine
with Gamay nose and fresh, grapy flavor, good in 2–4 years.
Octave Vallet

**Malvoisie de Cossan** w. s/sw.   ** 82 83
From Pinot Gris (here called Malvoisie) grown at Cossan, this golden-
copper wine needs 2 years to develop soft bouquet and smooth, *abboccato*
flavor with a light bitter undertone.
Institut Agricole Régional Aoste

**Malvoisie de Nus** am. s/sw.   ** 70 73 76 78 79
Dessert wine of ancient renown made from what seems to be a Pinot
called Malvoisie by the village priest at Nus E of Aosta. Aged 2–3 years
after fermenting in a sealed barrel, it becomes deep amber with rich
bouquet and off-dry, strong (17%), clean, highly personalized flavor
that remains attractive for decades. The few bottles made are costly.
Augusto Pramotton

**Moscato di Chambave** w. dr.   ** DYA
A rare dry Moscato from grapes grown at Chambave. Bright golden,
perfumed, its grapy, full flavor is most enjoyable inside a year.
Ezio Voyat

**Müller Thurgau** w. dr.
Although bottlings aren't in evidence, this high-altitude vine might do
famously on these lofty slopes. Proposed under the regionwide DOC.

**Passito di Chambave** w. s/sw.   ***
From semidried Moscato grapes, this long-lived wine is deep golden,
delicately aromatic, sweet but turning drier with age as its ample flavor
becomes suave. It can keep for decades.
Ezio Voyat

**Petit Rouge** r. dr.   **\*→\*\*\*** 78 79 82 83
Apparently of French origin, this dark variety makes several
distinguished red wines, including varietals. Deep ruby, almost purple,
its bouquet is enticingly flowery and its flavor, though dry, is generous
and lively young, becoming sedate with a decade of age.
Chateau St Pierre (Zanello)            Institut Agricole Régional Aoste
Clos Gerbore                              Gratien Montrosset

**Pinot Noir** r. dr.   ** 76 78 80 82 83
Proposed as a varietal under Valle d'Aosta DOC, scattered plantings
have given promising results, such as Aldo Perrier's Pinot Noir de
Charvensod and Sang des Salasses (see).
Aldo Perrier

**Sang des Salasses** r. dr.  ★★  79 81 82 83
From Pinot Noir grown at Cossan near Aosta, this ruby-garnet wine has
a fruity scent and dry, round flavor with light bitter background, to
drink in 2–5 years.
Institut Agricole Régional Aoste

**Torrette** r. dr.  ★★→★★★   71 74 78 79 80 82 83
DOC candidate for wine from Petit Rouge grown around St Pierre,
Sarre, and Aymaville W of Aosta. Torrette is deep ruby to violet, with
bouquet increasing wondrously with age (sometimes over a decade) and
dry, lightly acidic but clean, robust flavor with a hint of bitterness.
Filippo Garin

**Valle d'Aosta** or **Vallée d'Aoste**
This proposed regionwide DOC would take in the currently classified
Donnaz and Enfer d'Arvier and add to the list: Arnad-Montjovet, Blanc
de Morgex e La Salle, Chambave, Gamay, Müller Thurgau, Nus, Pinot
Noir, Torrette.

**Vin des Chanoines** r. dr.  ★★  82 83
From Gamay grown near Aosta, this bright ruby wine has balance in
light body and bouquet with flavor that improves for 2–4 years.
Institut Agricole Régional Aoste

**Vin du Conseil** w. dr.  ★★★  DYA
From Petite Arvine grown in the Vignoble de Prieuré de Montfleury
outside Aosta, this is the pride of Joseph Vaudan, priest and director of
the regional agricultural school. Aged briefly in barrel, it is bright straw
yellow with seductive scent of pear and dry but mouth-filling fruitiness.
Institut Agricole Régional Aoste

*Wine & Food*

Aostans thrive on rustic, generous fare; few specialities, but the
dishes they share with Piedmont taste unmistakably Aostan.
Pasta isn't at home here; instead, polenta, thick soups, rye bread
with butter. Meat is the essence of this hearty diet, with salami,
sausages and cold cuts, such as mountain *prosciutto*, the rare
*mocetta* (dried chamois meat), and the tasty stews and game
dishes cooked with wine. The vaunted cheeses are *fontina* and *tome*
(from ewe's milk). After cooked fruit and biscuits, each diner sips
from the *grolla*, a pot with spouts filled with coffee and grappa.

**Boudins** Blood sausages, a
speciality of Morgex.
  ★★  Petit Rouge.
**Capriolo alla valdostana**
Venison stewed with vegetables,
wine, grappa, and cream.
  ★★★  Torrette.
**Carbonade** Salted beef cooked
with wine in a rich stew served
with polenta.
  ★★★  Chambave Rouge.
**Costoletta alla valdostana**
Breaded veal cutlets with *fontina*,
and possibly truffles.
  ★★★  Donnaz.

**Polenta cùnsa** Polenta with
*fontina*, *toma*, melted butter, and
Parmesan.
  ★★  Gamay.
**Tegole** Crunchy almond biscuits.
  ★★★  Passito di Chambave.
**Trota** Trout from mountain
streams cooked in butter.
  ★★★  Vin du Conseil or ★★ Blanc
de Morgex.
**Zuppa valpellinentze** *Fontina*,
ham, black bread, cabbage, herbs,
and spices, cooked in what could
be defined loosely as soup.
  ★★  Vin des Chanoines.

## Restaurants

Recommended in the regìon: *Cavallo Bianco* at Aosta; *Parisien* at
Chatillon; *Le Vieux Pommier* at Courmayeur; *Maison de Filippo* at Entreves
de Courmayeur; *Hôtel Bellevue* at Pré St Didier; *Casale* at St Cristophe;
*Batezar-da Renato* at St Vincent; *Da Pierre* at Verres.

# Veneto

Veneto

Venice's region is leading Italian viniculture into the future, showing that wine can be a practical and profitable big business. The Veneto vies with Emilia-Romagna, Apulia and Sicily as volume leader and rivals Tuscany in DOC production with about 170 million liters a year. Much of the classified wine comes from Verona, where Soave ranks second to Chianti in prominence among DOCs with Valpolicella and Bardolino not far behind. The Veronese trio has far outdistanced Chianti in exports to become the most representative of Italian quality wines abroad. Efficient, modern production and astute marketing techniques lie behind the success of these three appealing, moderately priced wines for regular drinking. Verona also makes wines for special occasions, most notably Amarone, a limited-production red of dynamic dimensions.

The Veneto, which extends from the Austrian border S to the Po basin and from the Adriatic W to Lake Garda, is an enviably productive land. Vines flourish in its verdant hills and fertile flatlands. The range of grape varieties is remarkable. Among the natives are the light Garganega of Soave and the dark Corvina, Rondinella, Molinara, and Negrara of Valpolicella and

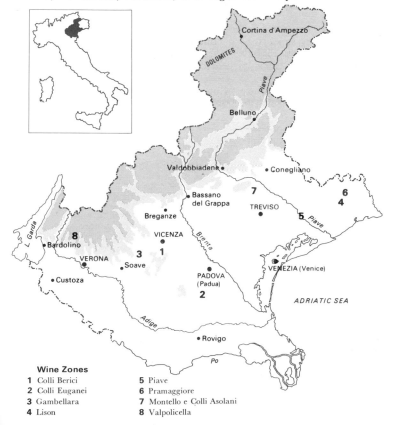

**Wine Zones**

| | |
|---|---|
| **1** Colli Berici | **5** Piave |
| **2** Colli Euganei | **6** Pramaggiore |
| **3** Gambellara | **7** Montello e Colli Asolani |
| **4** Lison | **8** Valpolicella |

Bardolino, as well as Piave's distinctive Raboso, Verduzzo, and Prosecco, the latter a source of growingly popular bubbly wines. The imports range even farther afield, from the aristocratic Cabernets, Pinots, Sauvignon and Merlot (the prevalent variety of the E Veneto) down to Clinton, an outlandish North American vine surviving here as an outlaw.

Quality covers the gamut from majestic estate bottlings to murky country wines to pasteurized products of assembly lines shipped all over Europe in outsized bottles with metal caps. It must be said, though, that industrial winemaking can be admirable here; some large houses make some of the best wine.

Visitors who wander into Venice's interior in quest of wine and some of Italy's finest food, will also find a heritage of art, architecture and history amidst landscapes that could still inspire Renaissance painters. Vinitaly, held each April in Verona, is the nation's premier wine fair. Wine roads lead through Verona's hills, as well as through Breganze, the Piave valley and the Marca Trevigiana north of Treviso. A local habit that the tourists take to is the little glass of wine called the *ombra* or *ombretta* sipped at intervals during the day. Impressive shops include the *Bottega del Vino* at Bassano and the *Enoteca Angelo Rasi* at Padova.

## Recent vintages

Most Veneto wines are good young, though the Cabernets and Merlots of the E Veneto and Amarone take aging.

1983 Size was cut by hail and drought, though natural thinning led to a very good year all over.
1982 Fine, bountiful crop, though whites lacked acidity.
1981 Sharply reduced, especially in Verona, where quality was acceptable at best; results elsewhere were modest.
1980 Uneven; below average except for wine from select grapes.
1979 Fine, abundant harvest; reds of superior quality should have above-average life spans.
1978 Down in size, but good, normal wines were made, somewhat better than normal in Pramaggiore.
1977 Good year around Verona; less satisfying to the east.
1976 Fair to good in Verona; very good in Piave and Colli Berici.
1975 Disappointing in Verona; fair to good elsewhere.
1974 Generally good harvest.
1973 Decent crop in Verona, with some exceptional red in Colli Berici.
Earlier fine vintages: (Amarone) '69, '67, '64, '62; (Cabernet-Merlot) '71, '69, '67, '64.

**Amarone**
See Recioto della Valpolicella under Valpolicella.

**Bardolino** DOC r. p. dr. ★→ ★★★ 82 83
Popular red and rosé from Corvina Veronese, Rondinella, Molinara, and Negrara grown on SE shores of Lake Garda, most noted in *classico* zone behind Bardolino. The *rosso* is light ruby, grapy, dry, round, and balanced, sometimes with a hint of prickle and light bitter undertone – to drink in 4 years. Guerrieri-Rizzardi makes a perfumed *classico superiore*. The *chiaretto*, cherry pink, is lighter, more fragile, to drink in 2 years. Ag. *superiore* 1 yr.

| | |
|---|---|
| Aldegheri | Colle dei Cipressi |
| Anselmi | Eleonora |
| Bertani | Fratelli Fibiano |
| Biscardo | Rosino Ferri |
| Bolla | Gardoni |
| Paolo Boscaini & Figli | Girasole |
| Ca' Bordenis (Santi) | Gorgo (Bricolo) |
| Innocente Campostini | Guerrieri-Rizardi |
| C.S. di Custoza | Il Colle |
| C.S. Veronese del Garda | Lamberti |

| | |
|---|---|
| Le Tende | Salvalai |
| Le Vigne di San Pietro | Santa Sofia |
| Gianni Lonardi | Sartori |
| Masi | Scamperle |
| Antonio Menegotti | Taborro |
| Montecorno | Fratelli Tedeschi |
| Montresor | Tenuta Ca' Furia |
| Pallavicino Disertori | Tenute San Leone |
| Fratelli Pasqua | Eugenio Tinazzi & Figli |
| Pegaso | Tommasi |
| Umberto Peretti | Tre Colline |
| Pergreffi | Villa Girardi |
| Fratelli Poggi | Visconti |
| Luigi Rossi | Aldo Zanon |
| | Fratelli Zenato |

**Bianco di Custoza** DOC w. dr. (sp.) ★→★★★ DYA
Increasingly noticed white from a zone bordering on Lake Garda and
Lombardy. From a mélange including Trebbiano Toscano, Garganega,
and Tocai, when well made it is pale and flowery, with clean, dry, softly
fruity lines but crisp finish, capable of matching good Soave. A *spumante*,
usually *charmat*, is increasingly seen.

| | |
|---|---|
| C.S. di Custoza | Albino Pezzini |
| C.S. Veronese del Garda | Silvio Piona |
| Cavalchina | Santa Sofia |
| Eleonora | Santi |
| Gorgo (Bricolo) | Scamperle |
| Le Tende | Tenute San Leone |
| Le Vigne di San Pietro | Eugenio Tinazzi & Figlio |
| Martini & Rossi | Tommasi |
| Antonio Menegotti | Villa Girardi |
| Montecorno | Villa Medici |

**Bianco Toara** w. dr. ★★ DYA
From Garganega grown at Toara in the Colli Berici, this light golden
wine is flowery and dry with refreshing almond finish.
Alessandro Piovene Porto-Godi

**Breganze** DOC
The glacial moraine of this zone N of Vicenza is well suited to vines, as
exemplified by the excellent modern wines of Maculan.
– **Bianco** w. dr. ★→★★★★ 82 83
Based on Tocai Friulano, this is pale lemon yellow, delicate in scent,
smooth, and buoyantly good inside 2 years. Maculan's Breganze di
Breganze and, particularly, the wood-aged Prato di Canzio rival the best
Tocai of Friuli.
– **Cabernet** r. dr. ★★→★★★★ 78 79 80 81 82 83
From Cabernet Franc or, less likely, Cabernet Sauvignon, this is usually
a good, sturdy red, superb from Maculan with its Palazzotto and Fratta
special vineyard bottlings. Rich yet supple, grassy but harmonious, they
rank with the finest Cabernet Franc made anywhere, after 3–6 years of
aging. *Superiore* must have 12% alcohol.
– **Pinot Bianco** w. dr. ★→★★★ 82 83
Light straw green, fresh and fruity, this can develop silky texture and
flowery fragrance in 2–3 years.
– **Pinot Grigio** w. dr. ★→★★ DYA
With a hint of copper in its pale straw color, it is limber and smooth.
– **Pinot Nero** r. dr. ★→★★ 82 83
Light ruby, fruity, and dry with light bitter undertone, it can be labeled
*superiore* if it has 12% alcohol.
– **Rosso** r. dr. ★→★★★ 80 81 82 83
Based on Merlot, this most heavily produced Breganze wine is ruby red,
grapy and nicely rounded with a hint of tannin. Maculan's Brentino
becomes smooth and sumptuous in 2–3 years.
– **Vespaiolo** w. dr. ★★ DYA
A local varietal, this is bright straw yellow, pleasantly scented, brisk,
almost lemony, with a hint of almond underneath. *Superiore* must have
12%.

| | |
|---|---|
| Cantina B. Bartolomeo | Villa Magna (Novello) |
| Maculan | |

**Cabernet** r. dr. ★★→★★★  71 75 77 78 79 80 82 83
DOC under Breganze, Colli Berici, Colli Euganei, Montello Colli
Asolani, Piave, and Pramaggiore, Cabernet also makes table wines both
as varietals and in blends with Merlot, Malbec and others. A cross of
Cabernet-Prosecco known as I.M.2,15 or Cabernet Manzoni is also
gaining favor. Styles vary. The following producers of non-DOC
Cabernet, in which Cabernet Franc often prevails, make wine of notable
quality.

Leone Agnoletti               Silvio Ermolao
Col Sandago                   Valdo
Costozza (Da Schio)           Villa Dal Ferro-Lazzarini
A. Cosulich

**Campo Fiorin** r. dr. ★★★  78 79 82 83
Basically a Valpolicella, it gains the body, color, and strength of a bigger
wine by being left with Recioto pressings. Deep ruby and ample in
bouquet, its dry flavor is robust and warm, with bitter background and
suave texture, impressive for 4–8 years.
Masi

**Capitel San Rocco** r. w. dr. ★★★  78 79 82 83
Distinguished table wines from San Rocco vineyards at Pedemonte in
Valpolicella. The *rosso*, like Campo Fiorin, is Valpolicella reinforced
with Recioto pressings. The *bianco*, from Garganega with a touch of
Durello, is bright straw green and flowery, with a dry, almondy finish.
Fratelli Tedeschi

**Capo del Monte** r. dr. ★★★  79 80 82 83
Unique mix by winemaker Gianni Spinazzè in which the aggressive
grass and pepper character of Cabernet is toned down by Marzemino in
a wine of depth and stature to drink in 2–5 years, sometimes more.
Fattoria di Ogliano

**Cartizze** or **Superiore di Cartizze**
Special subdenomination of Prosecco di Conegliano-Valdobbiadene.

**Castello di Roncade** r. dr. ★★→★★★  71 73 75 78 79 82 83
This classic composite of Cabernet Sauvignon, Cabernet Franc, Merlot,
Malbec, and Petit Verdot grown at Roncade in the Piave valley can be
remarkably close in character to certain Bordeaux. The 1971 (which
rated ★★★★ and hasn't been equalled since) combined extraordinary
power with finesse – a complete, intricate, ruby-garnet wine with
bouquet reminiscent of berries, tar, and flowers.
Barone Ciani Bassetti

**Clinton** r. (p.) dr. s/sw. (fz.) ★ DYA
Popular N American vine (barred because not *vitis vinifera*) makes
simplistic wines in E Veneto of inky-violet color and strawberry-like
aroma, usually dry with typically foxy flavor. Also pink and *frizzante*.

**Colli Berici** DOC
Zone historically noted for wine has seven DOC varietals, though some
top producers leave their wines unclassified (see Costozza and Villa Dal
Ferro).
– **Cabernet** r. dr. ★→★★★  78 79 82 83
From Cabernet Franc, sometimes Cabernet Sauvignon, this bright ruby-
garnet wine can show rich, herby bouquet with 3–7 years.
Ag. *riserva* 3 yrs.
– **Garganega** or **Garganego** w. dr. ★→★★ DYA
Pale yellow, subtly scented, the light, brisk, almondy traits of the zone's
most popular wine are attractive when young.
– **Merlot** r. dr. ★→★★  81 82 83
Fruity, full-bodied, and soft, from some producers it has enough stuff to
show well for 4–5 years.
– **Pinot Bianco** w. dr. ★→★★ DYA
Pale greenish yellow and flowery, its dry, smooth flavor has zestful bite.
– **Sauvignon** w. dr. ★→★★ DYA
Pale straw with fine varietal scent, its refreshingly crisp, gunflint qualities
are best young.
– **Tocai Italico** w. dr. ★ DYA
Pale lemon yellow and vinous, so far this Tocai doesn't match its
namesake in Friuli.

– **Tocai Rosso** r. dr. ★★ DYA
This native Tocai thrives here as a brilliant ruby-crimson wine, grapy
with a hint of licorice and a cleansing tannic bite, refreshing young.

| | |
|---|---|
| C.S. dei Colli Vicentini | Alessandro Piovene Porto-Godi |
| Castello di Belvedere | Claudio Pozzati |
| Cornelio Fabbian | Nani Cav. Rizzieri & Figli |
| Fratelli Montagna | Franceschetto Rizzieri |
| Severino Muraro & Figli | |

## Colli Euganei DOC

These dramatically sheer hills rising from the Po valley S of Padova have
been noted for wine since Roman times. The list takes in 7 types.

– **Bianco** w. dr. (s/sw.) (sp.) ★→★★ DYA
From Garganega, Serprina, Tocai and Sauvignon, this straw-yellow
wine is fruity in scent with dry, soft flavor, best young. An *amabile* is also
made. Both may be *spumante*.

– **Cabernet** r. dr. ★→★★ 82 83
From Cabernet Sauvignon and/or Franc, this is a tasty red when young,
taking on some class with age. *Superiore* must have 12.5%.
Ag. 1 yr.

– **Merlot** r. dr. (s/sw.) ★→★★ 82 83
Grapy, soft red to drink young – sometimes *abboccato*. *Superiore* must have
12%.
Ag. 1 yr.

– **Moscato** w. s/sw. sw. fz. (sp.) ★→★★ DYA
From Moscato di Canelli, this golden wine has aromatic sweetness,
whether still or bubbly.

– **Pinot Bianco** w. dr. (s/sw.) ★→★★ DYA
Though unproven, this could do well here as a dry wine. *Abboccato* is also
permitted. *Superiore* must have 12%.

– **Rosso** r. dr. (s/sw.) ★→★★★ 78 79 81 82 83
Based on Merlot with Cabernet, Barbera and Raboso, this singular red
has a fresh, grapy bouquet, sturdy structure and smooth, mellow flavor
that can improve for 3–6 years in the dry version. Villa Sceriman makes
a good example. *Amabile* is also made. *Superiore* must have 12%.

– **Tocai Italico** w. dr. (s/sw.) ★ DYA
Newly designated white will make mostly dry but also semisweet wine.
*Superiore* must have 12%.

| | |
|---|---|
| C.S. Cooperativa Colli Euganei | Luxardo de' Franchi |
| La Principessa | Villa Sceriman |

## Costozza

Prominent Colli Berici estate making non-DOC varietals. See Cabernet,
Pinot Nero, and Riesling.

## Durello w. dr. (sp.) ★★→★★★ DYA

The Durello grape grown in Vicenza and Verona provinces makes
brassy wines of high acidity and attractive scent and flavor. Well suited
to both still and bubbly wines, a bid is in for DOC for Durello from the
Lessini hills near Vicenza.

| | |
|---|---|
| C.S. Colli Vicentini | Santi |
| Col de' Fratta | Zonin |
| Marcato | |

## Gambellara DOC

The zone E of Soave in Vicenza province has three types of wine, all
based on Garganega with a dose of Trebbiano di Soave.

– **Gambellara Bianco** w. dr. ★→★★ DYA
Almost a twin of Soave, it provides a fresh alternative. Light straw-gold,
somewhat fruity in scent, its dry, balanced softness has a nice hint of acid
on the finish. *Superiore* must have 11.5%.

– **Recioto di Gambellara** w. sw. (sp.) ★★
From slightly raisined grapes, this golden dessert wine is intense in aroma
and flavor, whether still, *frizzante* or *spumante*.

– **Vin Santo di Gambellara** am. sw. ★★
A rarity from semidried grapes. After 2 years in barrel it is amber,
aromatic, sweet, smooth, and relatively strong (14%).

| | |
|---|---|
| C.S. di Gambellara | A. Menti & Figli |
| Fratelli Cavazza | Zonin |

**Le Pergole or Costa delle Pergole** r. dr.  ★★★  79 80 82 83
This Cabernet-Merlot blend gets a distinctive touch from Wildbacher, of
Austrian origin, which lends a berry-like richness. Smooth, structured,
but easy on the palate, its bouquet expands with 3–6 years of age.
Col Sandago

**Le Sassine** r. dr.  ★★→★★★  79 82 83
Special vineyard bottling of what is virtually a Valpolicella but with
10% of grapes from old vines added for character in this sturdy table
wine that improves with 4–5 years of age, sometimes more.
Le Ragose

**Lison-Pramaggiore**
Proposals to combine the current DOCs of Tocai di Lison and
Pramaggiore's Cabernet and Merlot, and to expand the listing to 12
types were being considered for a unified zone in E Veneto.

**Lugana**
Part of the DOC zone is in the Veneto. See under Lombardy.

**Malbec** or **Malbeck** r. dr.  ★→★★  81 82 83
A native of Bordeaux, it makes varietals in E Veneto. Dark ruby to
cherry red with peculiar grapy-fruity scent, the tannic harshness
smoothens with 3–5 years, sometimes more.

| | |
|---|---|
| Bertoja di Ceneda | Sant' Osvaldo |
| Deroà | Tenuta Sant'Anna |

**Masianco** w. dr.  ★★★  DYA
From Garganega, Trebbiano, and Durello grown in Valpolicella, this
straw-colored wine is among the most elegant whites of Verona, thanks
to masterful balance of fruit against ample acidity.
Masi

**Merlot** r. dr.  ★→★★★  79 82 83
DOC under Colli Berici, Colli Euganei, Montello e Colli Asolani, Piave,
Pramaggiore, and as Breganze *rosso*, the E Veneto's most popular variety
also makes table wines, often in the grapy, herby, lissome style, but truly
elegant from some. The Campo del Lago Merlot of Alfredo Lazzarini's
Villa Dal Ferro can achieve monumental heights, such as in '78 when it
rated ★★★★. It needs 3–6 years to reach its peak.

| | |
|---|---|
| Club Produttori Associati | Valdo |
| Col Sandago | Verga Falzacappa |
| Quarto Vecchio | Villa Dal Ferro-Lazzarini |

**Montello e Colli Asolani** DOC
Recently recognized, this zone is noted for Palladian villas and wine,
particularly Venegazzù (the finest reserve of which is not DOC).
 –**Cabernet** r. dr.  ★→★★  82 83
From Cabernet Sauvignon and/or Cabernet Franc, this ruby-garnet
wine is dry, warm, somewhat tannic, herby, and stylish in 3–6 years.
Ag. *superiore* 2 yrs (1 in barrel).
 –**Merlot** r. dr.  ★→★★  82 83
Ruby-garnet, grapy, supple when young, it can take on some refinement
over 3–5 years.
Ag. *superiore* 2 yrs (1 in barrel).
 –**Prosecco** w. dr. s/sw. fz. sp.  ★★  DYA
This typical white of Treviso province is usually *frizzante* or *spumante*. Pale
straw to light gold, whether dry or lightly sweet, it has delicate fruit in
aroma and flavor and a refreshing nut-like undertone.

| | |
|---|---|
| C.S. La Montelliana e dei Colli | Tomasella |
| Asolani | Venegazzù (Loredan Gasparini) |
| C.S. Valdobbiadene | |

**Montericco** r. dr.  ★★★  75 78 79
What would qualify as Valpolicella is reinforced with Recioto pressings,
making it bigger and sturdier after barrel age.
Le Ragose

**Piave** DOC
Large zone on either side of the Piave extending from the Marca
Trevigiana hills to the alluvial plains of Venice, which have become a
model of flatland viticulture. List recently expanded to take in 8 varietals.
 –**Cabernet** r. dr.  ★→★★★  79 82 83
Cabernet Franc and/or Sauvignon make a robust ruby to garnet wine

with bouquet and flavor gaining style over 3–6 years.
Ag. *riserva* 3 yrs.
– **Merlot** r. dr. ★→ ★★★  79 82 83
Soft, round and sapid when young, this can take on a persuasive bouquet
with 2–5 years. Some 10 million liters a year are made here.
Ag. *vecchio* 2 yrs.
– **Pinot Bianco** w. dr. ★→ ★★  DYA
Newly designated, this could be a winner as a full-bodied white.
– **Pinot Grigio** w. dr. ★→ ★★  DYA
A well-known entity in the Venezie, this could become one of the better
DOC versions.
– **Pinot Nero** r. dr. ★→★★  82 83
The climate of Piave could prove favorable for this difficult vine.
Ag. *riserva* 2 yrs.
– **Raboso** r. dr. ★→ ★★★  82 83
Though newly elevated, Raboso is noted in Piave for its warm, rich,
tannic wines that need time to mellow and develop bouquet.
Ag. 3 yrs.
– **Tocai Italico** w. dr. ★→ ★★  DYA
Pale and delicate, Tocai can develop some depth and tone.

– **Verduzzo** w. dr. ★  DYA
A pale green lightweight, it can be snappily fresh when young.

| | |
|---|---|
| Abbazia di Busco (Liasora) | Deroà |
| Bertoja di Ceneda | Enoteca Prof. Cescon |
| Bianchi Kunkler | Maccari |
| Cantina Colli del Soligo | Marcello del Majno |
| C.S. di San Donà | Rechsteiner (Stepski Doliwa) |
| C.S. Ormelle | Santa Margherita |
| C.S. Ponte di Piave | Tenuta Mercante |
| Castello di Roncade | |

**Pinot Bianco** w. dr. (sp.)  ★★→★★★  82 83
DOC in Breganze, Colli Berici, Colli Euganei and Piave, Pinot Bianco is
also used for table wines and *spumanti* in the Veneto. Producers listed are
noted for quality.

| | |
|---|---|
| Cantina Club | Piona-Cavalchina |
| Club Produttori Associati | Venegazzù (Loredan Gasparini) |
| Fattoria di Ogliano | Villa Dal Ferro-Lazzarini |

**Pinot Grigio** w. dr. ★→★★  DYA
DOC only in Breganze and Piave, numerous table wines labeled Pinot
Grigio del Veneto, delle Venezie, or with other vague allusions to origins
are processed or bottled in the Veneto. The vine is not heavily planted in
the region. Producers listed use locally grown grapes.

| | |
|---|---|
| Cantina Club | Bianchi Kunkler |
| Castello di Roncade | La Fattoria |

**Pinot Nero** r. p. dr. (fz.) ★→★★  79 81 82 83
Planted in various places, Pinot Nero is DOC only in Breganze and Piave
as a red wine. It is also used for rosé (Maculan's sterling Costa d'Olio, for
instance) and both pink and white *spumante*. Only rarely do red wines
from this variety rise above the ordinary, though the Rosso del Rocolo of
Villa Dal Ferro can rate ★★★ from some vintages.

| | |
|---|---|
| Abbazia di Busco (Liasora) | Villa Dal Ferro-Lazzarini |
| Costozza | Zonin |
| Verga Falzacappa | |

**Pinot** (and **Chardonnay**) **Spumante** w. dr. sp.  ★★→★★★  DYA
Much sparkling wine from Pinots and Chardonnay (sometimes with
Prosecco, as in Zardetto Brut) is processed in the Veneto by both *charmat*
and *champenoise* methods. The base wines generally originate in the Tre
Venezie, though the sources are rarely clear. *Méthode champenoise* is
marked *m.c.*

| | |
|---|---|
| – **Accademia Brut** | – **Tenuta Sant'Anna Brut (m.c.)** |
| Maculan | Tenuta Sant'Anna |
| – **Bolla Brut Riserva** | – **Venegazzù Brut (m.c.)** |
| Bolla | Conte Loredan Gasparini |
| – **Brut di Pinot** | – **Zardetto Brut** |
| Col Sandago | Pino Zardetto |
| – **Ruggeri Nature (m.c.)** | |
| Ruggeri | |

**Pramaggiore** DOC
The zone in the flatlands of E Veneto around Portogruaro and
Pramaggiore extends into Friuli-Venezia Giulia. This area of Cabernet
and Merlot coincides with Tocai di Lison; they may soon be combined
into a single zone called Lison-Pramaggiore.
– **Cabernet di Pramaggiore** r. dr. ★→★★★ 78 79 80 82 83
From Cabernet Sauvignon and/or Cabernet Franc with 10% Merlot
permitted, the color is deep ruby tending to brick red with 3–5 years, as
bouquet heightens and full, rather tannic flavor becomes velvety.
Ag. *riserva* 3 yrs.
– **Merlot di Pramaggiore** r. dr. ★→★★ 80 82 83
From Merlot with 10% Cabernet permitted, it is attractively grapy and
herby when young, becoming fairly robust over 2–4 years.
Ag. *riserva* 2 yrs.

| | |
|---|---|
| C.S. di Portogruaro | Morassutti |
| Castello di Porcia | Russolo |
| Club Produttori Associati | Sant'Osvaldo |
| Paolo De Lorenzi | Santa Margherita |
| Dialma | Tenuta La Brighina |
| La Fattoria | Tenuta Sant'Anna |
| La Frassinella | Villa Frattina |

**Prosecco di Conegliano-Valdobbiadene** DOC w. dr. s/sw. sw. fz. sp.
★→★★★ DYA
The fortunes of this seductive white from the native Prosecco vine have
risen with the demand for light, bubbly wines. Grown in the Marca
Trevigiana hills N of the Piave between Conegliano and Valdobbiadene,
production averages 6 million liters a year. Some 750,000 liters of this are
Superiore di Cartizze or simply Cartizze, from a delimited plot near
Valdobbiadene where wines are noted for finesse. Prosecco, whether still,
*frizzante*, or *spumante*, is pale white to light golden, with a hint of almond
in its fruity scent. The *spumante* may be *brut*, *demisec*, or *amabile*. It is not
always sold as DOC.

| | |
|---|---|
| Adami | Carpenè Malvolti |
| Augusto Agostini | Col Sandago |
| Antica Quercia (Riello) | Deroà |
| Walter Balliana | Fattoria di Ogliano |
| Desiderio Bisol & Figli | Maschio |
| Bortolomiol | Museo del Vino (Cosulich) |
| Canavel | Mario Rossi |
| Adamo Canel & Figli | Ruggeri |
| Cantina Club | Santa Margherita |
| Cantina Colli del Soligo | Tenuta Sant'Anna |
| C.S. di Valdobbiadene | Torre Collalto (Trevisiol) |
| Cantine Nino Franco | Valdo |
| Cardinal | Pino Zardetto |
| Emilio Carnio | |

**Quarto Vecchio** r. dr. ★★→★★★ 77 78 79 81 82 83
From Cabernet and Merlot grown in the Po flatlands, this table wine is
bright ruby, full-bodied, turning toward brick red with 5–8 years and
becoming suavely balanced with rich bouquet.
Quarto Vecchio

**Raboso** r. dr. ★★→★★★ 78 79 80 82 83
The indigenous variety makes reds of distinction in Piave, where it
recently became DOC. It is still often sold as *vino da tavola* whether alone
or mixed with Cabernet. Garnet to brick red, very dry, rather tannic,
and acidic, with 5 years it becomes warmly elegant with unique bouquet
of herbs, berries, and warm earth.

| | |
|---|---|
| Abbazia di Busco (Liasora) | Enoteca Prof. Cescon |
| C.S. di San Donà | Maccari |
| C.S. Ponte di Piave | Tenuta Sant'Anna |
| Deroà | |

**Recioto Bianco di Campociesa** am. sw. ★★★★ 78 79 81 82 83
From select semidried Garganega and Trebbiano of the Campociesa
vineyard at Valgatara N of Verona, this amber-gold dessert wine is rare
and exceptional. Amply perfumed of ripe fruit and flowers, it is warm on
the palate, silky, and exquisitely sweet.
Masi

**Recioto della Valpolicella, Recioto di Soave**
See under Valpolicella and Soave.

**Riesling** w. dr.  ★→★★★  DYA
Both Riesling Italico and Renano are grown in the Veneto, though not
prominently enough to have gained DOC. Pieropan makes a fine
Riesling Italico at Soave. The Renano is notable from Antica Quercia
near Conegliano, and Costozza and Villa Dal Ferro in the Colli Berici.

| | |
|---|---|
| Antica Quercia (Riello) | Ruggeri |
| Costozza (Da Schio) | Santa Margherita |
| Deroà | Villa Dal Ferro-Lazzarini |
| Pieropan | |

**Rosso San Pietro** r. dr.  ★★★  82 83
From partially dried grapes for Bardolino grown at Ca' dell'Ara
vineyards, this red table wine combines sturdy structure and depth of
flavors with a sensational floral bouquet after a couple of years.
Guerrieri-Rizzardi

**Ruzante** r. dr. fz.  ★★  DYA
Impishly lively red table wine based on Refosco mixed with other dark
grapes of E Veneto. Crimson to ruby, grapy with mouth-cleansing
acidity and a hint of bitter, it is best very young.
Santa Margherita

**Sauvignon** w. dr.  ★★  DYA
DOC only in Colli Berici, Sauvignon is being planted elsewhere in the
Veneto, notably in well-drained vineyards where its smoky bite is well
expressed.

| | |
|---|---|
| Tenuta Sant'Anna | Villa Sceriman |
| Verga Falzacappa | |

**Serègo Alighieri Vaio Armaron** r. dr.  ★★★★  79
An Amarone from vineyards owned by descendants of Dante Alighieri,
this made its first appearance in '79 as the ultimate example of what can
be achieved with Valpolicella's grapes. Of bright ruby color with a
brilliant array of perfumes, it has fine balance between ripe fruit, refined
wood tannins and the typically bitter Amarone finish. It should peak
between 5 and 8 years.
Masi

**Soave** DOC w. dr. (sp.)  ★→ ★★★  DYA
This basically simple, unpretentious wine, which not long ago was
Verona's "local" white, has enjoyed miraculous success in recent times.
Second in volume to Chianti among DOCs with 52 million liters a year.
Soave is Italy's best-selling DOC wine in the U.S. and other nations. It
shows that popular acclaim is worth more than approval by experts, who
tend to downgrade it for lack of character. Though much Soave is
uninspiring – especially after being treated for shipping – some wine from
the *classico* area in view of the town's castle can be remarkably attractive
in its youth. Pieropan's *classico* consistently stands out, as do Bolla's
Castellare and the Capitel Foscarino of Anselmi, both limited-
production *crus*. From Garganega with up to 30% Trebbiano di Soave, it
is straw yellow, sometimes with green glints, lightly fragrant, dry, of
medium body, and delicately fruity – ideally with an acidic bite and a
hint of almond at the finish. A *spumante naturale* is also permitted. Soave of
11.5% may be called *superiore* if aged 9 months.

– **Recioto di Soave** w. or am. sw.  ★★→★★★  79 81 82 83
Dessert wine from semidried grapes for Soave, it is light golden to amber
and, after 2–3 years of aging, is moderately strong (14%), with raisiny
aroma, smooth, rich texture, and rather sweet flavor. This Recioto may
also be *spumante* or, if fortified with alcohol, *liquoroso*. (Producers do not
include all bottler and shipper brands, which could also be dependable.)

| | |
|---|---|
| Aldegheri | Capitel Foscarino (Anselmi) |
| Anselmi | Fratelli Castagna |
| Bertani | Castellaro (Bolla) |
| Biscardo | Fratelli Fabiano |
| Ottavio Bixio | Finatello |
| Bolla | Gottardo |
| G. Campagnola | Guerrieri-Rizzardi |
| Cantina del Castello | Lamberti |
| C.S. Cooperativa di Soave | Marcato |
| C.S. di Gambellara | Masi |

Montresor
Orio
Fratelli Pasqua
Pegaso (Premiovini)
Pergreffi
Pieropan
Salvalai
Santa Sofia
Santi

Sartori
Scamperle
Fratelli Sterzi
Fratelli Tedeschi
Tommasi
Villa Girardi
Fratelli Zenato
Zonin

**Tocai** w. (r.) dr. ★→★★ DYA
The white Tocai Friulano or Italico is DOC under Colli Berici, Colli
Euganei, Piave and Tocai di Lison, and is the base of Breganze *bianco*.
The rare Tocai Rosso, DOC in Colli Berici, is occasionally grown
elsewhere. Good non-DOC Tocai Friulano is produced in several parts
of the Veneto.

Antica Quercia (Riello)
Castello di Roncade

Pietro Tomasi
Villa Dal Ferro-Lazzarini

**Tocai di Lison** DOC w. dr. ★→ ★★ DYA
The zone in E Veneto extending into Friuli-Venezia Giulia coincides
with Pramaggiore, with which it will soon be unified in a single DOC
called Lison-Pramaggiore. *Classico* is around the town of Lison. Pale
lemon, delicately fragrant, it is finely dry and fruity with a hint of
almond and clean finish.

Castello di Porcia
Club Produttori Associati
Paolo De Lorenzi
Guarise
La Fattoria
La Frassinella
Morassutti

Ruggeri
Russolo
Santa Margherita
Sant'Osvaldo
Tenuta Sant'Anna
Villa Frattina

**Torcolato** w. s/sw. ★★★★ 77 78 79 80 82 83
From semidried Vespaiolo, Tocai, and others of Breganze, this superb
dessert wine has a crystal-clear golden color, flowery aroma, and fruitily
*amabile* flavor with extraordinary balance of components and a long,
clean finish. Some prefer it young when it is opulently fruity, others after
6–10 years when it develops an almost Sauternes-like mellow warmth.
Maculan

**Turà** w. dr. fz. ★★ DYA
Recently concocted melange of Garganega, Durello, Trebbiano and
Pinot grown in Treviso, Verona and Vicenza provinces and aimed at the
light white market. With 10.5% alcohol and a hint of fizz, this is clean,
refreshing and, presumably, *di moda*.

Ca' Donini
De Baj
Della Torre

Lamberti
Santi

**Valdadige**
Part of the DOC zone is in the Veneto. See under Trentino-Alto Adige.

**Valpolicella** DOC r. dr. ★→ ★★★ 80 82 83
From Corvina Veronese, Rondinella, and Molinara grown in the last
wave of Alpine foothills above where the Adige River swings E through
Verona, Valpolicella is similar in composition to Bardolino but sturdier,
deeper, and usually longer-lived. An all-purpose wine of bright ruby
hue, medium body, and attractively grapy scent and flavor with a bitter
almond aspect, it shows balance that can approach elegance from some
producers. The *classico* zone, known historically as Valpolicella – around
Sant'Ambrogio, Fumane, San Pietro Incariano, Negrar, and Marano –
tends to make the best wine. But the DOC zone extends E almost to
Soave through the Valpantena, Valsquaranto, Valmezzane, Val Illasi,
and Valtramigna. With 30–35 million liters a year (including Recioto),
Valpolicella is fourth (with Marsala) behind Chianti, Soave, and
Moscato d'Asti in DOC production.
Ag. *superiore* 1 yr.
– **Recioto della Valpolicella** r. s/sw. sw. (sp.) ★★→★★★ 77 78 79 80 82
83
Select grapes for Valpolicella semidried may be used either for this
dessert wine or the dry Amarone (see below). The classic Recioto is
purple tending to garnet red with ample bouquet and fat structure: rich,
strong (14%), with concentrated semisweet flavor that has a bitter
undertone, it is rather pulpy when young but becomes smoother with

age. Masi, Giuseppe Quintarelli and Fratelli Tedeschi make outstanding bottles. A *spumante* is popular locally. There is also a *liquoroso* of 16%.

– **Recioto della Valpolicella Amarone** or **Amarone** r. dr.
★★→★★★★   74 77 78 79 80 82 83

The most prized Veronese wine is widely appreciated for the way it combines raw power with an almost Burgundian softness. Dark ruby purple when young, it tends to garnet with 4–5 years of age as its aroma deepens and its youthful largesse becomes austere and ethereal, though still retaining the *amaro* (bitter) dry finish that gives it its name. Capable of lasting 20 years, some connoisseurs prefer it inside 5 years when its fruity buoyancy is unsuppressed. Bertani and Bolla have deserved international reputations; Masi, Quintarelli and Domenico Vantini (with Tramanal) are rated tops with smaller scale production. (Producers do not include all bottler and shipper brands, which could also be dependable.)

| | |
|---|---|
| Aldegheri | Pegaso (Premiovini) |
| Allegrini | Pergreffi |
| Anselmi | Giuseppe Quintarelli |
| Bertani | Luigi Righetti |
| Biscardo | Salvalai |
| Bolla | Sanperetto |
| Brigaleara | Santa Sofia |
| Ca' del Monte (Zanconte) | Santi (Castello d'Illasi) |
| G. Campagnola | Sartori |
| C.S. Valpolicella | Scamperle |
| C.S. Veronese del Garda | Fratelli Speri |
| Fratelli Fabiano | Fratelli Sterzi |
| Girasole | Tramanal (Vantini) |
| Guerrieri-Rizzardi | Fratelli Tedeschi |
| Lamberti | Tommasi |
| Le Ragose | Villa Girardi |
| Masi | Fratelli Zenato |
| Montresor | Zonin |

**Venegazzù della Casa** r. dr.   ★★★→★★★★   71 76 78 79 82 83
Classic Bordeaux mix in a ruby-garnet wine that needs 5–10 years of aging to show its eloquent bouquet and austere breed, making it outstanding in its genre in Italy.
Conte Loredan Gasparini

**Verdiso** w. dr. fz.   ★ DYA
The native Verdiso makes a bone-dry, platinum-green wine around Conegliano with skittish fragility that needs to be savored in its infancy.
Pino Zardetto

**Villa Dal Ferro**
Estate in the Colli Berici with distinguished varietals, each given a special name: Cabernet (Le Rive Rosse), Merlot (Campo del Lago), Pinot Bianco (Bianco del Rocolo), Pinot Nero (Rosso del Rocolo), Riesling Renano (Busa Calcara), and Tocai Friulano (Costiera Granda).

*Wine & Food*

Whether the setting is a smart *ristorante* on the Grand Canal or a country *trattoria* with a spit turning before an open fire in the *fogher*, dining in the Veneto is a civilized pleasure. No other region has such equilibrium in food sources – from fertile plains, lush hillsides, woods, lakes, streams and the Adriatic – and no other cooks combine them with such easy artistry. Dishes can be lavish, ornate, and/or exotic (the Venetians introduced spices to Italy), but the elements that bind the regional cooking are simple: rice, beans, polenta, sausages, salame, poultry, game, mushrooms, and mountain cheeses. Venice is the showcase, but the food is every bit as delicious in the interior provinces, in Verona, Vicenza, Padua, Belluno, Rovigo, and perhaps most of all in Treviso, which some consider the sanctuary of Italian gastronomy. Listed are but a few of the delights.

**Asparagi in salsa** Tender white asparagus of Bassano del Grappa with sauce of hard-boiled eggs chopped with vinegar and oil.
★→★★ Breganze *bianco*.

**Bigoli con l'anara** Thick hand-made spaghetti with duck ragout.
★★→★★★ Valpolicella.

**Fegato alla veneziana** Calf's liver cooked with onions and wine.
★★ Cabernet di Pramaggiore.

**Granseola alla veneziana** Spider crab with oil and lemon.
★★★ Bianco di Custoza.

**Pasta e fasioi** Soups of pasta and beans are popular in the Veneto.
★★ Merlot or ★★ Bardolino.

**Pastissada di manzo** Beef (or horse meat) stewed with wine and served with gnocchi or polenta.
★★★ Venegazzù della Casa
or ★★★ Castello di Roncade.

**Risi e bisi** Rice and peas cooked together Venetian style.
★★ Tocai di Lison.

**Risotto nero** The rice is cooked with squid, blackened by its ink.
★★★ Soave *classico*.

**Sopa coada** Thick soup – stew really – of pigeon meat, bread, wine, and vegetables.
★★→★★★ Merlot del Piave.

**Torresani alla perverada** Spit-roasted pigeons with a sausage-liver-anchovy-herb sauce on a bed of polenta.
★★★ Raboso or
★★★→★★★★ Amarone.

## Restaurants

Recommended in or near wine zones: **Breganze** *Al Sole* at Bassano del Grappa. **Colli Berici** *Da Remo* at Vicenza. **Colli Euganei** *La Montanella* near Arquà Petrarca; *Rifugio Monte Rua* at Torreglia Alta. **Montello e Colli Asolani** *Villa Cipriani* at Asolo; *Agnoletti* at Giavera del Montello; *Da Celeste alla Costa d'Oro* at Volpago del Montello. **Piave** *Tre Panoce* at Conegliano; *Da Paolo Zanatta* at Maserada sul Piave; *Da Gigetto* at Miane; *Miron* at Nervesa della Battaglia; *Relais Toulà* at Paderno di Ponzano; *Gambrinus* at San Polo di Piave; *Da Lino* at Solighetto; *Alfredo El Toulà* at Treviso. **Verona area** *San Vigilio* at Garda; *Groto di Corgnan* at Sant'Ambrogio di Valpolicella; *Al Cavallo* at Torri del Benaco; *12 Apostoli*, *Arche* and *Il Desco* at Verona.

# Index

Note: Wines from different regions/zones but bearing the same name occur throughout the text (e.g. Cabernet, Moscato). To aid readers in locating them, the following abbreviations for regions (in parentheses) have been used preceding the relevant page number(s).

Ab *Abruzzi*; Ap *Apulia*; Bas *Basilicata*; Cal *Calabria*; Cam *Campania*; E-R *Emilia-Romagna*; F-VG *Friuli-Venezia Giulia*; Lat *Latium*; Lig *Liguria*; Lom *Lombardy*; Mar *Marches*; Mol *Molise*; Pie *Piedmont*; Sar *Sardinia*; Si *Sicily*; T-AA *Trentino-Alto Adige*; Tus *Tuscany*; Umb *Umbria*; VdA *Valle d'Aosta*; Ven *Veneto*.